MARTYRDOM

DR JON COLE &
DR BENJAMIN COLE

First published in hardback 2009
by Pennant Books

Text copyright © Dr Jon Cole and Dr Benjamin Cole 2008

The moral right of the authors has been asserted.

British Library Cataloguing-in-Publication Data:
A catalogue record for this book is available on request from
The British Library

ISBN 978-1-906015-20-6

Design & Typeset by Envy Design Ltd

Printed and bound in Turkey by Mega Printing

Pictures reproduced with kind permission of PA Photos and Getty Images.

Pennant Books
A division of Pennant Publishing Ltd
PO Box 5675
London W1A 3FB

www.pennantbooks.com

Acknowledgements

The authors would like to thank Jacintha Moore, Louise Cole and Laurence Alison for their generous assistance with the research and proofreading of this book.

Editorial Note

All names appear correctly to the best of our knowledge, but within our research material variant spellings inevitably appear, and we have not attempted to conform these to our own style.

contents

Glossary

Al Ghuraba: radical Islamist political group, successor to
al Muhajiroun.

Al Muhajiroun: radical Islamist political group led by Omar Bakri
Mohammed.

Al Qaeda: 'The base', transnational terrorist network led by
Osama bin Laden.

Barelwi: one of the main traditions of Islam followed by Muslims
in Britain, whose followers are predominantly among the South
Asian community. It originated in the Indian sub-continent,
and is spiritual and apolitical in nature.

Biradri system: an unwritten law of social conduct in South Asian
communities, revolving around ideas of honour where individual
interests are subordinated to those of the community, informally
administered by community elders.

Caliphate: the name given to a historical Muslim super state which
covered much of the Middle East and North Africa and first
emerged 1400 years ago. The *caliphate* was governed according
to *sha'ria* law. *Islamists* believe that the *caliphate* was only finally
abolished on the dissolution of the Ottoman Empire in 1924.

Dar al-Harb: the land of conflict. This term is classically used to refer to countries where Muslim law is not in force in respect of worship and the protection of the faithful.

Dar al-Islam: the land of Islam.

Dar al-Kuffar: non-Muslim countries.

Deen: the laws of Islam.

Deobandi: one of the main Islamic traditions in Britain. Fundamentalist in nature, its adherents advocate the creation of Islamic states governed by *sha'ria* law.

Fatwa: religious ruling or edict.

Hadith: the collected actions and sayings of the Prophet Mohammed. Hadith collections are regarded as important tools for determining the *Sunnah*, or Muslim way of life, by all traditional schools of Islamic jurisprudence. They are the second most important writings in Islam, after the *Qur'an*.

Hafiz: a person who can recite the *Qur'an* from memory.

Hajj: Muslim pilgrimage to Mecca in Saudi Arabia. A religious obligation that all Muslims must complete at least once in their lives.

Halal: (Arabic) permitted.

Hamas: *Harakat al-Muqawamah al-Islamiyya* or 'Islamic Resistance Movement'. Has political and military wings. The military wing has been responsible for numerous attacks on military and civilian targets in Israel, including suicide bombings. Its political wing participates in the Palestinian elections, and in 2007 took control of the Gaza Strip.

Haram: (Arabic) forbidden.

Harkat-e-Jihad-e-Islami: 'The Movement for Islamic Jihad', Pakistan-based *jihadi* group operating in Indian-controlled Kashmir.

Harkat ul-Ansar: 'Movement of the Helpers' (an historical reference to the citizens of Medina who helped the Prophet Mohammed and his companions on their arrival in the city after their migration). Formed from a merger between *Harkat ul-Mujahideen* and *Harkat-e-Jihad-e-Islami* in 1993. It was labelled a terrorist organisation by the US in 1997. To avoid the repercussions of the ban, it was dissolved back into two separate groups the same year.

Harkat ul-Mujahideen: 'Movement of Holy Warriors' or the 'Islamic Freedom Fighters Group', formed by a splinter group of *Harkat-e-Jihad-e-Islami* in 1985. It initially fought in the war against the Soviet Union in Afghanistan. After the war ended it joined the *jihad* in Indian-controlled Kashmir. According to British defence sources, it is, in effect, an international brigade composed mainly of Afghans, Pakistanis and Arabs. Inspired by *Wahhabism* and the *Deobandi* tradition of Islam, and advocates the implementation of *sha'ria* law.

Hezbollah: 'Party of God', Lebanese Islamist resistance movement formed to liberate Lebanese territory from Israeli military control. Controls much of southern Lebanon.

Hijab: a veil worn by Muslim women.

Hizb ut-Tahrir: radical Islamist political group. The UK branch was founded by Omar Bakri Mohammed in the 1990s. It is banned in many countries but not the UK. Its primary objective is to re-establish the Islamic *caliphate*.

Islamic Army of Aden: Islamist terrorist group operating in Yemen, whose goal is to establish an Islamist state in Yemen.

Islamism/Islamist: A school of Islam that is an offshoot of Fundamentalism. Islamists aim to establish a 'pure' Islamic society by means of the appropriation through activism of modern state structures, and the imposition of *sha'ria* law.

Jaish-e-Mohammed: 'Army of God', Pakistan-based *jihadi* group fighting in Indian-controlled Kashmir.

Jamaat-e-Islami: 'Islamic Block', an Islamist group founded in India and Pakistan. It has similar ideas to the Muslim Brotherhood, in wanting to spread the governance of *sha'ria* law to both Muslims and non-Muslims, but is primarily focused on South Asia. Non-violent and advocates gradual change through the takeover of the structures of the state.

Jihad: there are different perceptions of *jihad* which stem from the *Qur'an*. These differences are rooted in Islamic history and reflect the diversity of Islamic thought. These ambiguities have led Muslim scholars to emphasise either the peaceful or the violent nature of *jihad* depending upon their own understanding of the sacred texts as well as the historical and political contexts in which they wish to apply the concept. For contemporary militant Islamists, violent *jihad* is a means of challenging oppression and establishing the rule of Islam.

Jilbab: a long, loose-fitting coat or garment worn by Muslim women. It covers the entire body except the hands, feet, face and head. Women who wear the *jilbab* often also cover their heads with a scarf or wrap.

Jundullah: 'Army of God', *jihadi* group operating in Indian-controlled Kashmir.

Kafir (*plural* Kuffar): (Arabic) unbeliever (i.e. non-Muslim), culturally it is used as a derogatory term.

Lashkar-e-Taiba: 'Army of the Pure' or 'Army of the Righteous'. Pakistan-based *jihadi* group fighting to liberate Indian-controlled Kashmir. It also has a wider agenda to re-establish the Islamic *caliphate*.

Madrassas: religious schools where students learn about Islam and the *Qur'an*.

Mirpuri: from, or of, the Mirpur district of the Pakistan province of Azad Kashmir.

Mujahid (*plural* Mujahideen): 'struggler', often used to mean holy warrior. Its wider meaning includes a Muslim involved in *jihad*, or who is fighting in a war or involved in other forms of struggle.

Pir: holy elders of the *Barelwi* tradition.

Qur'an: the Koran, the Muslim holy book.

Salafism: *Salafis* believe that contemporary society should emulate that of Mohammed and the early believers, who are known as the *Salaf*. Their vision of society is therefore very traditional and conservative. They advocate replacing manmade laws with *sha'ria* law.

Saved Sect: one of the successor groups to *al Muhajiroun*.

Shahid (*plural* Shaheed): (Arabic) martyr.

Sha'ria law: (Arabic) God's law.

Shi'a Islam: the second largest denomination of Islam. *Shi'as* believe that the family of the Prophet Mohammed, including his descendants known as Imams, have special spiritual and political rule over the Muslim community.

Sufism: spiritual, apolitical form of Islam, the opposite of Islamism. Its adherents do not advocate the use of violence.

Sunnah: the religious actions that were instituted by the Prophet Mohammed.

Sunni: the largest denomination of Islam.

Supporters of Sha'ria: radical Islamist group, formerly led by Abu Hamza.

Tablighi Jamaat: Fundamentalist missionary movement, non-violent in nature. Part of the *Deobandi* tradition. It advocates that Muslims should live separately from non-Muslims.

Takfir wal-Hijra: 'Excommunication and Exodus', a militant Islamist group which emerged in Egypt in the 1960s as an offshoot of the Muslim Brotherhood. Members of the group are not bound by the usual religious constraints. They adopt a non-Islamic appearance, drink alcohol and even eat pork, in order to deceive their enemies. The word *takfir* means to judge somebody to be a *kafir*, based on their behaviour resembling that of infidels. To commit *takfir* is to claim that a society is *kafir* for having deviated from the teachings of Islam. *Hijra* means flight or emigration. If a society is pronounced to be *kafir*, the members of *Takfir wal-Hijra* see it as their duty to separate from it and seek to destroy and conquer it.

Ummah: (Arabic) the global community of Muslims that transcends national and racial boundaries.

Wahhabi: Fundamentalist Islamic movement originating in Saudi

Arabia. The terms *Wahhabism* and *Salafism* are often used interchangeably, but *Wahhabism* has also been called a particular orientation within *Salafism*.

Zakat: (Arabic) alms, or charity, for the poor.

Zulm: tyranny or oppression.

Chapter 1

The shaheed

In November 2001, two young Englishmen, Richard Reid and Saajid Badat, flew to Pakistan and travelled overland to the North West Frontier region bordering Afghanistan. It was not the best time of the year for tourism; the mountainous environment is extremely harsh and unforgiving, with strong winds and freezing temperatures. Nor is it the safest of places; it is a region where the Pakistani police force has little control and where traditional forms of justice are dispensed by tribal and village elders.

But Reid and Badat were not there to admire the scenery or experience the local culture; they were there to plan a terrorist attack on transatlantic American airliners. They quietly slipped over the border into Afghanistan where they made contact with their *al Qaeda* handlers. They were given casual footwear which had explosives built into the soles, and the pair then returned separately to the UK in early December 2001.

After returning to the UK, Badat made his final preparations for carrying out the attack. He booked a flight from Manchester to Amsterdam, from where he intended to catch a US-bound flight. But soon afterwards he had second thoughts. He emailed his handler, 'You will have to tell Van Damme [i.e. Reid] that he could be on his own.' He then cut off all contact and returned to his parents'

1

house in Gloucester, where he dismantled the bomb and kept the parts in a cupboard.

In contrast, Reid did not falter. On 21 December 2001, he turned up at Charles de Gaulle airport in Paris to catch an American Airlines flight to Miami. Standing six feet three inches tall, lank haired and dishevelled, he immediately drew the attention of security officials. The fact that he was travelling alone, had paid for his ticket in cash and his only luggage was a small backpack containing a *Qur'an*, a Walkman with religious tapes and a magazine raised an automatic warning flag. Reid told them that he was visiting relatives and explained his lack of luggage by claiming that his family had plenty of clothes for him. He was questioned for so long that he missed the flight. The following morning, Reid turned up two hours early for the flight. The security staff, recognising him from the previous day, waved him through and he boarded American Airlines Flight 63 to Miami.[1]

A few hours later, as the plane cruised at more than 30,000ft, Reid put the plan into action. He waited until the woman sitting next to him went to the toilet before trying to light detonator cords trailing out of his shoes. He then intended to place his foot against the fuselage, blowing a hole the size of a tractor wheel in the plane.[2]

Other passengers complained of a smoke smell in the cabin and flight attendant Hermis Moutardier walked the aisles of the plane, trying to find the source. She found Reid attempting to light a match. Moutardier warned him that smoking was not allowed on the airplane, and he promised to stop. A few minutes later, Moutardier found Reid hunched over in his seat with a shoe in his lap and a lit match in his hand. She tried grabbing Reid but he pushed her to the floor, and she screamed for help. When another flight attendant, Cristina Jones, arrived to try to subdue him, they fought and he bit her thumb. With the events of 9/11 fresh in their minds, other passengers quickly got involved and Reid was overpowered. He was restrained using plastic handcuffs, seatbelt extensions and headphone cords, and a doctor administered Valium for good measure. When the plane landed in Boston, Reid was arrested.[3]

A major terrorist incident had been prevented by a combination of pure luck, Reid's reliance on matches and the diligence of the cabin staff on the aircraft. It had been a cold, wet day in Paris which had made the detonator cords damp so they would not ignite straight away.[4] Reid had only brought matches to light the fuses; if he had invested in a cheap disposable lighter, he might have been successful.

However, Reid's arrest was not the end of the matter. Two years later in November 2003, police in Gloucester arrested Badat. On 25 February 2005, Badat pleaded guilty to involvement in the conspiracy and was sentenced to 13 years' imprisonment. The reasons why he pulled out of the plot are not entirely clear but he told the police that he wanted to 'get away from danger and introduce some calm into his life'.[5] Other Muslims who were previously members of terrorist groups and have renounced violence tend to emphasise religious reasons for their change of heart. Badat did not, and nor did he renounce Islamism or *al Qaeda*. More damningly, he had not warned the police of Reid's impending attack.

Reid and Badat were both members of the *al Qaeda* terrorist network, but apart from that they could not have been more different. Reid was born a Christian, to a white English mother and a Jamaican father. He grew up in Bromley, South London, in the 1990s where he spent his youth smoking marijuana, spray-painting graffiti and chasing after girls. His father was incarcerated in prison for most of his childhood, and his parents eventually split up. Reid then fell out with his mother.

Despite this unsettled early family life, there was nothing particularly unusual about Reid at this time. One of his former teachers recalled that 'he was never rude, or disruptive, or aggressive. And always polite. Although he was quiet, you could get him to laugh. I felt he needed more of that really.'[6] Reid eventually left school aged 16 with no qualifications and few prospects. His mother then moved to the West Country with her new partner and Reid's younger brother, leaving him to live alone in a hostel.[7] He soon joined a gang called the FRF crew and fell into a life of petty crime, marijuana dealing and car theft, which was to land him in a number of prisons, and it was during a stint in Feltham Young Offenders Institution that he converted to Islam.[8]

After being released from Feltham, Reid began to worship at Brixton mosque, which has a reputation as a moderate institution that assists former offenders in their rehabilitation. He seemed to settle in well, becoming involved in the life of the mosque and learning Arabic. The Chairman of Brixton mosque, Abdul Haqq Baker, described Reid as an 'affable kid, keen to learn and quick at picking up things'.[9]

Another worshipper at Brixton mosque at that time was Zaccarias Moussaoui, a French citizen who is often referred to as the '20th hijacker' of the 9/11 attacks, and who would later be convicted in the US of conspiring to commit acts of terrorism with the 19 men who carried out the attacks.[10] Moussaoui was a known militant and was asked to leave the mosque shortly after Reid arrived. The precise nature of the relationship between Moussaoui and Reid is unclear, but it seems that they became friends and began attending Finsbury Park mosque in North London, which at that time was dominated by adherents of *Takfir wal-Hijra*, the Islamist ideology influential among European operatives of *al Qaeda*.[11] From this time, Reid appears to have become a changed man and he gradually drifted away from Brixton mosque. He took the name Abdel Rahim and on his trips back to Brixton mosque harangued listeners with his newfound radical views.[12]

A number of other convicted terrorists are also known to have worshipped at Finsbury Park mosque in the 1990s, including Nizar Trabelsi, a Tunisian who in 2003 was convicted in Belgium of plotting to bomb US targets. It would later be alleged that Trabelsi was Reid and Badat's handler.[13] The sermons of Abu Hamza al Masri, the mosque's Imam, continually stressed the importance of violent *jihad* as a religious obligation, although Hamza never publicly encouraged the use of terrorist violence in the UK itself. Reid and Moussaoui are believed to have left the UK together in 1998 and travelled to

Afghanistan where they attended the *jihadi* training camp at Khalden.[14] Reid subsequently spent most of 1999 and 2000 in Pakistan and possibly Afghanistan.

Khalden, however, was not an *al Qaeda* training camp, and it is possible to argue that it was not even a terrorist training camp. It was operated by Abd al Rab al Rasul Sayyaf, an Afghan warlord and Islamic scholar. Its curriculum was largely based on the training regimen that had been established in the 1980s to train *mujahideen* for the war against the Soviet Union, and comprised mainly ideological instruction and basic military training.[15] It was other camps in Afghanistan that provided specialist terrorist training. Nevertheless, Sayyaf and bin Laden knew each other and had fought together against the Soviets. Bin Laden is known to have visited Khalden, and *al Qaeda* is known to have recruited from the camp. It is not known exactly how Reid and Badat graduated from Khalden to *al Qaeda*; however, it can be assumed that they were spotted by *al Qaeda* recruiters and subsequently given more intensive terrorist training in one of *al Qaeda*'s specialist terrorist training camps. It is alleged that they met *al Qaeda* military commander Mohammed Atef, and that Reid reported to Khalid Sheikh Mohammed, the former chief of *al Qaeda*'s military committee who would later become the most senior *al Qaeda* figure held in the US prison camp at Guantanamo Bay.[16]

Reid reappeared in London in 2000, and attempted to attend a debate at Brixton mosque, forcing Baker to ask him to leave. His activities in London at this time are unknown, but he kept in close contact with Moussaoui by telephone.[17] In late 2000, both men returned to Afghanistan. Captured *al Qaeda* fighters would later identify Reid as the 'highly strung' trainee suicide bomber that they met at a training camp near Kandahar in early 2001.[18]

In contrast, his fellow conspirator Badat was the son of Asian immigrants from Malawi, and had always been a devout Muslim. He was a *hafiz*, someone who could recite the *Qur'an* from memory, and often led prayer services at his local mosque in Gloucester. Neighbours and associates described him as being quiet, softly

5

spoken and respectful.[19] One senior member of Gloucester's Muslim community added, 'He's a good boy. He comes down to the mosque and teaches the basics of Islam. During the month of Ramadan, he came down to the mosque and during our prayer sessions he would lead some of them. He used to say the prayer and we used to follow him. He's very intelligent, very smart, very helpful. He respects his elders.'[20]

After leaving school, Badat briefly trained to be an optometrist before deciding to study to become an Islamic scholar and teacher. In 1999, he attended a religious school, or *madrassa*, in Pakistan, and it is believed that during his time there he crossed the border into Afghanistan to receive training at Khalden. After completing his training, Badat returned to the UK in early 2001 and settled back into everyday life, enrolling at the College of Islamic Knowledge and Guidance in Blackburn. But he also set about obtaining replacement passports from British consulates in order to hide his movements.

Meanwhile, in early 2001, Reid continued life as a full-time *jihadi*. By the summer, he was back in London but he was soon on the move again. In July he obtained a new British passport in Amsterdam, claiming that he had accidentally put his old one through a washing machine. He then flew to Israel on an El Al flight. It is believed that his purpose was to check out El Al security, a shopping mall and office complex called the Azrieli Center, as well as local bus and train stations. He is also thought to have visited the western wall of the Temple Mount in Jerusalem. After 10 days in Israel, Reid crossed into Egypt, from where he flew to Turkey and back to Pakistan in August. He was subsequently debriefed by his handlers in Afghanistan, but he did not stay there long. On 9 August 2001, he was back in Amsterdam where he spent much of his time in internet cafes sending emails to addresses in Pakistan. It was during these months that the shoe-bomb plot is believed to have been planned.[21]

On 5 December, Reid travelled to Brussels, where he applied for another new passport. Several pages of his old one had been ripped out, probably to remove potentially incriminating immigration stamps, but the replacement was issued without question.[22] By 17 December, Reid was finally in Paris, but where and who he stayed with remains unknown. After missing his initial flight to Miami on 21 December, he emailed his handler who urged him to try again the next day.[23] French sources say that many of Reid's emails were sent to an address in Peshawar, Pakistan, which they believe provided postal-drop and forwarding services for *al Qaeda* operatives in Europe.[24]

On 30 January 2003, Reid was found guilty of terrorism charges at a federal court in Boston, Massachusetts. During his trial, Reid was given the opportunity to explain his actions. He described himself in court as a soldier and claimed that bombing the plane was necessary to 'prevent the destruction of Islam'.[25] He went on to declare:

I further admit my allegiance to Osama bin Laden, to Islam, and to the religion of Allah. With regards to what you said about killing innocent people, I will say one thing. Your government has killed two million children in Iraq. If you want to think about something, against two million, I don't see no comparison. Your government has sponsored the rape and torture of Muslims in the prisons of Egypt and Turkey and Syria and Jordan with their money and with their weapons. I don't know, see what I done as being equal to rape and to torture, or to the deaths of the two million children in Iraq. So, for this reason, I think I ought not apologize for my actions. I am at war with your country. I'm at war with them not for personal reasons but because they have murdered more than, so many children and they have oppressed my religion and they have oppressed people for no reason except that they say we believe in Allah. This is the only reason that America sponsors Egypt. It's the only reason they sponsor Turkey. It's the only reason they back Israel. As far as the sentence is concerned, it's in your hand. Only really it is not even in your hand. It's in Allah's hand. I put my trust in Allah totally and I know that he will give victory to his religion. And he will give victory to those who believe and he will destroy those who wish to oppress the people because they believe in Allah. So you can judge and I leave you to judge. And I don't mind. This is all I have to say. And I bear witness to Muhammad this is Allah's message.[26]

Not surprisingly, Reid was sentenced to life imprisonment.

Reid and Badat were, and are, not alone. As time goes by, it is increasingly obvious that some British Muslims are politically radicalised to the point that they become violent extremists. The purpose of this book is to analyse why individuals born or raised in the UK would seek to perpetrate acts of terrorism. We are not seeking to examine the transnational threat posed by Islamist terrorism as there are already numerous excellent analyses in the public domain. This analysis is deliberately restricted because we want to avoid complicating factors that may not be relevant to the situation in the UK. Ultimately, if we are to tackle the issue of Islamist terrorism in the UK, we need solutions specifically aimed at the problems faced in the UK and not those faced in other parts of the world. The key to any solution will be why Reid tried to blow up a plane over the Atlantic, while Badat returned home and put his bomb in a cupboard. We will do this by analysing the publicly available information on 54 British-born or -raised Muslims who have been convicted of acts of terrorist violence, or preparing for such acts, as well as those who died in suicide-bomb attacks. This information comprises a set of data (or dataset) on the personal histories of these 54 individuals. The dataset comprises the following cells and individuals:

The 'Yemen 8' cell were **Mohammed Kamel, Mohsin Ghalain, Samad Ahmed, Shahid Butt, Malik Nasser Harhara, Iyad Hussein, Shazad Nabi** and **Ghulam Hussein**. They were arrested in Yemen in 1998 and convicted in March 1999 of conspiracy to conduct a bombing campaign. The alleged targets were the UK consulate in Sa'na, an Anglican Church, a Swiss-owned hotel and a nightclub frequented by homosexuals. They were trained and armed by the Islamic Army of Aden. Wires, fuses, a global positioning system, mobile phones, two anti-tank missiles, TNT, Yemeni army uniforms, training videos and militant Islamic literature were discovered in their car, hotel rooms and rented villa. A video of Kamel and Ghalain handling weapons was also discovered. All of them confessed to the plot, but later retracted their confessions, arguing that they had been extracted under torture.[27]

Moinul Abedin was arrested in 2000 and convicted in 2002 of 'doing an act with intent to cause an explosion'. In a flat that had been rented by Abedin, police discovered large quantities of chemicals that could be used to make the high-explosive hexanethylene triperoxide diamine (HTMD), detonators and a 'terrorist handbook' with details on bomb making and urban warfare. Police failed to uncover any direct links to a wider conspiracy.[28] Abedin refused to co-operate with the police so little is known about his pathway into terrorism.

Omar Sheikh was arrested and convicted in Pakistan in 2002 of involvement in the murder of the US journalist Daniel Pearl. Sheikh was a member of the Pakistani militant group *Jaish-e-Mohammed* (Army of God), and had a record of involvement in terrorist activity in South Asia stretching back to the mid-1990s. He is suspected of handling money for *al Qaeda* and has been linked to an attack on the American Centre in Calcutta. Indian police have also linked Sheikh to a payment of $100,000 that was made to Mohamed Atta, the suspected ringleader of the 9/11 hijackers. After fighting in Bosnia, he joined *Harkat ul-Ansar* (Movement of the Helpers), a militant group fighting against the Indian army in Kashmir. In 1994, he was sent to India to kidnap foreigners who could be used to bargain for the release of *Harkat* fighters held in Indian jails. He kidnapped four Westerners, but was soon captured by the Indian security forces and spent the next five years in an Indian jail. In December 1999, *Harkat* fighters hijacked an Indian Airlines jet to Kandahar in southern Afghanistan, and as part of their demands forced India to release three militants from jail, including Sheikh and Maulana Masood Azhar. Azhar subsequently set up *Jaish-e-Mohammed*, which took a lead in the Kashmir insurgency, and Sheikh joined the group.[29]

Asif Hanif and **Omar Sharif** were suicide bombers who died in Israel on 1 April 2003. They initially travelled from the UK to Damascus where they met activists from the Palestinian group *Hamas*, and travelled to Gaza. From Gaza they travelled to Tel Aviv. Hanif detonated his bomb in a bar, killing three people and injuring 60. Sharif waited outside to set off his bomb among the rescuers but it failed to detonate. He drowned later that evening while trying to make his escape. For the purposes of this dataset, Sharif is treated as a suicide bomber, because he attempted to detonate his device.

Andrew Rowe was arrested in 2003 while returning to the UK via the Channel Tunnel, and convicted in September 2005 of possessing items which could be used in terror attacks. He had travelled the world for 10 years fighting for Muslim causes, notably in Bosnia and Chechnya. He was linked to an *al Qaeda* cell in Belgium headed by Lionel Dumont. Raids on his home uncovered a handwritten guide to firing battlefield weapons, videos of the 9/11 atrocities and tapes of Osama bin Laden. Police also discovered a coded sheet in which he had used the names of specific models of Nokia mobile phones as code for words and phrases such as 'airline crew', 'explosives' and 'army base'. His socks carried traces of TNT, the plastic explosives PETN and RDX, and nitro-glycerine.[30]

The 'Ammonium Nitrate' cell were arrested in 2004 and convicted in 2007 of conspiracy to cause explosions. The cell were led by **Omar Khyam**, and included **Salahuddin Amin, Jawad Akbar, Waheed Mahmood** and **Anthony Garcia**. They had purchased a tonne of ammonium nitrate fertiliser and aluminium powder, which are component parts of a fertiliser bomb. Their proposed targets were shopping centres and nightclubs in and around the London area.

The '7/7' cell were suicide bombers who all died detonating bombs on the London transport system on 7 July 2005. The cell were led by **Mohammed Siddique Khan**, and the other members were **Shehzad Tanweer, Germaine Lindsay** and **Hasib Hussain**.

The '21/7' cell attempted to replicate the attacks of the 7/7 cell on 21 July 2005. The cell were led by **Muktar Said Ibrahim**, and also included **Ramzi Mohammed, Yassin Omar, Hussain Osman, Manfo Asiedu** and **Aadel Yahya** (who was responsible for procuring the ingredients for the bombs but was not one of the bombers). The bombs failed to explode and the suspects were arrested shortly afterwards and convicted in 2007.

Abu Mansha was convicted in January 2006 of possessing information 'likely to be useful to a person committing or preparing an act of terrorism'. He had acquired the address of a British soldier who had been decorated for bravery in Iraq, after reading media stories about his exploits, and had also sought details of Hindu and Jewish businessmen who, the prosecution argued, Mansha was intending to target for religious reasons. When the police raided his flat, they recovered a blank-firing gun which was in the process of being converted to fire live rounds, along with anti-Western DVDs which featured Osama bin Laden, the beheading of British hostage Ken Bigley in Iraq, Iraqi rebels attacking allied troops, and calls for Muslims to take part in a holy war following the allied attack on the city of Fallujah.[31] Even though he never faced a charge of conspiracy to kill, he was being groomed to conduct such an attack, and when he acquired the address of the soldier he was making a preparatory step to perpetrating an act of violence.

The 'Gas Limos' cell, who were arrested in August 2004, were led by **Dhiren Barot**, who was allegedly one of *al Qaeda*'s leading operatives in the UK. The cell also comprised **Qaisir Shaffi, Nadeem Tarmohamed, Mohammed Naveed Bhatti, Junade Feroze, Zia Ul**

11

Tarmohamed, **Mohammed Naveed Bhatti**, **Junade Feroze**, **Zia Ul Haq**, **Abdul Aziz Jalil** and **Omar Abdur Rehman**. Barot was convicted in October 2006 and the others in July 2007. The main plan, which Barot called the 'Gas Limos Project', involved packing three limousines with gas cylinders and explosives and detonating them in underground car parks. The cell also had three other plans, including one that Barot called the 'Radiation (Dirty Bomb) Project'. Barot had wanted the attacks to be synchronised with the main 'Gas Limos Project'. It was intended for the Radiation Project to be an independent plot in its own right which Barot hoped would cause 'injury, fear, terror and chaos'. Barot also pleaded guilty to planning attacks against the International Monetary Fund, World Bank and financial institutions in New York, Washington and Newark.[32]

Kazi Rahman, the alleged leader of a terrorist cell in East London, was convicted in 2007 of attempting to purchase three Uzi sub-machine-guns and ammunition. He had also enquired about procuring Rocket Propelled Grenades and Surface to Air Missiles.[33]

Parviz Khan was arrested in January 2007 and convicted in 2008 of planning to kidnap and behead a British Muslim soldier, which he intended to video and upload on to the internet. Khan was a fixer who ran a logistic network sending ingredients similar to those used in the 7 July bombs, outdoor equipment, cheap electronic goods and other kit that could be used for a military purpose to *jihadi* groups in Pakistan and Afghanistan. Khan's handlers refused to sanction his getting involved in violent activity so he acted independently by trying to arrange the beheading plot. However, he failed to convince anyone else to take part. Four others, Zahoor Iqbal, Basiru Gassama, Mohammed Irfan and Hamid Elasmar, were also found guilty of involvement in the logistics network, and Gassama was also guilty of not informing police of the beheading plot. None of them was convicted of involvement in the beheading plot, so they are not included among the dataset.[34]

The 'Training' cell were arrested in 2006 and convicted in February 2008. They were led by **Mohammed Hamid**, and the other members were **Atilla Ahmet, Mohammed Al Figari, Kibley Da Costa** and **Kader Ahmed**. They ran terrorist training camps in various locations in the UK, including organised paintballing for their recruits. They also claim to have arranged for some of their recruits to attend military training camps overseas and facilitated contacts with *jihadi* groups based in Pakistan. Hundreds of young Muslims are believed to have attended these camps, including the 21/7 cell. These training camps were probably the earliest stages in the process of selecting and indoctrinating recruits.[35]

Mohammed Kyriacou, Yassin Mutegombwa and **Hassan Mutegombwa** were all convicted in February 2008 of receiving terrorist training from the Training cell. Hassan Mutegombwa was stopped at Heathrow as he tried to catch a flight to Nairobi with military fatigues in his luggage. He was en route to become a suicide bomber in Somalia and was sentenced to 10 years in prison for seeking money for terrorism.[36]

The 'Airline' cell were arrested in 2006 and convicted in 2008. They were led by **Abdulla Ahmed Ali** (also known as Ahmed Ali Khan) who, together with **Tanvir Hussain** and **Assad Sarwar**, was convicted of conspiracy to murder. The other members of the cell, **Umar Islam** (previously known as Brian Young), **Arafat Waheed Khan, Ibrahim Savant** and **Waheed Zaman**, were convicted of conspiring to cause a public nuisance. However, the central allegation of the prosecution, that they intended to destroy eight airliners in mid-air using liquid explosives containing hydrogen peroxide, was not proven.[37]

There are other British citizens who have committed acts of terrorism abroad, such as Mohammed Bilal, who became the first British suicide bomber in Kashmir, in 2001. Others have died unreported deaths in various *jihads* around the world. However, because very little is known about these individuals, they are not included in this analysis.

ANALYSING THE BEHAVIOUR OF VIOLENT EXTREMISTS

How do we go about understanding why these individuals became violent extremists and what can we do to stop them? Every one of us is a naive psychologist in that we are continually trying to explain events that happen around us. As you are reading this book it is likely that you have already given some thought to why people raised in the UK would seek to kill their fellow countrymen. There is much speculation in this area around cause and effect. Do these individuals know what they are doing or are they simply being manipulated by others such as Osama bin Laden?

Causal Attribution theory was developed by psychologists to explain how we analyse the causes of human behaviour. Observers of human behaviour basically face a dichotomous choice: is the observed behaviour the result of the actor's disposition (i.e. the internal cause) or the situation in which they found themselves (i.e. the external cause)? Do you fail an exam due to its difficultly (external cause) or your lack of knowledge (internal cause)? How you attribute the cause of behaviour will have potentially significant impacts. For example, depressed patients attribute negative outcomes to their own failings and positive outcomes to external causes. This pattern of causal attributions contributes to their depressed psychological state. Therefore, causal attribution theory is central to how we analyse the behaviour of our dataset. The most obvious and tempting causal attribution is that our dataset are simply evil and/or abnormal. This narrative is easy to dismiss as the rhetoric of the tabloid media. Unfortunately, it is not that simple as 'normality' is a relative concept. In 1973, the American Psychiatric Association 'cured' millions of people of their psychiatric disorder overnight by simply removing homosexuality from the psychiatric disorders classified in the *Diagnostic and Statistical Manual of Mental Disorders* that is used to diagnose psychiatric patients. There are countless other examples in the field of abnormal psychology that illustrate how concepts of normality are culturally determined and subject to change. We have to analyse our dataset bearing in mind that there is no universally agreed definition of what is 'normal'.

Before we begin our analysis of the dataset, we must appreciate how our thinking about them can be distorted by systematic errors in judgement. Such errors can be either explicit (i.e. deliberate) or implicit (i.e. unconscious), so it is not always obvious when we are making them.

The first and probably most obvious systematic error will be the **Hindsight Bias**. As we all know, hindsight allows us to know everything about the past, including information that was not available to us at the time. This means that, with hindsight, many decisions, judgements and actions may appear stupid or ill-conceived. For example, we could argue that the security personnel at Charles de Gaulle airport should have searched Reid more thoroughly or detained him for longer. However, they must stop numerous people like Reid who are perfectly innocent and it is only because we now know he attempted to destroy an airliner that we scrutinise their decision to let him through. Our analysis is not seeking to apportion blame to individuals and/or organisations that 'should' have noticed that something was wrong and tried to prevent the members of our dataset from engaging in terrorist activities. Instead, we are attempting to identify what we should look for as other people become violent extremists in the future.

The **Fundamental Attribution Error** occurs when we overestimate the role of disposition and underestimate the role of the situation in observed behaviour. This is not surprising as the individual we are observing is always more salient than the environment in which we observe them. **Actor-Observer Differences** occur when the actor tends to attribute their behaviour to the situation and the observer tends to attribute the same behaviour to the disposition of the actor. As we shall see in later chapters, situational factors play an enormous role in influencing behaviour, but they are often overlooked by observers.

Priming Effects will occur when prior information distorts our judgement of the individual's behaviour. This is very pertinent to our analysis as we know before we start that our dataset have all been convicted of terrorist offences. The most controversial source of priming effects will be **Stereotypes**. Most of us think of stereotypes as wholly negative representations of individuals and groups within society. In psychological terms, a stereotype is simply a mental shortcut that allows us to make assumptions about an individual from salient characteristics of the social group to which they belong. In this context, stereotypes are neither positive nor negative; they are simply mental representations of the typical member of the group facing us, for example police officers or school teachers. Stereotypes are powerful psychological processes and are heavily implicated in prejudice and discrimination. (Although an in-depth discussion of the role of stereotypes in prejudice and discrimination is beyond the scope of this book, we must be aware that stereotypes may influence our analysis of the dataset.)

Expectancy Effects will occur when our prior knowledge of the individual influences which information we attend to. The most common expectancy effect is **Confirmation Bias**, where we only focus on information which supports our view of the world and ignore that which contradicts it.

Finally, the limitations of the information that we have used for our analysis should be acknowledged. We have only used open source information and have no access to covert intelligence or direct interviews with the members of the dataset. It is possible that access to either source of intelligence could dramatically alter our analysis as new evidence may come to light. We must also be careful not to place too much emphasis on interviews with convicted terrorists as it is likely that their explanations for their behaviour will be subject to some of the systematic errors described above. If they are still seeking to gain capital from their criminal activity, it is likely that they will overemphasise their role in the ideological struggle. If they are seeking redemption, they may overemphasise the role of others in their crimes. This is called the **Halo Effect**, where the individual seeks to put themselves in the best possible light as a form of impression management. As we will discuss later, the social behaviour of our dataset was central to their movement into violent extremism.

Some similarities between the members of our dataset are obvious, for example, they are mostly young men. However, the overwhelming majority of young men are not violent extremists, so attempting to profile our dataset by their age and gender will not be particularly useful. There must be something that is different between the members of our dataset and other young British Muslims, so that is where we will start our analysis.

Notes and references

1 Elliott M & Amendola E, 'The Shoe Bomber's world', *Time Magazine*, 16 February 2002; 'The making of a human timebomb', War on Terrorism: Observer Special, *Observer*, 30 December 2001, http://observer.guardian.co.uk/waronterrorism/story/0,,625868,00.html.

2 'The making of a human timebomb', War on Terrorism: Observer Special, *Observer*, 30 December 2001, http://observer.guardian.co.uk/waronterrorism/story/0,,625868,00.html.

3 Booth Thomas C, 'Courage in the air', *Time Magazine*, 1 September 2002.

4 'The making of a human timebomb', War on Terrorism: Observer Special, *Observer*, 30 December 2001, http://observer.guardian.co.uk/waronterrorism/story/0,,625868,00.html.

5 Jacobsen M, 'The bombers who weren't', *Washington Post*, 23 March 2008.

6 'At school with the shoe bomber', *Guardian*, 28 February 2002, http://www.guardian.co.uk/g2/story/0,3604,659184,00.html.

7 'At school with the shoe bomber', *Guardian*, 28 February 2002, http://www.guardian.co.uk/g2/story/0,3604,659184,00.html.

8 'Richard Reid', Wikipedia, http://en.wikipedia.org/wiki/Richard_Reid_(shoe_bomber).

9 'I saw the change in shoe bomb suspect', *South London Press*, 28 December 2001, http://icsouthlondon.icnetwork.co.uk/0100news/0400lambeth/tm_method=full%

26objectid=11502384%26siteid=50100-name_page.html#story_continue. (Accessed April 2008.)

10 'Q&A: Moussaoui trial', BBC NewsOnline, 3 May 2006, http://news.bbc.co.uk/1/hi/world/americas/4471019.stm.

11 Elliott M & Amendola E, 'The Shoe Bomber's world', *Time Magazine*, 16 February 2002.

12 Elliott M & Amendola E, 'The Shoe Bomber's world', *Time Magazine*, 16 February 2002.

13 'Saajid Badat', Wikipedia, http://en.wikipedia.org/wiki/Saajid_Badat.

14 'The making of a human timebomb', War on Terrorism: Observer Special, *Observer*, 30 December 2001, http://observer.guardian.co.uk/waronterrorism/story/0,,625868,00.html.

15 Burke J, *Al-Qaeda: The True Story of Radical Islam* (London: Penguin, 2004), pp 169–71.

16 'Sources: Reid is al Qaeda operative', CNN, 6 December 2003, http://www.cnn.com/2003/WORLD/asiapcf/southeast/01/30/reid.alqaeda/.

17 'The making of a human timebomb', War on Terrorism: Observer Special, *Observer*, 30 December 2001, http://observer.guardian.co.uk/waronterrorism/story/0,,625868,00.html.

18 'The making of a human timebomb', War on Terrorism: Observer Special, *Observer*, 30 December 2001, http://observer.guardian.co.uk/waronterrorism/story/0,,625868,00.html.

19 'Bright student suspected of falling under al-Qa'eda spell', *Daily Telegraph*, 29 November 2003, http://www.telegraph.co.uk/news/main.jhtml?xml=/news/2003/11/29/nterr329.xml.

20 'Terror suspect held in Gloucester', *Daily Telegraph*, 28 November 2003, http://www.telegraph.co.uk/news/main.jhtml?xml=/news/2003/11/28/nterr128.xml.

21 'The making of a human timebomb', War on Terrorism: Observer Special, *Observer*, 30 December 2001, http://observer.guardian.co.uk/waronterrorism/story/0,,625868,00.html. After the invasion of Afghanistan, a file was discovered on a captured *al Qaeda* computer which contained a detailed account of the travels of Abdul Ra'uff during the summer of 2001. Ra'uff had flown from the Netherlands to Israel, Egypt and Turkey scouting out locations for terrorist attacks. Ra'uff's itinerary

matched one known to have been taken at the same time by Reid, and the FBI believe that Reid and Ra'uff are the same man. Elliott M & Amendola E, 'The Shoe Bomber's world', *Time Magazine*, 16 February 2002.

22 'The making of a human timebomb', War on Terrorism: Observer Special, *Observer*, 30 December 2001, http://observer.guardian.co.uk/waronterrorism/story/0,,625868,00.html.

23 Elliott M & Amendola E, 'The Shoe Bomber's world', *Time Magazine*, 16 February 2002.

24 Elliott M & Amendola E, 'The Shoe Bomber's world', *Time Magazine*, 16 February 2002.

25 'Exchange between Reid and judge follows life sentence', CNN, 6 December 2003, http://www.cnn.com/2003/LAW/01/31/reid.transcript/.

26 'Exchange between Reid and judge follows life sentence', CNN, 6 December 2003, http://www.cnn.com/2003/LAW/01/31/reid.transcript/.

27 'On Yemen's Death Row', *Guardian*, 17 January 1999, http://www.guardian.co.uk/yemen/Story/0,2763,209259,00.html; 'Terrorists or tourists', *Guardian*, 26 June 1999, http://www.al-bab.com/yemen/artic/gdn42.htm.

28 'Was Midlands man first Al Qaida bomber in UK?', *Birmingham Post*, 14 August 2006, http://icbirmingham.icnetwork.co.uk/birminghampost/news/tm_method=full%26objectid=17558114%26siteid=50002-name_page.html#story_continue; 'Accused denies bomb claims', *Birmingham Post*, 8 February 2002, http://icbirmingham.icnetwork.co.uk/0100news/0100localnews/tm_method=full%26objectid=11602344%26siteid=50002-name_page.html#story_continue.

29 'Manhunt for public school kidnapper', *Guardian*, 9 February 2002, http://www.guardian.co.uk/pakistan/Story/0,2763,647495,00.html.

30 'British Muslim convert jailed for terrorism offences', *Guardian*, 24 September 2005, http://politics.guardian.co.uk/terrorism/story/0,15935,1577303,00.html.

31 'Market trader found guilty of plotting to kill British soldier', *Guardian*, 23 December 2005, http://www.guardian.co.uk/military/story/0,,1673290,00.html.

32 'Muslim was planning dirty bomb attack in UK', *Daily Telegraph*, 13 October 2006, http://www.telegraph.co.uk/news/main.jhtml?xml=/news/2006/10/13/nterr13.xml.

33 'Plumber "planned to bring down jet" in rocket attack', *The Times*, 1 May 2007, http://www.timesonline.co.uk/tol/news/uk/crime/article1729047.ece.

34 'The jihadi and the beheading plot', 18 February 2008,
http://news.bbc.co.uk/1/hi/uk/7241778.stm.

35 'How the terror camp gang were bugged and caught', *The Times*, 26 February
2008,
http://www.timesonline.co.uk/tol/news/uk/crime/article3437865.ece?token=null
&offset=12; 'Hamid, Ahmet and their associates may well have been the last
graduates of Abu Hamza's Finsbury Park terrorist finishing school', *The Times*,
26 February 2008,
http://www.timesonline.co.uk/tol/news/uk/crime/article3441588.ece.

36 '"Osama bin London" groomed 21/7 bombers', *Daily Telegraph*, 27 February
2008,
http://www.telegraph.co.uk/news/main.jhtml?xml=/news/2008/02/26/nterror52
6.xml&page=3; 'How the terror camp gang were bugged and caught', *The Times*,
26 February 2008,
http://www.timesonline.co.uk/tol/news/uk/crime/article3437865.ece?token=null
&offset=12.

37 'Key conspirator "took on new identity to join in transatlantic bomb plot"',
The Times, 8 April 2008,
http://www.timesonline.co.uk/tol/news/uk/crime/article3702430.ece; 'Alleged
bomb plotters' urban "bomb factory"', *Daily Telegraph*, 4 April 2008,
http://www.telegraph.co.uk/news/main.jhtml?xml=/news/2008/04/04/nterror90
4.xml; 'Police in crisis after jury rejects £10m terror case', *The Times*, 9
September 2008,
http://business.timesonline.co.uk/tol/business/law/public_law/article4710879.ece;
'The eight in the dock', *The Times*, 9 September 2008,
http://www.timesonline.co.uk/tol/news/uk/crime/article4707712.ece.

Chapter 2

British Muslim Identity

The most obvious shared experience of our dataset is that of being a British Muslim. As we outlined in the previous chapter, we are analysing the behaviour of a very small, select group of individuals, who have been involved in terrorist offences. Some of them have consciously invoked the Muslim identity and experience to rationalise their behaviour, but it would be wrong to argue that this is a problem within the British Muslim population as the numbers involved are so small that it cannot be a widespread community-related problem. Having said that, the various communities that comprise the British Muslim population are the ones in which our dataset were born and/or raised, or, in the case of the converts among them, the communities which they joined later in life. To understand them, we therefore need to examine the social identity of British Muslims.

Our membership of various groups within society defines who we are, referred to by psychologists as our social identity. In fact, many people utilise their membership of groups to describe who they are. As most of us have a mental representation of the average member of most groups within society (i.e. a stereotype), we have some basic understanding of other people. The use of stereotypes based on group membership facilitates social interaction as it forms a basis on which to communicate without our exhaustively trawling for information, and helps prevents us from inadvertently saying or doing something which may be deemed inappropriate when we first meet people. The use of stereotypes is fraught with many problems and prejudicial stereotypes often form the basis of discrimination against specific groups. However, the dynamics of prejudice and discrimination within society are beyond the scope of our analysis as we need to examine the social processes that occurred within our dataset, and to examine their behaviour we need to retain our focus on the real and perceived conflicts between social groups within the UK.

The basic assumption of social identity is that most people want to have high self-esteem and to believe that others think good things about them. As a result, most people will transfer their desire on to the social groups to which they belong. Following social comparison theory, we would expect most of us to evaluate our social groups by comparing them to other groups of which we are not members. To maintain high self-esteem, it is necessary for these comparisons to demonstrate that our social group is superior to the others, and this superiority is then transferred on to us by virtue of our membership. Social identification is defined by two facets: cognitive and emotional identification with the group. Cognitive identification is the extent to which an individual classifies themselves as a member of a specific group, and emotional identification is the emotional commitment that an individual has to the group, reflecting the feelings that they hold about it. The social status of an individual's social group is therefore important to them.

We can understand the importance of social status by looking into our evolutionary past. All species that display any kind of social behaviour develop social structures based on social status or dominance. In simplistic terms, we can divide these species into colonial and territorial. Colonial species will live as large social groups, typically of mixed sex, with a dominance hierarchy, the most dominant animals having unfettered access to food, water and mates. The dominant animal will subordinate all others to maintain their position and restrict access to the available resources, and those lowest in the social hierarchy will have a difficult time due to their inability to access such resources. These dominance hierarchies are maintained through aggressive behaviour, although fighting may be very infrequent once the hierarchy is established. Territorial animals, on the other hand, tend to be solitary and they defend their solitude by attacking any same-sex intruders. Territories are defended because they have access to resources, such as food and water, and territorial defence is signalled through marking, either physically or through scent. Ethologists have found that scent marking assists the territorial male in fighting off intruders as it increases anxiety in the intruder. Dominant animals will also defend their colonies but they are more tolerant of others already within it, which is essentially the difference between colonial and territorial animals.

The key to understanding the relevance of such animal behaviour for humans is that it is the *function* of behaviour that has survived through evolution rather than the behaviour itself. Dominance serves a central function in every social species as it ensures access to necessary resources and therefore we can expect dominance hierarchies to form within human groups. However, human dominance hierarchies are not necessarily based on aggression alone and therefore social status is much more difficult to definitively define. For the purposes of our analysis, we will operate with two different types of social status: personal status, based on an individual's characteristics and resources (for example, people with lots of money are generally considered to have a higher social status than those with less money); and role status, based on the role that the individual occupies (for example, the military officer has a higher social status than the troops they command).

Real and perceived status inequalities can generate significant inter-group animosity and conflict. Realistic Group Conflict theory proposes that, when groups are in conflict for scarce resources, the potential success of one group threatens the wellbeing of the others resulting in negative out-group attitudes within all of the groups.[1] If the goals of competing groups are at variance, the resulting conflict will increase the solidarity of the in-group and widen the in-group/out-group distinction, thus creating inter-group hostility. The original research conducted by Sherif and colleagues in the 1960s divided children in a summer camp into two groups and then had them compete against each other in a series of sporting activities. As the success of one group was at the expense of the other, each group felt threatened by the other. As the competitions continued, hostility between the groups escalated to the point that violence occurred in some cases. The important point to this experiment is that the children were randomly allocated to the newly created groups so therefore this inter-group hostility developed as a direct result of the competition. When the tasks required inter-group co-operation, the level of hostility decreased. Such hostility is not dependent on the individual feeling directly threatened, as threats to the group as a whole will be perceived as threats to the individual even though their self-interest is not impacted.

Symbolic Threat occurs when the out-groups violate and therefore threaten values that are important to the in-group.[2] In this theory, the conflict between groups is the result of divergent values and beliefs, rather than direct competition for resources or contradictory goals. As the perceived gap between the values and beliefs of the in- and out-groups decreases, so do the negative attitudes towards the out-groups.

Integrated Threat theory brings together Realistic and Symbolic Threat with two additional sources of inter-group threat: inter-group anxiety and negative stereotypes.[3] Inter-group anxiety reflects awkwardness and uneasiness felt in the presence of out-group members because of uncertainty about how to behave towards them, and this makes such contacts seem threatening to the individual. Hostility and the desire to avoid contact with out-group members will increase as inter-group anxiety increases. Expectations about members of out-groups will be formed by stereotypes and negative ones will influence social information processing and, subsequently social judgements. Integrated Threat theory has been well supported, by research into a range of different inter-group contexts, such as attitudes towards immigrants or ethnic groups. High levels of perceived inter-group conflict, negative contact between groups and in-group identification are predictors of high levels of perceived threat.

THE ETHNIC AND CULTURAL BACKGROUND OF BRITISH MUSLIMS

The Muslim population of the UK can be differentiated by ethnicity and nationality, as well as by the different traditions of Islam that they follow. In turn, these factors give rise to a range of different cultural traditions within different Muslim communities in the UK. Most Muslims in Britain belong to the *Sunni* tradition of Islam, but a small proportion are *Shi'a*. However, they have a diverse ethnic and national heritage: 43 per cent are of Pakistani descent, 17 per cent are of Bangladeshi descent, nine per cent are of Indian descent, six per cent are black, four per cent are white and 21 per cent are of other descent. Around a quarter of Muslims in Britain have origins in the Middle East and North Africa.[4]

Within the wider Islamic community, there are further smaller communities following different traditions of Islam. Most South Asians follow the *Barelwi* and *Deobandi* traditions, but there are also followers of other traditions or schools of Islam such as *Sufism*, *Salafism*, *Wahhabism* and *Islamism*. The *Barelwi* and *Sufi* traditions are mystical orders which focus on meditation and prayer, and generally eschew politics. In contrast, the *Deobandi*, *Salafi* and *Wahhabi* traditions are part of the Fundamentalist school of Islam, which leans towards scriptural literalism and is more overtly political. These traditions are revivalist in nature, seeking to recreate the Islamic world's former glory, and therefore their vision of society is very traditional and conservative. They reject manmade laws, which they believe oppress mankind, and advocate replacing them with Allah's law, or *Sha'ria* law, which they believe will bring freedom, purity and justice to mankind.[5] *Salafis*, in particular, reject modernity and believe that society should be restructured to emulate that of the Prophet Mohammed and the early believers, the *Salaf*. There is also an Islamist movement within the UK, which advocates a highly politicised form of Islam. The groups that comprise this movement see Islam not just as a religion but as a political, social and economic system, and a whole system of life for the believer. Their aim is to establish a 'pure' Islamic society by gaining control of the structures of the modern state.

As first-generation Muslim immigrant communities became more firmly established in the UK, they became increasingly fragmented according to village, kinship, tribal, ethnic and sectarian affiliation, and each established their own mosques and religious schools.[6] Sectarian diversity became the norm in the major towns and cities of Britain, adding to the social and theological fragmentation of the Muslim population by national origin, ethnicity, language, age, class, education, doctrine and practice that was characteristic of most British Muslim communities.[7]

In particular, Mirpuris make up around 70 per cent of the British population of Pakistani descent, with sizeable communities living in Northern towns such as Bradford, Leeds, Derby and Huddersfield. First-generation British Mirpuris mainly came from rural and conservative parts of the Pakistani province of Azad Kashmir. The vast majority of Mirpuris adhere to the *Barelwi* tradition of Islam, which revolves around holy elders known as *pirs*.[8] However, *Barelwism* has struggled to translate itself effectively into contemporary British urban life. Its mosques are tightly controlled by patriarchal elders who hire Urdu-speaking Imams from their home villages. Consequently, there are very few English-speaking *Barelwi* Imams, which has made it difficult for them to communicate with English-speaking second- and third-generation Mirpuris.[9]

The first generation of British Mirpuris brought the *biradri* system with them and it remains integral to Mirpuri culture in Britain. This is an unwritten law of social conduct revolving around notions of honour where individual interests are subordinated to those of the community, and it is informally administered by community elders, whose authority cannot be challenged.[10] Under this system, a family unit will stick together and parents will normally arrange marriages for their sons and daughters with close relations. In Pakistan, it ensures that, in very poor rural areas where little or no state provision exists, villagers can provide themselves with the basic structures of a community, such as healthcare, justice, childcare and security.[11] But the underpinning rationale for the *biradri* system is redundant in the UK, given that all British citizens have free access to public services. As a consequence, the younger generations have increasingly begun to question why they should live according to the strict requirements of such a system.

In contrast, other traditions of Islam have adapted well to the British milieu. By 2007, *Deobandis* ran more than 600 of Britain's 1,350 mosques. Their success is in part due to the fact that they have trained a generation of British-born Imams, who understand what it is like to be a Muslim in Britain and, most importantly, who preach in English. The *Deobandi* tradition is strongest in the towns and cities of the Midlands and Northern England, with 59 of the 75 mosques in Blackburn, Bolton, Preston, Oldham and Burnley being run by *Deobandis*.[12]

Because the Muslim population of the UK is not homogeneous, but rather comprises a number of distinct communities, mainstream religious and political discourse within the Muslim population is fractured. In addition, Islam is not a hierarchical religion, so there is no single Imam or group with the authority to speak on behalf of all Muslims in the UK. Instead, individual Imams have authority within their respective mosques. Some organisations such as the Muslim Parliament, the Muslim Council of Britain, the Muslim Association of Britain and the Muslim Public Affairs Committee claim to represent the Muslim population, but there is no individual or national body which can legitimately claim to speak for all British Muslims.

There is clearly no single British Muslim social identity that can adequately capture the complexity of the Muslim community in the

UK. British Muslims have multiple ethnic and cultural backgrounds, varying from person to person and community to community. For some British Muslims, there are strong transnational kinship and community ties that make what happens abroad as relevant to their day-to-day lives as that which happens in their local communities. As we shall see in Chapter 4, this may explain the importance of British foreign policy for the British Muslim population.

This diversity of social backgrounds is reflected in the individuals in our dataset. The majority are of Pakistani descent, but there are also Bangladeshis, North Africans, East Africans, other black and Asian Africans, a Yemeni, one mixed Egyptian/white European, and eight of them are reported to be converts to Islam. They came from communities throughout the UK, although the majority are from in and around the London area. This illustrates how violent extremism has crossed the boundaries of the diverse communities that comprise the Muslim population of the UK, although radicalisation in the Pakistani communities is proportionately greater than among communities of other ethno-national background.

THE GENERATION GAP AND THE REJECTION OF TRADITIONAL IDENTITY

One of the other common features of the dataset is that they are predominantly young men: the average age at the time of their arrest was approximately 25, a handful were teenagers and a few of them were over 30. It is unknown when they actually became politically radicalised and subsequently involved in terrorist activities, but it is evident that the average age was lower than when they were arrested or killed, and that a significant number of the dataset at least began the process of radicalisation as teenagers. Omar Khyam, for instance, first became aware of the war in Kashmir at the age of 17, when he began attending meetings of the radical *al Muhajiroun* group (which will be discussed in greater detail in Chapter 5).[13] The young age at which the dataset were initially radicalised hints at the role that generational conflict might have played in their journey into violent extremism.

Family problems are a marked feature in the personal histories of many individuals in British *jihadi* networks. Indeed, there have been suggestions that radical recruiters specifically target such individuals. Abd Samad Moussaoui, the brother of Zaccarias Moussaoui, argued that *al Qaeda* recruiters looked for 'young people who have become estranged from their families, the strong moral anchors that are their father, mother, brothers and sisters, and even friends'.[14] Estrangement from family is a theme in the lives of several members of our dataset. In several cases, this led to their leaving the family home and its protective influence, after which they appear to have become radicalised. This was particularly evident with Saajid Badat who was well integrated into the local community in Gloucester, before falling out with his father in the late 1990s. He then moved to London where he began the process of radicalisation.[15]

As with Richard Reid, some of the others also had chaotic family lives. Germaine Lindsay's natural father played little role in his life and it appears his first stepfather was hard on him. Lindsay was closer to his second stepfather but he only stayed with the family until 2000. Two years later, when Lindsay was 16, his mother moved to the US to live with another man, leaving Lindsay alone in Huddersfield. This has been described as a traumatic experience for the teenager.[16] Muktar Said Ibrahim had also fallen out with his family in his teenage years. He was sleeping on friends' floors and had already been in trouble with the police for committing sexual assault and robbery.[17] Yassin Omar lived with his elder sister until she married a man who took a dislike to him, and she then passed him into the care of social services. He was subsequently fostered but, when he reached the age of 18, his foster parents were no longer allowed to care for him and he was given a council flat on the ninth floor of a tower block. Isolated and lacking adult guidance, he dropped out of college.[18]

However, it is not just individuals who are estranged from their parents who experience this generation gap, and a significant proportion of the dataset had seemingly normal home and family lives, with no evidence of their being estranged from their families.

An unstable family background does not therefore appear to be an essential prerequisite for the radicalisation process to begin, although it is a common element for many members of the dataset.

The root cause of this generation gap is typically the rejection of their parents' traditionalism, and the sense of identity that goes with it. For some first-generation Muslim immigrants, preserving their identity led to their congregating in communities which enabled them to maintain their traditional way of life, including the *biradri* system, as much as possible. But the role of the community elders in the *biradri* system effectively disenfranchises the young,[19] which makes it difficult for the younger generations, who are struggling to adapt their often traditional upbringing to the realities, difficulties and opportunities afforded by life in a modern secular country. These problems are often compounded by the traditionalism of the mosques in many communities. The fact that many foreign-born Imams cannot particularly relate to life in the UK, and frequently do not speak English, means that younger Muslims often do not understand much of what they see or hear in their traditional mosques and as a result gradually drift away.[20]

Hassan Butt, a former recruiter for the radical Islamist group *al Muhajiroun*, argues that traditional communities often push their young into the arms of the radicals through their traditional attitudes towards jobs, dress, schooling, and socialising.[21] In particular, Butt identifies arranged marriages as being one of the major issues which alienates the younger generation from their families. He claims that a lot of people he knew became politically radicalised, or took the initial steps towards becoming radicalised, as a result of their families trying to force them to marry someone they didn't want to.[22]

This experience was reflected among some members of the dataset. In particular, Mohammed Siddique Khan began his journey into radical Islamism after his mother died, and the *Barelwi* tradition he grew up in was forcing him into an arranged marriage. In reaction, he converted to *Wahhabism*, and fell in love with a woman he met at Leeds Metropolitan University in 1997. Her family were *Deobandis*, a tradition that was diametrically opposed to the Khan family's *Barelwism*. However, the Fundamentalist and Islamist Imams offer a way out to those in this situation, because one of the central tenets of their ideology is that Muslims should not be divided by race or nationality, since they are all part of one global community called the *ummah*. Consequently, they do not proscribe who should marry who, as long as they are Muslim.[23] After Khan married in October 2001, his links with his father were finally cut.[24] Several others also married outside of their communities, which can be taken as a potential indicator that they faced family difficulties over who they married.[25]

However, this explanation does not cover all members of the dataset, particularly because not all of them are of Pakistani-Kashmiri descent. Aadel Yahya of the 21/7 cell entered an arranged marriage with a Yemeni woman in June 2005. The same is also true for some of those who were of Pakistani descent, who were apparently content in their arranged marriages. Junade Feroze of the Gas Limos cell, for instance, had a happy arranged marriage with a cousin from Pakistan.[26] Equally, it is not true of the converts to Islam in the dataset.

The issue of arranged marriage, therefore, is just one aspect of the profound rift that has opened up between the different generations in many Muslim communities. There is also a strong sense among some young Muslims that the traditional teachings of their parents' generation are too passive for dealing with the problems of racism and Islamophobia that they face in their everyday lives. Unlike their parents, second- and third-generation Muslims are much more prepared to confront prejudice, and as a result have proved more willing to embrace traditions of Islam which empower them to do so. Therefore, in rejecting the sense of identity offered by their parents' traditionalism, many of them end up seeking an alternative form of identity which can help them to reconcile living as Muslims in a modern, secular, urban society, and also help them deal with life as part of a religious and ethnic minority population. A common observation of many young British Muslims of Pakistani descent is that they feel neither British nor Pakistani, because they do not feel accepted in Britain, but do not have strong ties to Pakistan either. For many, this has led to an identity crisis which extremists can exploit.

For some of those members of the dataset who did not come from traditional Muslim backgrounds, their identity crises took different forms. Richard Reid's closest friend at school has suggested that, after Reid's mother met a new, white partner, Reid suffered a crisis of identity from being part of a white family. Unsure of what being black meant, his confusion deepened. Another friend recalled that 'he seemed to identify with the other black boys but they didn't seem accepting of him. He always walked behind – bringing up the rear ... He just didn't belong.'[27] However, his conversion to Islam seemed to resolve these issues. Abdul Haqq Baker felt that Reid was at ease with himself, an enthusiastic young man who was happy with his identity.[28] Yet, despite this, Reid still gravitated towards radical Islamist groups.

Nevertheless, not all young Muslims are troubled by their sense of identity. A report by the Joseph Rowntree Foundation in 2006 discovered that among a small dataset of Muslim men living in Bradford, their sense of identity was strong. They provided a picture of individuals for whom their Muslim, Pakistani and British identities were maintained alongside each other. There were tensions for some of them, but managing these tensions on a day-to-day or longer-term basis appeared to be relatively straightforward.[29] This was confirmed by the findings of a MORI poll of British Muslims in July 2005, which showed that 86 per cent of the respondents felt fairly or very strongly that they belonged to Britain, and 96 per cent of the respondents felt fairly or very strongly that they belonged to Islam.[30] This indicates that the majority of the respondents saw no incompatibility between being British and Muslim. These findings are reflected in some members of the dataset, for whom there is no evidence of their having experienced a crisis of identity prior to their radicalisation. This was particularly true of Omar Sheikh, whose journey into terrorism began when he watched a film about the suffering of Muslims in Bosnia.

This evidence suggests that the tensions between traditional religious and cultural beliefs and living in a secular Western society can create problems for some young people trying to reconcile these two aspects of their lives. For the overwhelming majority, these problems are easily solved, but for some they appear to lead to an increasing sense of alienation from their family and wider community. For this latter group, the search for a new social identity is a factor that may promote radicalisation and this is something that we will return to later in our analysis (see Chapter 5). However, the fact that there is no evidence of these tensions in some members of the dataset indicates that it is not just the alienated or those suffering identity crises who are vulnerable to being radicalised.

RELIGIOUS OBSERVANCE

Research commissioned by the government in 2007 suggested that extremist groups successfully recruit by exploiting a combination of alienation and lack of religious knowledge among young people.[31] This suggests that individuals with limited religious knowledge and a desire to know more are particularly vulnerable to the influence of radical ideologies, but equally it implies that individuals who are properly schooled in Islam would not be vulnerable. It is possible to categorise the majority of the dataset as having limited knowledge of Islam, or as having turned away from Islam to some extent, prior to their radicalisation. As part of the radicalisation process, they rediscovered Islam through a radical ideology. The most obvious cases are the converts to Islam, who seem to have been radicalised either during their conversion or shortly afterwards, while they were still learning about Islam. In particular, Richard Reid was politicised during his conversion to Islam in Feltham Young Offenders Institution. A friend recalled how he began to challenge the world around him: 'We talked about stuff that no one else would. Richard talked about Africa, and places no one knew about: Libya, the Congo – no-go areas. He wanted to know why governments do what they do. We talked about the

Iran–Iraq war. He was particularly taken by the time a million Iranian women and kids went into war – it was suicide basically – armed with nothing. He asked me, "What must you go through to get there? Where life doesn't matter any more?"'[32]

Similarly, former schoolfriends of Germaine Lindsay recalled that, after he converted to Islam at the age of 15, he suddenly became extremely thoughtful and serious about world affairs, religion and politics, and he began to hand out leaflets in support of *al Qaeda*.[33]

Several other members of the dataset discovered militant Islam as teenagers, after being brought up with secular, Western lifestyles.[34] Omar Sharif, for instance, quickly became devout after attending meetings of the radical Islamist group *Hizb ut-Tahrir* while he was a student at King's College in London (this group will be discussed in more detail in Chapter 5).[35] Zaheer Khan, who was a friend of Sharif's at King's, says Sharif was 'like an empty bowl' when he first arrived at King's in 1994. He recalled that 'Omar didn't know much about the culture of his own family, his background … He didn't have a clue about Islam. He knew how to pray and this and that, but an in-depth understanding was not there at all.' Sharif was impressed and excited by the diversity he found among the young Muslims at the university, and, about three months into his course, he began attending meetings organised by *Hizb ut-Tahrir*. Zaheer Khan observed, 'Stick in a few out-of-context verses from the *Qur'an* and from the *Hadith* to back themselves up, and people with that vulnerability will buy in … Omar Sharif was that type.'[36]

When he was growing up, Omar Sheikh was not noted by his friends as being particularly religious, but, after watching a film about the war in Bosnia at the London School of Economics, he started to become religious and began to quote the *Qur'an*.[37] There is no evidence that he had become an Islamist at that time, but after going to Bosnia in 1993 he seems to have embraced an Islamist ideology. In 1994, he told a journalist that he had spent two years taking part in *jihad* in Bosnia,[38] and, after being sentenced to death for his part in the murder of journalist Daniel Pearl in 2002, he declared that his trial was a waste of time in a 'decisive war between Islam and infidels'.[39] Indian investigators reported that 'he is the kind of person who came across with very strong views, a very strong commitment to using Islam for political purposes'.[40]

The majority of the dataset, however, seem to have grown up in traditional, religious families, and then turned away from Islam during their teenage years to live more secular lifestyles, before rediscovering Islam. For instance, in a media interview, Abu Hamza confirmed that some members of the Yemen 8 cell had only recently returned to Islam prior to their mission in Yemen.[41] It therefore seems that it was during this process of rediscovering Islam that they became radicalised with a militant ideology. The extent to which members of the dataset integrated into wider, secular society will be explored in more detail in subsequent chapters.

But, while a significant number of the dataset had limited religious knowledge and displayed little religious observance in their earlier lives, a small number had always been devout and had been well schooled in mainstream, non-radical mosques. As discussed in Chapter 1, Badat fits into this category, as does Tanweer, who had been serious about religion from an early age. Tanweer is said to have become even more religiously observant after dropping out of university. He appeared to devote the majority of his time to religious study and observance, including at a religious school in Dewsbury, although those around him saw no signs that his strict religious observance had turned to extremism.[42] Asif Hanif was also very religious, having been brought up in a *Sufi* tradition. He was an active member of the Light Study, an international *Sufi* group whose apolitical non-violent philosophy is directly opposed to that of *al Qaeda*, and whose British base is at Hounslow mosque. The Hanifs' house was often used to hold gatherings of the group because of its close proximity to the mosque.[43]

Finally, a small number of the dataset do not appear to have been overtly religious. A high-level Yemeni source suggested that, among the Yemen 8 cell, Ghalain and Harhara were not Islamic fundamentalists, and that Ghalain was not even a Muslim. Prison guards were surprised that the two were not practising Muslims. During interrogation, Ghalain, who dyed his hair red, stated that he had no religion, but shortly afterwards changed his mind and claimed to be a Muslim. He did not know how many times a day a Muslim is supposed to pray and showed no interest in which wall of his cell faced Mecca. In addition, both he and Harhara requested food during daytime at the height of Ramadan, when Muslims are supposed to fast. Abu Hamza confirmed that his stepson Ghalain was not a devout Muslim: 'When he was here he was not even wearing the proper Islamic dress ... I wanted him to learn the *Qur'an* but he chose to learn about electronics instead. He's not a bad boy but I wanted him to be a cleric like me.' Hamza continued, 'I would have loved him if he had made a stand like Abu al-Hassan [the leader of the Islamic Army of Aden] because his people are religiously motivated. They stand firm even if they get killed. This is why I don't even bother to defend my stepson.'

Friends who knew Harhara at Westminster University remember him as a formidable drinker.[44]

Ghalain's and Harhara's actions may just have been a charade to try to prove that they were not Islamists, and therefore not part of an Islamist plot. However, it is entirely possible that some of the dataset were secular terrorists working with Islamists. For Khyam, Garcia and Amin, their initial interest in the cause of Kashmir might well have been political in nature, simply to liberate Kashmir from Indian rule and possibly to integrate it with Pakistan.

A review of the individuals in the dataset suggests that British Muslims with a limited knowledge of Islam may be more vulnerable to radicalisation and becoming violent extremists than those who are more educated in Islam. However, it also indicates that even individuals who have been well schooled in Islam by mainstream Imams are still capable of being indoctrinated with violent ideologies. It also shows that increased religious observance has been a feature

36

of the radicalisation of the majority of these individuals and, as we shall discuss later, in their motivations to commit violent acts. However, it is not strict adherence to traditional Islamic teachings *per se* which is problematic; it is increased religious observance driven by a belief in a violent politico-religious ideology which is the key, and it is important that we do not fall into the trap of equating increased religious observance with an increased risk of becoming a violent extremist. This is a classic example of stereotyping and confirmation bias. The key to understanding the motivations of the dataset is their politico-religious ideology. A lack of knowledge about Islam may have made some of the dataset more vulnerable to the ideas presented to them by the militant groups, which was confirmed by Omar Nasiri, an informant for the security services, who noted that Abu Hamza's militant followers at Finsbury Park mosque were 'younger, less settled in their lives, ignorant. Nobody truly educated in Islam would have listened to Hamza. He knew nothing at all.'[45]

THE IDEOLOGICAL CONFLICT WITHIN ISLAM

The tensions between the different generations that have been outlined above are exacerbated by a battle for supremacy between four broad schools in contemporary Islam, Traditionalism, Fundamentalism, Modernism and Islamism, which has been playing out across the Muslim world for decades.[46] The ideology of violent extremism does not exist in a vacuum, but sits alongside the mainstream political, cultural and religious discourse between these four broad schools. The extent to which violent militant ideologies converge and diverge with elements of this mainstream discourse on a range of issues helps to explain why they have appeal to some people.

The Traditionalists and Fundamentalists both lean towards scriptural literalism. The main difference between the two groups is how they regard the 1,400 years of theological innovation since the death of the Prophet Mohammed. Traditionalists draw upon centuries of scholarly argument, evolution in *Sha'ria* law and changes in accepted Islamic practice. In contrast, Fundamentalist movements, of which the Saudi-backed *Wahhabis* and *Deobandis* are the most important in the UK, reject all theological innovation since the life of Mohammed and his closest companions, arguing that Muslims should only pay attention to the *Qur'an* and the *Hadith* (the collected deeds and sayings of the Prophet Mohammed). For example, the *Deobandi* seminary in the town of Bury outlaws art, television, music and chess, demands that women should cover up in public, and views football as 'a cancer that has infected our youth'.[47]

There are a number of Fundamentalist organisations operating in the UK. For example, the *Ahle Hadith* is a *Wahhabi* organisation which runs a number of extremist camps and *madrassas* in Pakistan and Kashmir. It runs four dozen centres in England and a similar number of *madrassas*. Its website tells Muslims that their fellow citizens are *kuffar* [unbelievers] and warns them to 'be different from the Jews and Christians. Their ways are based on sick or deviant views concerning their societies.'[48] Other organisations which promote a Fundamentalist view of Islam include the *al Muntada al Islami*, a Saudi-funded and -run foundation in London, promoting *Wahhabism* in Africa, and *al Sunnah*, which is based at the Birmingham Centre for Islamic Studies.[49]

The third and smallest group are the theological modernisers who argue that Muslims should look beyond the literalism of the *Qur'an* and seek out the meaning behind the words. For this group, what counts in the modern world are not the actions of Mohammed in seventh-century Arabia, but the principles that inspired them. Most liberal Muslims belong to this group, but they are a small minority within Muslim societies.[50]

The fourth school, Islamism, is a relatively recent offshoot of Fundamentalism, and is the term given to an extreme form of politicised Islam. It emerged in response to the fall of the Ottoman Empire after the First World War, but harks back 1400 years to the early days of the Islamic *caliphate*, a super-state which governed the Muslim world according to *Sha'ria* law. Islamism sees Islam not just as a religion, but as a political, social and economic system for governing the world, and a total way of life for the individual.[51] Its adherents pick and choose teachings from across the ages, and, while they read script literally and share the same religious ideas as Fundamentalists, they are more akin to an ideological movement than a religious one.[52] Islamism originates from a number of organisations which all believe that Islam is in a state of war with both the West and insufficiently pious Muslims around the world.

The first of these groups is the *Tablighi Jamaat* which is part of the *Deobandi* tradition, which believes that Muslims must return to the basics of Islam, establish the *ummah* and separate themselves from non-Muslims. It also emphasises that Muslims are obliged to live as responsible citizens in the countries in which they live.[53] Despite the group describing itself as being non-violent and apolitical, the FBI has alleged that it is a major recruiter for violent *jihad* across the globe: '*Tablighi Jamaat* has always adopted an extreme interpretation of Islam, but in the last two decades it has radicalised to the point where it is now a driving force of Islamic extremism.'[54] The French intelligence services call it the 'antechamber of fundamentalism', and claim that 80 per cent of all Islamists in France are members.[55] There is even concern about *Tablighi Jamaat* within the Muslim population. Dr Irfan al-Alawi, European director of the Centre for Islamic Pluralism, has expressed grave concerns about the spread of the group because he sees it as a separatist organisation.[56] *Tablighi Jamaat* has a presence in London and a number of cities in the North of England and Scotland. It has expressed no political ambitions *per se*, but its goal is to win over the whole of Britain to Islam.[57]

Among the dataset, Reid as well as members of the 7/7, 21/7 and Airline cells have all been linked to *Tablighi Jamaat*.[58] However, there is no indication that any of them were actually members of the group at the time when they were engaged in terrorist activities. Instead, their involvement with *Tablighi* might well have been a stepping stone to involvement with a more militant Islamist group.

The second group is the Muslim Brotherhood, a *Salafi* organisation that was founded in Egypt in 1928. The Brotherhood's stated goal is to instil the *Qur'an* and the *Sunnah* (the religious actions that were instituted by the Prophet Mohammed) as the 'sole reference point for … ordering the life of the Muslim family, individual, community … and state'. The Brotherhood officially opposes the use of violence, but with some notable exceptions, such as in the Israeli–Palestinian conflict or efforts to overthrow the secular *Ba'athist* regime in Syria. However, this official position has been questioned, and members of the Brotherhood have been involved in political violence.[59] The Muslim Brotherhood operates in the UK through a series of interlocking organisations, including the Muslim Association of Britain, the Muslim Welfare Trust, Interpal, the Palestinian Reform Centre, the Institute of Islamic Political Thought, Mashreq Media Services and the Centre for International Policy Studies, among others.[60]

The third group is the *Jamaat-e-Islami*, which was founded in India and Pakistan. It has similar ideas to the Muslim Brotherhood, in wanting to spread the governance of *Sha'ria* law to both Muslims and non-Muslims,[61] but is primarily focused on South Asia. Unlike some more radical Islamist groups, *Jamaat-e-Islami* advocates gradual change through the takeover of parliament, the military and the various arms of the modern state. Ed Husain, a former member of *Jamaat-e-Islami* and *Hizb ut-Tahrir*, describes his early adherence to the *Jamaat-e-Islami* ideology as emotional Islamism, because the group lacked a practical programme to achieve political change.[62] The main centre for *Jamaat-e-Islami* in the UK is the Islamic Foundation in Leicester, but it also has a strong presence in the East End of London.[63]

Despite the consistencies in the ideologies and objectives of these Islamist groups, they are not a homogeneous movement, and relations between them have at times been marked by fierce competition for ideological supremacy and recruits; for instance, there has been strong competition between *Jamaat-e-Islami*, *Tablighi Jamaat* and the radical group *Hizb ut-Tahrir* in East London.

A major factor in the growing popularity of Fundamentalism and

Islamism in the UK is that Traditionalist mosques tend to recruit Imams from their home countries, deliver their sermons in Urdu and other Asian languages and do not publish material to engage their English-speaking congregations.[64] Research conducted in 2007 showed that only eight per cent of Imams preaching in British mosques were born in the UK, and almost 45 per cent had been in the UK for less than five years. Only six per cent of Imams in Britain spoke English as a first language, and 52 per cent gave sermons in Urdu. In general, they are a deeply conservative body of individuals who are typically qualified in the traditional Islamic curriculum, which has changed little since medieval times.[65] Yet even Imams who are born in the UK and can relate to the problems of young Muslims living in Britain cannot necessarily prevent individuals becoming Islamists. The Imam of Brixton mosque, Abdul Haqq Baker, is British-born, yet Richard Reid still drifted away from that mosque to join *al Qaeda*.

In contrast, *Wahhabis* and Islamists give their sermons in English and take their recruitment on to the streets. Most importantly, they have encouraged the training of British-born Imams. In 2007, 17 of Britain's 26 Islamic seminaries were run by *Deobandis* and they produced 80 per cent of British-trained Imams.[66] The *Wahhabis* and Islamists have also learned to exploit the potential of the internet and have generally come to understand what makes second-generation British Muslims tick. They win new members by contrasting their galvanising message of world Islamic justice with the inactivity of the first-generation Traditionalists, who are struggling to come to terms with the realities of life in modern, secular, urban Britain. They also argue that the saint worship, mysticism and arranged marriages of the Traditionalists are evidence of corruption by weakness and Hinduism.[67] Crucially, their messages are clear and straightforward, and delivered in a fashion which connects with young British Muslims, in contrast to the more intellectual and complicated nature of preaching in Traditionalist mosques.

Their other advantage is that they are centrally funded. It is estimated that, over the last two decades, Saudi Arabia invested $2–3 billion per year in promoting *Wahhabism* in other countries. It is not known how much of that money has come to *Wahhabi* groups in Britain. Islamist groups like the Muslim Brotherhood and *Hizb ut-Tahrir* are also centrally funded; they gather money from members and pass it to a central administration which then hands it back out again. These groups' lack of local community focus means that they have to compete harder for recruits, which has made them hungrier and more efficient.[68]

The Fundamentalists and Islamists identified a constituency in disaffected young British Muslims who they called 'orphans of Islam', and set about winning them over.[69] Evidence of the spread of Fundamentalism and Islamism can be found in a study published in January 2007, which found evidence of young Muslims between the ages of 16 and 24 adopting more Fundamentalist beliefs on key social and political issues than their parents or grandparents. 40 per cent of those questioned in that age group said they would prefer to live under *Sha'ria* law in Britain, compared to 17 per cent of over-55s. One in eight of that age group said they admired groups such as *al Qaeda* that were prepared to fight the West, and 36 per cent said they believed that a Muslim who converts to another religion should be punished by death, compared to 19 per cent of the over-55s. Three out of four of that age group preferred Muslim women to choose to wear the veil or *hijab*, compared to only a quarter of over-55s.[70] Many of the dataset fall within this 16- to 24-year-old age group.

MUSLIM SEPARATISM

There is an influential strand of thought within the mainstream discourse in the British Muslim population which rejects Western culture and society, which are perceived to be corrupt and immoral, and encourages segregation and separation in order to maintain the purity of Islam. This was neatly summed up by the leading British *Deobandi* Imam, Riyadh al Huq, who reminded his congregation:

'Allah has warned us in the *Qur'an*, do not befriend the *kuffar*, do not align yourselves with the *kuffar*.'[71] He went on to preach:

> In one verse Allah says: 'Oh believers, do not take the *Yahoud* and the *Nasara*, the Jews and the Christians, as *awliya*.' Now the word *awliya* is the plural of *wali*. The word *wali* means many different things. It means friend, it means guardian, it means protector, it means master, it means ally and many other things. So when Allah says do not take the *Yahoud* and *Nasara* as *awliya*, it doesn't just mean do not take them as friends. Do not take them as your guardians, your protectors, your allies, your friends, your masters. In no way should there be this alliance with the *kuffar*. Allah says they are allies, they are the *awliya*, of one another. And whoever makes them a friend, then that person is of them. Allah does not guide those who are sinful.[72]

While some *Deobandi* preachers have a more cohesive approach to interfaith relations than Riyadh al Huq, Islamic theologians suggest that they do not represent mainstream *Deobandi* thinking in the UK.[73] Similar views have been articulated by a number of other mainstream Muslim religious and political leaders. Zubair Dudha, an Imam from Dewsbury, has previously told parents that allowing their children to mix with non-Muslims is an evil that is 'bringing ruin to the holy moral fabric of Muslim society'.[74] Dr Taj Hargey, Chairman of the Muslim Education Centre in Oxford, has confirmed that: 'We see it from the time you're a child, you're given this idea that those people they are *kuffar*, they're unbelievers. They are not equal to you, they are different to you. You are superior to them because you have the truth, they don't have the truth. You will go to heaven, they will go to hell.'[75]

These separatist elements are reflected in public demands for official recognition of Islamic family law and the creation of a parallel Islamic legal system. An opinion poll of Muslims in July 2005 showed that 14 per cent of respondents either fairly or strongly agreed that Islam is incompatible with Western democracy.[76] Another poll, in

February 2006, found that 40 per cent of respondents supported the introduction of *Sha'ria* law in those areas of Britain which are predominantly Muslim. This constitutes a significant minority, but when set against the 41 per cent of respondents who opposed the notion it also indicates deep fissures within the opinions of the Muslim population.[77]

Yet these separatist elements co-exist with strong integrationist elements within this mainstream discourse. During the 2004 elections, militant Muslim political groups threatened Muslim candidates and voters across the country, claiming that democracy is against Islam. In response, mosques in Luton made announcements encouraging people to vote. Zafar Khan, a prominent local Muslim and chairman of the Luton Council of Faiths, declared that it was a sacred duty to choose a representative to serve the community: 'As a minority community Muslims need to play a constructive part in the wider community and one way of doing that is to take part in politics and in all spheres of public life ... To do otherwise is to the detriment of the Muslim community.'[78] However, the concern is that, as Fundamentalists and Islamists become more influential within Britain, these voices will become less powerful.

ATTITUDES TOWARDS VIOLENT *JIHAD*

Among Muslims, there are different perceptions of the concept of *jihad*. These stem from the *Qur'an* itself, in which the concept of *jihad* develops over time in a divergent and apparently contradictory fashion. These ambiguities have led Muslim scholars to stress either the peaceful or the violent nature of *jihad* depending upon their own understanding of the sacred texts, as well as on the historical and political contexts in which they wish to apply the concept. These differences, rooted in Islamic history, reflect the diversity of Islamic thought. Some Muslim scholars, including those from the *Sufi* tradition, emphasise the concept of higher *jihad*, the spiritual struggle for purification against one's baser instinct, for moral self-improvement, while, for contemporary militant Islamists, violent *jihad* is a means of challenging oppression and establishing the rule of Islam, believing it to be a struggle to help the oppressed against atrocities perpetrated by aggressors.[79]

At various points in the *Qur'an*, Muslims are commanded to fight in self-defence and, in certain circumstances, to fight unbelievers. Militant Islamist ideologues typically cite the 'sword verses' in the *Qur'an* to justify attacks against non-Muslims. One verse states, 'When the sacred months have passed, slay the idolaters wherever you find them, and take them and confine them, and lie in wait for them at every place of worship.'[80] Islamist teachings also declare that 'those who adamantly refuse to convert to Islam are, to all intents and purposes, enemies of Allah Himself'.[81] However, other verses of the *Qur'an* state that women and children should not be killed.

Views on violent *jihad* in the mainstream discourse of British Muslims are heavily influenced by Islamic views of justice and self-defence. In a speech entitled 'On our responsibilities as Muslims', which he delivered in May 2006, Riyadh al Huq reminded his audience of the religious obligation imposed upon Muslims to assist Allah, to assist Allah's religion and to assist fellow Muslims, and their duty to establish and maintain justice and to stand up in defence of the truth.[82] This is reflected in the attitudes of many British Muslims, who view the conflicts in the occupied Palestinian territories, Chechnya, Iraq and Afghanistan as wars of national liberation, and define the fighters in these conflicts as freedom fighters. The prevalence of such views has been reflected in comments made by young Muslims to the media. In responding to questions about Omar Sharif and Asif Hanif's suicide-bomb attack in Israel, one young man from Derby argued that 'killing people is wrong, obviously, but if he was doing it for God himself – then fair enough',[83] while another teenager declared that his parents would be proud of him if he were to blow himself up for the Palestinian cause.[84]

In articles in the *Muslim Weekly*, Palestinian groups fighting against Israel have been referred to as 'resistance fighters'. A joint statement by groups including the Association of Muslim Lawyers, the Islamic Human Rights Commission, the Muslim Association of Britain and *Q-Magazine* (a popular Muslim magazine) stated that 'the Muslim Community in Britain has unequivocally denounced acts of terrorism. However, the right of people anywhere in the world to resist invasion and occupation is legitimate.'[85] Similarly, the Muslim Council of Britain has previously refused to denounce suicide bombings.[86] Sir Iqbal Sacranie, the former Secretary General of the council, declared of suicide bombers that 'those who fight oppression, those who fight occupation, cannot be termed as terrorist, they are freedom fighters'.[87] These views reflect the dichotomy at the heart of all debates about terrorism – the absence of a universally agreed definition, which enables different people and communities to apply the label according to their own value systems and political interests.

Al Sunnah, the *Wahhabi* organisation based at the Birmingham Centre for Islamic Studies, maintains a low profile in Britain but is known for its hardcore stance over the occupation of Palestine and the involvement of Western governments in the support of Israel. It has published leaflets urging Muslims to become suicide bombers which have been found in the occupied Palestinian territories. It publishes books, leaflets and a monthly magazine that is distributed across the Muslim world, including the Palestinian territories. One leaflet published just before the war in Iraq stated: 'when this sudden explosion of American-Zionist violence is aiming to eradicate a nation's existence, eliminating its vitality and sites of resistance, the only way to protect this nation is through acts of martyrdom.'[88] This clearly urges Muslims to become martyrs.

These views are also given legitimacy by the pronouncements of some mainstream Imams. Sheikh Taher, the Imam of the Leeds Grand Mosque, condemned the 7 July bombings, declaring that 'such acts have no place in Islam',[89] yet he does not condemn the use of violence *per se*. In a sermon in March 2004, he declared that the taking of life was justified if it was done for preserving the *deen* [the laws of Islam]: 'If the forces of evil stop and intervene between the people and them entering this *deen* as Allah, exalted is He, loves for them, it is legislated for them to sacrifice themselves for the sake of this *deen* and for the sake of making the *da'wah* of Islam reach every heart ... The preservation of the *deen* comes before the preservation of life.' He went on to justify the killing of Israelis because of the killing of the *Hamas* spiritual leader Sheikh Yassin by the Israeli army.[90]

Similarly, in a speech entitled 'The globalised suffering of the Muslims', the leading *Deobandi* Imam, Riyadh al Huq, argued that:

And no one dare utter the J word. The J word has become taboo. The J word can never be mentioned and if someone mentions it even Muslims look at one another. So much is happening and yet we are expected to remain silent. The J word is *jihad* in the way of Allah. When the Chechnyans rise, when the Palestinian Muslims rise, when the Kashmiri Muslims rise, when any Muslim force rises against the oppressors they are branded extremists, fanatics. Not only is their blood made *halal* [permitted], but anyone who is affiliated to them in any way, his blood is made *halal*, the honour and dignity of their women folk is snatched from them. Allah says: 'and why should you not fight in the way of Allah and in defence of those poor, weak and oppressed men, women and children who are calling out and pleading to Allah "Oh Allah, remove us from this city whose inhabitants and occupants are so tyrannical against us and so oppressive against us. And oh Allah, grant us a guardian from unto yourself and raise from amongst us one who will assist us."' Allah says: 'those who believe, fight in the way of Allah and those who disbelieve, fight in the way of evil.' Fight the friends of *Shaitan* [the devil]. I'm not suggesting that we should rise here. I'm sure we are all sensible and intelligent enough to know that. I speak of those Muslims who are in the situation that Allah has described in these verses of the *Qur'an*, yet when they rise they

47

are branded terrorists, extremists, fanatics. Everything is legitimised against them and we cannot even as much as speak in their favour.[91]

However, there are also powerful voices among community leaders which oppose participation in violent *jihad* abroad. The news that three Muslims from Luton had been killed in Afghanistan in 2001 provoked a backlash against extremist elements among the Muslim population of Luton.[92] Local leaders pledged to drive Taliban supporters from the streets and supporters of the radical Islamist group *al Muhajiroun* were banned from all Islamic buildings in the town. The fury of Luton's Muslim leaders was underlined by another community leader who declared: '*al Muhajiroun* have been warned in no uncertain terms that their activities will no longer be tolerated in Luton ... Muslims are sick and tired of their provocative remarks, if we see *al Muhajiroun* on the streets spreading their poison, we will drive them off the streets.'[93] Councillor Mohammed Bashir said, 'They are so stupid attempting to poison the minds of our young men. We don't allow them at the central mosque and we don't want them trying to mobilise anything. Most people completely disapprove of them and we want them out of our area, their views are stupid and they're living in a foolish world.'[94] However, these comments could also reflect broader generational divisions within the Muslim population, with community leaders tending to be more moderate, and extremist views being more prevalent among young people.

There is some evidence that mainstream views supporting violent *jihad* overseas influenced some members of the dataset prior to their indoctrination with a violent Islamist ideology. Omar Khyam claimed that all of his family, with the exception of his mother, were pleased that he had gone to Kashmir to fight,[95] while Junade Feroze of the Gas Limos cell first met Dhiren Barot through his family's involvement in the cause of Kashmir. Feroze's defence counsel noted that: 'The struggle of the people for independence in Kashmir was the backdrop for his involvement in this conspiracy. It was through that he came to meet Barot. Barot expressed a commitment to the Kashmir issue. He claimed he had interests in the funding of the struggle in Kashmir.'[96]

This illustrates how the concept of violent *jihad* is firmly rooted within mainstream discourse in the Muslim population of the UK. It is reflected in general attitudes towards the use of violence for political and social ends. Opinion polls suggest that a significant minority of Muslims in the UK support the use of political and religious violence. One poll in November 2004 found that 11 per cent of respondents felt that it was acceptable for religious or political groups to use violence for political ends,[97] although in the immediate aftermath of the 7 July bombings this figure dropped to four per cent.[98] While this is a small percentage, four per cent of the UK Muslim population equates to approximately 64,000 people. Although this indicates that there is at least rhetorical support for political violence within a significant minority of the Muslim population, what cannot be gauged from opinion polls is the correlation between rhetorical support for violence and an actual willingness to engage in acts of violence, as well as the age distribution of those that support its use. These views are so significant because they link mainstream discourse in the Muslim population with the ideology of radical Islamist groups, and the concept of *jihad* has been co-opted by terrorist networks in their ideological rationale for terror attacks in the UK.

ATTITUDES TOWARDS TERRORISM

There has been strong condemnation of the 7 July bombings and terrorism in general from spokespeople within the Muslim population, such as the British Muslim Forum, which issued a *fatwa* against terrorism:

Islam strictly, strongly and severely condemns the use of violence and the destruction of innocent lives. There is neither place nor justification in Islam for extremism, fanaticism, or terrorism.

Suicide bombings, which killed and injured innocent people in London, are *haram* – vehemently prohibited in Islam – and those who committed these barbaric acts in London are criminals not martyrs. Such acts, as perpetrated in London, are crimes against all of humanity and contrary to the teachings of Islam.[99]

In April 2004, the Muslim Council of Britain wrote to the Imams of all mosques in the UK, urging them to appeal to worshippers at Friday prayers to co-operate with the police in the fight against terrorism. Secretary General Sir Iqbal Sacranie said, 'We are facing a major crisis in the country and world over. We have to exercise our duty, an Islamic duty, which is to convey the message to the community that they have responsibilities as well.'[100]

It also printed booklets which reminded Muslims of their obligation to help safeguard Britain's security.

Opinion polls indicate a slight difference in attitudes towards terrorism, as opposed to other forms of violence, which some Muslims consider to be justified on religious or political grounds. In February 2006, 14 per cent felt it was right to attack Danish embassies in Muslim countries in response to the global controversy over the publication of cartoons of the Prophet Mohammed, 12 per cent felt it was right for Muslim demonstrators to carry placards calling for the killing of those who insult Islam, and 13 per cent felt that it was right to exercise violence against those who are deemed by religious leaders to have insulted them. Yet only four per cent felt that it was right for *al Qaeda* and those affiliated with it to attack Western targets. This number fell to one per cent in respect of the attacks on 7 and 21 July 2005.[101] But the picture is further complicated by the findings of a poll in March 2004, which showed that 13 per cent of respondents believed that further attacks on the US were justified. In an ICM poll for the *Sunday Telegraph* in February 2006, seven per cent agreed that Western society is decadent and immoral and Muslims should seek to bring it to an end, if necessary by violence.[102]

Public reactions to the 7 July bombings were mixed. In the immediate aftermath of the bombings, a poll found that five per cent of respondents felt that further attacks by suicide bombers in the UK were justified.[103] Another poll, in February 2006, indicated that eight per cent felt sympathy with the feelings and motives of those who carried out the 7 July attacks,[104] but this contrasts markedly with a poll for Channel 4 television in 2006, which showed that nearly a quarter of respondents thought that the 7 July bombings were justified because of Britain's foreign policy, and almost one in five respected Osama bin Laden to some extent.[105] These polls indicate that there is very little support for terrorism within the Muslim population, but they also suggest that there could be a significant minority which is potentially capable of being recruited into terrorist cells.

FORGING A NEW SOCIAL IDENTITY

Family and generational conflict are characteristic of the search for a social identity that all of us go through during our lives, and this is no different for second- and third-generation British Muslims. Disconnected from the beliefs and culture of their parents' generation, many young Muslims have sought out new social identities that they feel can reconcile their faith and Islamic identity with life in a secular, multicultural, Western democracy. However, these alternative social identities are not necessarily violent in nature; some are non-extremist, non-violent and perhaps even non-religious. Maajid Nawaz, a former member of the extremist group *Hizb ut-Tahrir*, for instance, initially immersed himself in a counter-culture based on American rap music before gravitating towards *Hizb ut-Tahrir*,[106] while others have formed street gangs and engaged in criminality. For others, however, their reaction has been to look for an alternative brand of Islam to the one their parents taught them, and embrace a more prominent form of Islamic social identity.

The more strident and confrontational attitude of the Fundamentalists and Islamists is perceived by some young Muslims to be better suited to dealing with the situations which they encounter in their everyday lives and to offering solutions to them. Islamism offers the young a political alternative to the *biradri* system, which empowers them and challenges some of the most traditional elements of Asian culture; for instance, it encourages the active participation of women, rejects arranged marriages and opposes honour killings. Neither fully Western nor Eastern, this discourse of Islamist identity is supra-cultural and identifies with an idealised global *ummah*.[107] It is also highly confrontational. Abdul Haqq Baker commented that 'there are hundreds of disaffected young Muslims tired of their parents' understanding of Islam and how it is taught in the mosques ... They like the fiery rhetoric of *jihad*; they like to hear they are living among the infidel.'[108] This new identity is not one of integration, but one that rejects the modern secular world of UK society.

Embracing Fundamentalism or Islamism is not necessarily problematic *per se*, but Ed Husain, a former member of *Hizb ut-Tahrir*, argues that the path to becoming a terrorist begins with a less extreme shade of Islamism or *Wahhabism*.[109] Evidence to support this contention can be found in the case of Mohammed Siddique Khan.

In the mid-1990s, Khan fell under the influence of *Wahhabi* preachers at local mosques in Beeston, having found that his local traditional, community-run mosque had nothing to offer him. The people who ran the mosque had no idea how to connect with the second generation; they spoke and wrote in Urdu, and the only time they interacted with the younger Muslims was when they taught them to recite the *Qur'an* by rote in Arabic. The *Wahhabis* did things differently; they delivered sermons and printed publications in English. Khan's Urdu was poor, so the only available literature on Islam he could read were *Wahhabi*-approved publications. His progression to *Wahhabism* was reinforced by the fact that some of his friends were converting too.[110]

In 1999, his family persuaded him to see their *pir*, in an attempt to get him to conform to their beliefs and marry his cousin, but Khan told the *pir* that his views on Islam had changed and he wanted to travel to Afghanistan to train for *jihad*.[111] Over the following years, his life became focused on the mosques where he prayed, the buildings where he helped run Muslim youth groups, his youth-work supervisor's office and the Iqra bookshop where he gave talks. All of these venues were located within a quarter of a mile of the centre of Beeston Hill's Pakistani community.[112]

The influence that Fundamentalist teachings had on Khan is evident in the second part of his 'martyrdom' video, which comprised three-quarters of his message and is addressed to British Muslims:

> our so-called scholars today are content with their Toyotas and semi-detached houses. They seem to think that their responsibilities lie in pleasing the *kuffar* instead of Allah. So they tell us ludicrous things, like you must obey the law of the land. Praise be God! How did we ever conquer lands in the past if we were to obey this law ? ... By Allah these scholars will be brought to account, and if they fear the British government more than they fear Allah then they must desist in giving talks, lectures and passing *fatwas*, and they need to sit at home and leave the job to the real men, the true inheritors of the prophets.[113]

Similarly, his last will and testament focuses on the importance of *jihad* and martyrdom as supreme evidence of religious commitment, as well as containing anti-Semitic comments.[114]

This is the context within which the members of our dataset lived, and within which radical political groups and terrorist cells operate. While the elements of this mainstream discourse, which might be defined by outsiders as militant or radical, do not necessarily have widespread support, they are still nevertheless part of the discourse. As a consequence, there are a number of critical issues on which the ideology of militant and radical groups intersects with elements of the mainstream discourse in the Muslim population. As we shall see in later chapters, this is exploited by Islamist ideologues and recruiters.

This analysis also indicates that there is no simple profile of British Islamist terrorists; while some social characteristics might be shared by the majority of the dataset, individuals with a wide range of social characteristics can become involved in terrorism. Alienation from family and community can create individuals who are vulnerable to radicalisation, but those who have not experienced such estrangement may also be susceptible. It also suggests that a belief in Islamism or Fundamentalism can be one end of a spectrum of faith, the other end of which is ideologically driven terrorist violence. Yet not everyone who embraces Fundamentalism or Islamism becomes a terrorist, and the majority live peacefully within the UK. The following chapters look at how and why individuals make the transition to being prepared to use terrorist violence for ideological ends.

Notes and references

[1] Riek BM, Mania EW & Gaertner SL, 'Intergroup threat and outgroup attitudes: A meta-analytic review', *Personality and Social Psychology Review*, No. 10, 2006, pp 336–53.

[2] Riek BM, Mania EW & Gaertner SL, 'Intergroup threat and outgroup attitudes: A meta-analytic review', *Personality and Social Psychology Review*, No. 10, 2006, pp 336–53.

[3] Stephan WG & Stephan CW, 'Predicting prejudice', *International Journal of Intercultural Relations*, No. 20, 1996, pp 409–26; Stephan WG & Stephan CW, 'An integrated threat theory of prejudice', in Oskamp S (ed), *Reducing Prejudice and Discrimination* (The Claremont Symposium on Applied Social Psychology) (New Jersey: Lawrence Erlbaum Associates, 2000).

[4] Commission for Racial Equality, Briefing on Islamophobia.

[5] 'Yemen: The British link', *Observer*, 19 January 1999, www.al-bab.com.

[6] Ansari H, *The Infidel Within* (London: C. Hurst & Co, 2004), p 343.

[7] Ansari H, *The Infidel Within* (London: C. Hurst & Co, 2004), p 346.

[8] 'Orphans of Islam, The history of Britain's Mirpur population may help to explain why some became suicide bombers', *Guardian*, 18 July 2005, http://www.guardian.co.uk/attackonlondon/comment/story/0,,1530640,00.html.

9 'Orphans of Islam, The history of Britain's Mirpur population may help to explain why some became suicide bombers', *Guardian*, 18 July 2005, http://www.guardian.co.uk/attackonlondon/comment/story/0,,1530640,00.html.

10 Maher S, 'Campus radicals', *Prospect*, September 2006, http://www.prospect-magazine.co.uk/article_details.php?id=7742.

11 Malik S, 'A community in denial', *New Statesman*, 25 July 2005.

12 'Hardline takeover of British mosques', *The Times*, 7 September 2007, http://www.timesonline.co.uk/tol/comment/faith/article2402973.ece.

13 'Terror accused "ran away" to join jihad', *The Times*, 14 September 2006, http://www.timesonline.co.uk/article/0,,2-2357829.html.

14 '"A kind, really nice boy", What drives Western Muslim adolescents into the arms of fundamentalism and deliberate death?', *Observer*, 4 May 2003, http://observer.guardian.co.uk/comment/story/0,,949024,00.html.

15 'British-born Muslim admits plot to blow up airliner', *Independent*, 1 March 2005.

16 Report of the Official Account of the Bombings in London on 7 July 2005, HC1087 (London: The Stationery Office), 11 May 2006.

17 'Muktar Said Ibrahim: From robbery and indecent assault to bomb plot leader', *The Times*, 10 July 2007, http://www.timesonline.co.uk/tol/news/uk/crime/article2051428.ece.

18 'Yassin Hassan Omar: Rebellious foster child turned to radicalism', *The Times*, 10 July 2007.

19 Maher S, 'Campus radicals', *Prospect*, September 2006, http://www.prospect-magazine.co.uk/article_details.php?id=7742.

20 'Orphans of Islam, The history of Britain's Mirpur population may help to explain why some became suicide bombers', *Guardian*, 18 July 2005, http://www.guardian.co.uk/attackonlondon/comment/story/0,,1530640,00.html.

21 Taseer A, 'A British jihadist', *Prospect*, August 2005, http://www.prospect-magazine.co.uk/article_details.php?id=6992; Malik S, 'My brother the bomber', *Prospect*, June 2007, http://www.prospect-magazine.co.uk/article_details.php?&id=9635.

22 Taseer A, 'A British jihadist', *Prospect*, August 2005, http://www.prospect-magazine.co.uk/article_details.php?id=6992; Malik S, 'My brother the bomber', *Prospect*, June 2007, http://www.prospect-magazine.co.uk/article_details.php?&id=9635.

[23] Taseer A, 'A British jihadist', *Prospect*, August 2005, http://www.prospect-magazine.co.uk/article_details.php?id=6992; Malik S, 'My brother the bomber', *Prospect*, June 2007, http://www.prospect-magazine.co.uk/article_details.php?&id=9635.

[24] Malik S, 'My brother the bomber', *Prospect*, June 2007, http://www.prospect-magazine.co.uk/article_details.php?&id=9635.

[25] Jawad Akbar, Ghulam Hussein and Shahid Butt are known to have married outside of their traditional communities.

[26] 'Al Qaeda boss visited Blackburn', *Lancashire Evening Telegraph*, 15 June 2007, http://www.lancashireeveningtelegraph.co.uk/display.var.1474143.0.al_qaeda_boss_visited_blackburn.php.

[27] 'At school with the shoe bomber', *Guardian*, 28 February 2002, http://www.guardian.co.uk/g2/story/0,3604,659184,00.html.

[28] 'At school with the shoe bomber', *Guardian*, 28 February 2002, http://www.guardian.co.uk/g2/story/0,3604,659184,00.html.

[29] Alam MY & Husband C, 'British-Pakistani men from Bradford: Linking narratives to policy', Joseph Rowntree Foundation, November 2006, http://www.jrf.org.uk/knowledge/findings/socialpolicy/1960.asp.

[30] 'Attitudes of British Muslims', MORI, 23 July 2005, http://www.ipsos-mori.com/polls/2005/s050722.shtml. (Accessed March 2008.)

[31] 'Moves to marginalise extremists', BBC NewsOnline, 5 April 2007, http://news.bbc.co.uk/1/hi/uk_politics/6528305.stm.

[32] 'At school with the shoe bomber', *Guardian*, 28 February 2002, http://www.guardian.co.uk/g2/story/0,3604,659184,00.html.

[33] 'He was a quiet lad. It's unbelievable', ICHuddersfield, 16 July 2005, http://ichuddersfield.icnetwork.co.uk/0100news/0100localnews/tm_headline=he-was-a-quiet-lad-it-s-unbelievable%26method=full%26objectid=15748856%26page=6%26siteid=50060-name_page.html.

[34] Omar Khyam, Omar Sheikh, Omar Sharif, Salahuddin Amin and Omar Rehman, in particular, all had secular upbringings and only started to become interested in religion when they were teenagers. 'Terror accused "ran away" to join jihad', *The Times*, 14 September 2006, http://www.timesonline.co.uk/article/0,,2-2357829.html; 'The plotters uncovered', *Sun*, 15 June 2007, http://www.thesun.co.uk/article/0,,2-2007270793,00.html. Similarly, Omar Rehman's family was described as being 'culturally rather than religiously' Muslim, and Rehman led a secular existence until his late teens when he became more interested in Islam and, in June 2004, met Dhiren Barot who recruited him into his terrorist cell. Similarly, the young

Salahuddin Amin was not particularly religious; he rarely prayed and his only trips to the mosque were to celebrate festivals. 'Profile: Salahuddin Amin', BBC News Online, 30 April 2007, http://news.bbc.co.uk/1/hi/uk/6149790.stm.

35 'How radical preachers turned a young man into a suicide bomber', *The Times*, 18 November 2006, http://www.timesonline.co.uk/article/0,,2-2458970.html.

36 Malik S, 'Society NS Profile – Omar Sharif', *New Statesman*, 24 April 2006.

37 Lévy B, *Who Killed Daniel Pearl?* (New York: Melville House, 2003), pp 76, 87.

38 'Face to face with Omar Sheikh', BBC NewsOnline, 7 February 2002, http://news.bbc.co.uk/1/hi/world/south_asia/1806001.stm.

39 'Brother says killer is no terrorist', BBC NewsOnline, 16 July 2002, http://news.bbc.co.uk/1/hi/uk/2131286.stm.

40 'Manhunt for public school kidnapper', *Guardian*, 9 February 2002, http://www.guardian.co.uk/pakistan/Story/0,2763,647495,00.html.

41 'Terrorists or tourists', *Guardian*, 26 June 1999, http://www.al-bab.com/yemen/artic/gdn42.htm.

42 Report of the Official Account of the Bombings in London on 7 July 2005, HC1087 (London: The Stationery Office), 11 May 2006.

43 'Making of a martyr: From pacifism to jihad', *Observer*, 4 May 2003, http://www.guardian.co.uk/terrorism/story/0,12780,949104,00.html.

44 'Briton held in Yemen is not Muslim', *Observer*, 31 January 1999, http://www.al-bab.com/yemen/artic/gdn41.htm.

45 'Focus: My life as a spy at the heart of *al-Qaeda*', *Sunday Times*, 19 November 2006.

46 Malik S, 'My brother the bomber', *Prospect*, June 2007, http://www.prospect-magazine.co.uk/article_details.php?&id=9635.

47 'Hardline takeover of British mosques', *The Times*, 7 September 2007, http://www.timesonline.co.uk/tol/comment/faith/article2402973.ece.

48 Phillips M, *Londonistan* (London: Gibson Square Books, 2006), p 41; Alexiev A, 'Violent Islamists in the UK and Europe', *Internationale Politik* (Berlin), September 2005.

49 Phillips M, *Londonistan* (London: Gibson Square Books, 2006), p 42.

[50] Malik S, 'My brother the bomber', *Prospect*, June 2007, http://www.prospect-magazine.co.uk/article_details.php?&id=9635.

[51] Malik S, 'My brother the bomber', *Prospect*, June 2007, http://www.prospect-magazine.co.uk/article_details.php?&id=9635.

[52] Phillips M, *Londonistan* (London: Gibson Square Books, 2006), p 37.

[53] Sikand S, 'The origins and growth of the Tablighi Jamaat in Britain', *Islam and Christian–Muslim Relations* 9:2, 1998, pp 171–92.

[54] Phillips M, *Londonistan* (London: Gibson Square Books, 2006), p 156.

[55] 'Prevention and Suppression of Terrorism', *Hansard*, Column 490, 20 July 2006.

[56] 'Muslims oppose vast mosque plan', *The Times*, 27 November 2006, http://www.timesonline.co.uk/article/0,,2-2473884.html.

[57] Sikand S, 'The origins and growth of the Tablighi Jamaat in Britain', *Islam and Christian–Muslim Relations* 9:2, 1998, pp 171–92.

[58] The other members of the dataset who have been linked to *Tablighi Jamaat* are: Mohammed Siddique Khan, Tanweer, Ibrahim, Asiedu, Ali, Sarwar and Zaman. 'Muslims oppose vast mosque plan', *The Times*, 27 November 2006, http://www.timesonline.co.uk/article/0,,2-2473884.html; 'Airliner bomb trial: Fears raised over fundamentalist Islamic group in Britain', *Daily Telegraph*, 9 September 2008, http://www.telegraph.co.uk/news/majornews/2708409/Airliner-bomb-trial-Fears-raised-over-fundamentalist-Islamic-group-in-Britain.html.

[59] 'Muslim Brotherhood', Wikipedia, http://en.wikipedia.org/wiki/Muslim_Brotherhood.

[60] Phillips M, *Londonistan* (London: Gibson Square Books, 2006), p 41; Whine M, 'The penetration of Islamist ideology in Britain', in *Current Trends in Islamist Ideology*, Hudson Institute, Washington DC, Vol. 1, April 2005.

[61] Phillips M, *Londonistan* (London: Gibson Square Books, 2006), p 37.

[62] Husain E, *The Islamist* (London: Penguin, 2007), pp 51, 91.

[63] Ansari H, *The Infidel Within* (London: C. Hurst & Co, 2004), p 350.

[64] Malik S, 'My brother the bomber', *Prospect*, June 2007, http://www.prospect-magazine.co.uk/article_details.php?&id=9635.

65 'Few UK Imams "come from Britain"', BBC NewsOnline, 6 July 2007, http://news.bbc.co.uk/1/hi/uk/6275574.stm.

66 'Hardline takeover of British mosques', *The Times*, 7 September 2007, http://www.timesonline.co.uk/tol/comment/faith/article2402973.ece.

67 Malik S, 'My brother the bomber', *Prospect*, June 2007, http://www.prospect-magazine.co.uk/article_details.php?&id=9635.

68 Malik S, 'My brother the bomber', *Prospect*, June 2007, http://www.prospect-magazine.co.uk/article_details.php?&id=9635.

69 'Orphans of Islam, The history of Britain's Mirpur population may help to explain why some became suicide bombers', *Guardian*, 18 July 2005, http://www.guardian.co.uk/attackonlondon/comment/story/0,,1530640,00.html.

70 'Young, British Muslims "getting more radical"', *Daily Telegraph*, 29 January 2007, http://www.telegraph.co.uk/news/main.jhtml;jsessionid=tzvh0nw5nia3pqfiqmg sff4avcbqwiv0?xml=/news/2007/01/29/nmuslims29.xml.

71 Riyadh al Huq, 'Speech: Imitating the disbelievers', *The Times*, 6 September 2007, http://www.timesonline.co.uk/tol/comment/faith/article2401603.ece?token=nul l&offset=24.

72 Riyadh al Huq, 'Speech: Imitating the disbelievers', *The Times*, 6 September 2007, http://www.timesonline.co.uk/tol/comment/faith/article2401603.ece?token=nul l&offset=24.

73 'Hardline takeover of British mosques', *The Times*, 7 September 2007, http://www.timesonline.co.uk/tol/comment/faith/article2402973.ece.

74 'How bombers' town is turning into an enclave for Muslims', *The Times*, 21 October 2006, http://www.timesonline.co.uk/article/0,,2-2414708.html.

75 *Panorama*, BBC TV, 21 August 2005.

76 'Attitudes of British Muslims', MORI, 23 July 2005, http://www.ipsos-mori.com/polls/2005/s050722.shtml.

77 'ICM poll for the *Sunday Telegraph*', ICM, February 2006, http://www.icmresearch.co.uk/reviews/2006/Sunday%20Telegraph%20-%20Mulims%20Feb/Sunday%20Telegraph%20Muslims%20feb06.asp.

[78] 'Use your vote, Muslims urged', *Luton Today*, 5 May 2005, http://www.lutontoday.co.uk/ViewArticle2.aspx?SectionID=541&ArticleID=1017 063.

[79] Ansari H, 'Attitudes to Jihad, martyrdom and terrorism among British Muslims', in Abbas H, ed, *Muslim Britain: Communities under Pressure* (London: Zed Books, 2005), pp 146–49.

[80] *Qur'an*, 9:5.

[81] Taheri A, *Holy Terror: The Inside Story of Islamic Terrorism* (London: Hutchinson, 1987), p 191.

[82] Riyadh al Huq, 'Speech: On our responsibilities as Muslims', *The Times*, 6 September 2007, http://www.timesonline.co.uk/tol/comment/faith/article2401708.ece?token=nul l&offset=24.

[83] 'What drove 2 Britons to bomb a club in Tel Aviv?', *New York Times*, 12 May 2003, http://www.hvk.org/articles/0503/146.html.

[84] 'What drove 2 Britons to bomb a club in Tel Aviv?', *New York Times*, 12 May 2003, http://www.hvk.org/articles/0503/146.html.

[85] Phillips M, *Londonistan* (London: Gibson Square Books, 2006), p 136.

[86] Phillips M, *Londonistan* (London: Gibson Square Books, 2006), p 179.

[87] Phillips M, *Londonistan* (London: Gibson Square Books, 2006), p 153.

[88] 'Suicide bombing leaflets' UK link', *Observer*, 4 May 2003, http://observer.guardian.co.uk/uk_news/story/0,,949100,00.html.

[89] Leeds Grand Mosque Statement, 7 July 2005.

[90] Phillips M, *Londonistan* (London: Gibson Square Books, 2006), p 148.

[91] Riyadh al Huq, 'Speech: The globalised suffering of the Muslims', *The Times*, 6 September 2007, http://www.timesonline.co.uk/tol/comment/faith/article2401855.ece?token=nul l&offset=48.

[92] 'Muslims mass for moderation: Town groups team up to stress opposition to extremism', *Luton Today*, 27 April 2004, http://www.lutontoday.co.uk/ViewArticle2.aspx?SectionID=541&ArticleID=7809 83.

93 'We will drive Taliban supporters from our town: Muslim leaders speak out at fears of reprisals grow', *Luton Today*, 31 October 2001, http://www.lutontoday.co.uk/ViewArticle2.aspx?SectionID=541&ArticleID=279933.

94 'Terror group recruiters set sights on new target: Young whites "volunteer to join fanatics"', *Luton Today*, 30 October 2003, http://www.lutontoday.co.uk/ViewArticle2.aspx?SectionID=541&ArticleID=684009.

95 'Terror accused "ran away" to join jihad', *The Times*, 14 September 2006, http://www.timesonline.co.uk/article/0,,2-2357829.html.

96 'Al Qaeda boss visited Blackburn', *Lancashire Evening Telegraph*, 15 June 2007, http://www.lancashireeveningtelegraph.co.uk/display.var.1474143.0.al_qaeda_boss_visited_blackburn.php.

97 '*Guardian* Muslim poll', ICM, November 2004, http://www.icmresearch.co.uk/reviews/2004/Guardian%20Muslims%20Poll%20Nov%2004/Guardian%20Muslims%20Nov04.asp.

98 '*Guardian* Muslim poll', ICM, July 2005, http://www.icmresearch.co.uk/reviews/2005/Guardian%20-%20muslims%20july05/Guardian%20Muslims%20jul05.asp.

99 Phillips M, *Londonistan* (London: Gibson Square Books, 2006), p 137.

100 'Mosques in appeal to help police', BBC NewsOnline, 2 April, 2004, http://news.bbc.co.uk/1/hi/uk/3592115.stm. The full text of a letter from the Muslim Council of Britain to mosques across the UK, giving people advice on fighting terror.
Dear Respected Colleague

As salaamu 'alaikum wa rahmatullah

The last few weeks and days have been fraught with tragedies and dangers.

I am sure you are fully aware of the serious concerns expressed by the prime minister and the police authorities about the high probability of an imminent terrorist outrage in the UK.

I have no doubt that as a leader in the community you are already discharging your Islamic duty in helping to preserve the peace of the nation as well as protecting the community against falling into any trap or provocation.

Following the criminal terrorist attack on the Madrid trains, and despite our immediate, public and unequivocal condemnation of those atrocities some, however, continue to associate Islam with terrorism by using such misleading terms as 'Islamic terrorist'. The words of the Qur'an are clear:

'He who killed any person, unless it be a person guilty of manslaughter, or of spreading chaos in the land, should be looked upon as though he had slain all mankind, and he who saved one life should be regarded as though he had saved the lives of all mankind.'(5:32)

MARTYRDOM

We therefore urge you to take the following actions:
•To provide the correct Islamic guidance to the community, especially to our youth as to our obligation to maintain the peace and security of our country
•To observe the utmost vigilance against any mischievous or criminal elements from infiltrating the community and provoking any unlawful activity

•To liaise with the local police and give them the fullest cooperation in dealing with any criminal activity including terrorist threat
•'Help one another to virtue and God-consciousness and do not help one other to sin and transgression' (5:2)
•To proactively engage with the media in order to refute any misconception about Islam and the Muslim community
•To develop active contacts with other faith communities and civic organisations in order to help maintain social peace and good community relations
•In the event of any tragic incident taking place, give the fullest cooperation to the police and other concerned authorities
•Lastly, but most importantly, seek Allah's help and support and pray for His guidance and protection all the time.
We also urge you to convey the above message in your Friday sermon and bring awareness to our community of our duties and obligations in combating any threat to peace and stability.

By doing so, insha'Allah it will help to dispel the misrepresentation.

There is no need however to be daunted or intimidated by any Islamophobic propaganda and we should continue with our daily lives – normally and in accordance with the tenets of Islam.

All of us as Muslims will have been appalled to see some of the headlines in today's newspapers (for example 'Islamic Bomb Plot Foiled', *Daily Telegraph*; 'The Truck Bombers of Suburbia', *The Times* 2004).

This kind of sensationalised reporting has done immense damage to British Muslims as well as to community relations and we assure you that the MCB's Media Committee will be taking this matter up urgently with the editors concerned.

You will no doubt recall that in November 2002 the police made high-profile arrests of six Muslims accused of plotting to release cyanide gas into London's Underground system.

Yet nearly 18 months later, none of the men have been charged with any crime, let alone being convicted of terrorist activity.

There are other examples of incidents that have received prominent media attention only for the individuals to be subsequently released without any charges brought against them.

The impact of such ordeals on the persons concerned and their families is unbearable. Therefore we urge against hasty pronouncements of guilt.

The Muslim Council of Britain is planning to organise a number of events and meetings of which we shall keep you duly informed.

'O believers, be patient and let your patience never be exhausted. Stand firm in your faith and fear Allah, so that you may triumph.' (3:200)

May Allah protect and guide us.

Yours sincerely, Iqbal AKM Sacranie
Secretary General, The Muslim Council of Britain
'Fight terror' letter in full, BBC NewsOnline, 31 March 2004,
http://news.bbc.co.uk/1/hi/uk/3586703.stm.

[101] 'ICM poll for the *Sunday Telegraph*', ICM, February 2006,
http://www.icmresearch.co.uk/reviews/2006/Sunday%20Telegraph%20-
%20Mulims%20Feb/Sunday%20Telegraph%20Muslims%20feb06.asp.

[102] 'ICM poll for the *Sunday Telegraph*', ICM, February 2006,
http://www.icmresearch.co.uk/reviews/2006/Sunday%20Telegraph%20-
%20Mulims%20Feb/Sunday%20Telegraph%20Muslims%20feb06.asp.

[103] '*Guardian* Muslim poll', ICM, July 2005, http://www.icmresearch.co.uk/
reviews/2005/Guardian%20-%20muslims%20july05/Guardian%20Muslims%
20jul05.asp.

[104] 'ICM poll for the *Sunday Telegraph*', ICM, February 2006,
http://www.icmresearch.co.uk/reviews/2006/Sunday%20Telegraph%20-
%20Mulims%20Feb/Sunday%20Telegraph%20Muslims%20feb06.asp.

[105] Malik K, 'What Muslims Want', *Dispatches*, Channel 4 TV,
http://www.channel4.com/news/microsites/D/dispatches2006/muslim_survey/m
uslims.html. (Accessed March 2008.)

[106] 'Young Muslims and Extremism', Home Office-FCO Paper, 10 May 2004, p
10, http://www.timesonline.co.uk/article/0,,22989-1688872,00.html.

[107] Maher S, 'Campus radicals', *Prospect*, September 2006, http://www.prospect-
magazine.co.uk/article_details.php?id=7742.

[108] 'My son the fanatic', *Guardian*, 2 January 2002,
http://www.guardian.co.uk/ukresponse/story/0,11017,626641,00.html.

[109] 'I know how these terrorists are inspired', *Daily Telegraph*, 2 May 2007.

[110] Malik S, 'My brother the bomber', *Prospect*, June 2007,
http://www.prospect-magazine.co.uk/article_details.php?&id=9635.

[111] Malik S, 'My brother the bomber', *Prospect*, June 2007,
http://www.prospect-magazine.co.uk/article_details.php?&id=9635.

[112] Malik S, 'My brother the bomber', *Prospect*, June 2007,
http://www.prospect-magazine.co.uk/article_details.php?&id=9635.

[113] Malik S, 'My brother the bomber', Prospect, June 2007,
http://www.prospect-magazine.co.uk/article_details.php?&id=9635.

MARTYRDOM

114 Report of the Official Account of the Bombings in London on 7 July 2005, HC1087 (London: The Stationery Office), 11 May 2006.

Chapter 3

The British Muslim Experience

It is clear that some young British Muslims have become alienated from their own communities, as they have struggled to come to terms with adapting their often traditional upbringing to life as Muslims in a secular Western democracy. As a consequence, some have sought out an alternative social identity to that of their parents' generation. In addition to the issues surrounding social identity, there are a range of other, less personal, social, political and economic influences impacting on British Muslims. While life is not as hard as it is for Muslims in countries such as the occupied Palestinian territories or Chechnya, the Muslim population does experience various forms of alienation, discrimination and violence. As a consequence, Muslims consider themselves to be the most discriminated-against minority in the UK, and some have even defined themselves as the 'new blacks' of British society. It has therefore been argued in some quarters that this communal experience of political and economic dispossession has contributed to the profound disconnection that has opened up between many young British Muslims and the *Barelwi* tradition of Islam, which, being spiritual in nature, does not offer answers to these problems.[1]

SOCIO-ECONOMIC BACKGROUND

In many contexts, poverty is generally considered to be one of the main drivers of violent extremism. The absolute poverty of life in places such as Palestinian refugee camps, for example, presents a readily understandable explanation for why some inhabitants of the camps have resorted to violence. For oppressed people who have few life chances and no political means of redress, violent political action may appear to them to be the only way of improving their condition. And, although there are no estates or ghettoes in Britain comparable to the Palestinian refugee camps, this observation has also been made about the relative poverty of many British Muslims.

British Muslim communities are largely concentrated in areas of multiple deprivations, often living in dwellings designated as unfit or in serious disrepair. Compared to households of other faith groups, Muslim households are the most likely to be situated in socially rented accommodation, to experience overcrowding and to lack central heating.[2] However, this relative poverty or economic disadvantage is largely associated with the Pakistani and Bangladeshi communities, while Arab and Indian Muslim communities appear to be much less disadvantaged.[3]

The majority of the dataset could be loosely defined as having working-class backgrounds, and as coming from areas of relative deprivation in the UK,[4] but it is difficult to identify any of them as having grown up or lived in absolute poverty. The area of Beeston in which Mohammed Siddique Khan, Tanweer and Hussain grew up is considered to be deprived, with a low average income and over 10,000 of the 16,300 residents having living standards that are among the worst three per cent nationally.[5] Historically, the area used to have a strong sense of community until drug dealers arrived in the 1990s, after which the community's sense of neighbourliness disappeared and the area became known for its crack dens and wrecked houses. Largely unaware of how to deal with the drug problem, the older generation tended to move out of the area rather than confront it.[6] But, while Beeston is impoverished, Khan and

Hussain were not poor by the standards of the area, and Tanweer's father was a prominent local businessman.[7] Similarly, Omar Sharif and Omar Sheikh came from relatively affluent backgrounds, and a number of others came from middle-class backgrounds.[8]

The role of poverty in the radicalisation of members of the dataset is therefore unclear, but might have played a motivating role for at least some of them. Mohammed Siddique Khan is the only member of the dataset for whom there is any real indication that he may have been driven by the poverty that he experienced and witnessed around him. He is known to have expressed his discontent with the living conditions of the Muslim community in Beeston, saying he believed it would be many years before regeneration cash would transform the area.[9] Yet poverty and social marginalisation were not referred to in any of the 'martyrdom' videos produced by the dataset, interviews given to the police or statements made in court, and so it is difficult to argue with any certainty that any of them were primarily driven by poverty. This notion is supported by Hassan Butt, who rejects the argument that economic disadvantage is the root cause of the radicalisation of young British Muslims, and argues instead that radicalised individuals have witnessed and experienced Western life and have rejected it outright as having nothing to offer them.[10]

Among the key indicators of social and economic integration are education and employment. Educational under-achievement is a marked feature of the Muslim population of the UK, with Muslims more likely than other faith groups to have no qualifications, and over two-fifths having none. As a result, compared to other religious groups, Muslims constitute the highest proportion of people in the working-age population without any educational qualifications.[11] This is largely associated with the high level of disadvantage among the Pakistani and Bangladeshi communities.[12] But, despite this, nearly half of British Muslims of Pakistani descent between the ages of 18 and 30 were in higher education in 2006. For many British Muslims, Islam serves as the source of educational aspirations, providing a basis for upward mobility, where new career paths are negotiated with socially conservative parents.[13]

These facts are reflected in the members of the dataset, whose experience of education varied widely between those who achieved academically, those who failed to achieve at school and those who dropped out of higher education before fulfilling their potential. Overall, however, their level of educational achievement is well above the average level among the British Muslim population as a whole, and most of the dataset had access to good-quality education. In particular, Omar Sheikh, Omar Sharif and Salahuddin Amin went to fee-paying schools,[14] while many of the others went to good-quality state schools. Most significantly, 28 of the dataset are known to have accessed further or higher education, including six of the 22 actual and would-be suicide bombers.[15]

In contrast, Richard Reid and Anthony Garcia did poorly at school and left aged 16, as did Abu Mansha and Junade Feroze who both had very low IQs.[16] Four of the 21/7 cell had few or no qualifications, which may have proved to be a major factor in the failure of their mission: their bombs failed to explode because Muktar Said Ibrahim had mixed the explosives incorrectly. This illustrates why terrorist groups ideally need intelligent operatives. A small number of the dataset also dropped out before completing their education, primarily in order to commit themselves to *jihad*. For instance, Omar Khyam ran away to Pakistan at the age of 17, where he made his way to a *jihadi* training camp. Although his family brought him back from Pakistan and he returned to college, he failed to take his final exams. He subsequently enrolled on a foundation course at London Metropolitan University in 2001, but, before he joined his course, he went back to Pakistan and crossed into Afghanistan to visit the Taliban, before returning to England.[17]

The poor level of education among the Muslim population is reflected in the fact that Muslims have three times the unemployment rate of the population as a whole, and the lowest economic activity rates.[18] The higher levels of educational achievement among the dataset should have given them access to a greater range of employment opportunities than is available to the less educated members of their communities. However, despite this, their experience in finding employment reflects the experiences of their fellow Muslims, and only a small number of the dataset had stable employment. A small number of them were comfortably off, but most were not in particularly highly paid jobs.[19] The majority of the dataset were either unemployed or worked only sporadically in low-paid jobs,[20] which is particularly clear with the members of the 7/7 and 21/7 cells. Of the 7/7 cell, none really succeeded in the workplace and none of them was in employment at the time of the attack. Mohammed Siddique Khan was a learning mentor for special-needs children at a local primary school and a youth worker. However, the job came to an end in November 2004 following problems over extended sick leave, although he continued to be active as a youth worker.[21] Germaine Lindsay initially lived on state benefits after leaving school, doing occasional odd jobs selling mobile phones and Islamic books, but later found work as a carpet fitter. Shehzad Tanweer worked part-time in his father's fish and chip shop until late 2004, after which he did not have paid employment and was supported by his family while his father sought to set him up in business.[22] Only Ramzi Mohammed of the 21/7 cell was in stable employment at the time of their attempted attack.

In some cases, it seems that members of the dataset chose not to pursue regular employment in order to devote themselves to their militant activities – Omar Sheikh for instance, was a full-time *jihadi* – and it is also likely that others, such as Barot and Mohammed Siddique Khan, dropped out of regular, full-time employment specifically in order to commit themselves to their *jihad* pursuits.[23]

Employment is one of the activities which can facilitate contacts between individuals from different communities and break down social barriers, and the fact that the majority of the dataset were not in regular employment would have restricted their social contacts and exacerbated any sense of alienation that they might have been experiencing. As mentioned in the previous chapter, contact with other groups in society may have helped to reduce inter-group anxiety and challenge negative stereotypes, thereby reducing the perceived threat posed by those that they define as *kuffar*.

SOCIAL INTEGRATION

The government has placed a significant emphasis on the failure of Muslim communities to integrate with the wider population, and the consequent alienation of sections of the Muslim population, as one of the key drivers of political and violent radicalisation. In 2005, Trevor Phillips, the chief executive of the Commission for Racial Equality, claimed that maximising integration led to minimising extremism. This was reflected in draft documents that were leaked from the Department for Education in 2006, which warned that Muslims from 'segregated' backgrounds were more likely to hold radical views than those who have 'integrated into wider society'.[24]

Following riots in the Muslim communities of several Northern cities in 2001, Oldham Council commissioned the Cantle Report to assess the progress in building community cohesion. One of the main themes of the Cantle Report was the separation between communities:

> Whilst the physical segregation of housing estates and inner city areas came as no surprise, the team was particularly struck by the depth of polarisation of our towns and cities. The extent to which these physical divisions were compounded by so many other aspects of our daily lives, was very evident. Separate educational arrangements, community and voluntary bodies, employment, places of worship, language, social and cultural networks, means that many communities operate on the basis of a series of parallel lives. These lives often do not seem to touch at any point, let alone overlap and promote any meaningful interchanges.[25]

However, it would be wrong to assume that all Muslims live in the kind of parallel communities identified by the Cantle Report, or even that separate Muslim communities have an overwhelmingly negative impact on their residents. A report by the Joseph Rowntree Foundation in 2006 discovered that, despite perceived racism, poverty and other structural inequalities, a small dataset of Muslim men living in Bradford had a positive outlook on living in a viable and valuable multicultural city. They saw Bradford as a city of opportunity, reinforced by close and established support networks through family, friendship and local community links. Indeed, rather than feeling disempowered, disengaged, excluded or otherwise victimised, they were connected to their city, faith and heritage.[26]

Opinion polls have provided some general indicators of Muslim attitudes towards integration and social alienation. A poll in March 2004 showed that 33 per cent of respondents believed that the Muslim community needed to do more to integrate, while 26 per cent felt that it had integrated too much already, and 45 per cent expressed a preference to send their children to a Muslim school.[27] A poll in the immediate aftermath of the 7 July bombings found that 40 per cent of the Muslim respondents felt that the Muslim population needed to do more to integrate into mainstream British culture, while 18 per cent said it had integrated too much already.[28]

In an ICM poll in February 2006, 60 per cent of the respondents felt that, compared to a year previously, Muslims had become more alienated from British and Western society, 46 per cent believed that Muslims in the UK had become more radical in their views towards British and Western society, and 50 per cent believed that relations between Muslims and white British people were getting worse.[29] Yet, despite this, the polls also indicated a significant willingness to integrate; 80 per cent of respondents to another ICM poll believed that, while Western society might not be perfect, Muslims should live within it and not seek to bring it to an end; 52 per cent believed that most Muslims living in the UK were quite loyal to the UK and 29 per cent believed that most Muslims were very loyal, with 49 per cent of the respondents declaring that they themselves were very loyal.[30]

The majority of the dataset came from the kind of separate,

close-knit Muslim communities identified by the Cantle Report, which is particularly evident with the 7/7 cell. Mohammed Siddique Khan, Tanweer and Hussain grew up in Beeston and the neighbouring district of Holbeck on the outskirts of Leeds. Beeston has a Muslim population of only three per cent,[31] but Pakistanis make up 20 per cent of the population of Beeston Hill, the heart of Beeston, and form their own partially separate and cohesive community.[32] Khan moved a short distance away after his marriage in 2001, first to Batley then to Dewsbury, where Asians account for 24 per cent of the population, but Saville Town is 88 per cent Asian, almost all of whom are Muslims. It is possible for a Muslim child to grow up in Saville Town without coming into any contact with Western lifestyles, opinions or values.[33] Similarly, the members of the dataset who came from Birmingham all lived in predominantly Asian areas of the city. Luton and Walthamstow, where several of the Airline cell grew up and lived, both have sizeable Muslim populations of approximately 15 per cent, with the Muslim areas of Luton being particularly separate from the rest of city.

However, not all of the communities from which the dataset came can be classed as the sort of separate Muslim communities identified by the Cantle Report. This is particularly true of the eight converts who did not grow up in Muslim communities,[34] and the handful who came from middle-class neighbourhoods. A number of others came from towns and cities with relatively small Muslim populations. Crawley, where most of the Ammonium Nitrate cell came from, has a Muslim community of only 4,000. Similarly, Gloucester, where Badat grew up, has a Muslim population of 2,500, and he went to a predominantly white school in the city. Aylesbury, where Germaine Lindsay lived, has a Muslim population of 5,000.[35] Some others also lived outside of established Muslim communities, notably those who left home to go to university. In many mixed communities, relations are good, but, just because the community itself is not separated, it does not mean that individuals within it cannot be alienated or marginalised from mainstream society. Therefore, the evidence from the dataset indicates that living in a mixed community does not necessarily insulate an individual from militant influences.

Irrespective of where they lived, however, there is evidence that the majority of the dataset were integrated into their local communities to some extent. Shahid Butt, for instance, was a voluntary worker who established a youth club at Birmingham central mosque and was active in anti-drugs work,[36] while Mohammed Siddique Khan was linked into the local community through his teaching-assistant job and youth work. Even Richard Reid was at one time integrated into the community life around Brixton mosque, having initially fitted in well.[37] In addition, a significant number of the dataset were married, most of whom also had children,[38] which theoretically should have helped to root them more strongly within their communities, exposing them to the more moderate influences within the community. However, it seems the radicalised networks that they were part of were clearly more dominant than their other social contacts. Nevertheless, some of them were marginalised from both their own communities and wider society. This includes Naveed Bhatti who had poor social skills and had no friends, until Barot took him under his wing.[39]

THE INFLUENCE OF WIDER SOCIETY

A feature of the lives of many members of the dataset is that at some stage they had been Westernised and at some level could be argued to have been integrated into the wider population. Some of them, including Omar Sharif, Omar Sheikh and Omar Khyam, grew up in secular Westernised families and were always fairly well integrated, and some went to mixed schools where they had non-Muslim friends from an early age. Other members of the dataset, who came from a more traditional background and went to predominantly Muslim schools, had a more difficult transition in trying to interact with wider society, but many of them still seem to have managed it. Some of them embraced urban youth culture, going to nightclubs, chasing after women and using alcohol and drugs,[40] while others were exposed to wider society through their attendance at college and university, or in the workplace.

Some of the dataset had clearly engaged in what many would consider to be normal behaviour for young people in the UK. Many of us temporarily adopt several different social identities as we go through adolescence and enter adulthood, so it is not surprising that some of our dataset were involved with Western subcultures. However, this does not necessarily mean that these various social identities provide the social bonding and support that we all require, which is evident in the cases of several of the converts to Islam, who grew up outside of Muslim communities. For example, even before his conversion to Islam, Reid was socially marginalised. There can also be a dichotomy between appearance and reality in terms of being Westernised, as illustrated by Omar Khyam who, at the age of 11, became the 'man of the family' when his father left home and began to make decisions as to what his younger brother could do. The decisions he reached were puritanical and austere, including forbidding him from going to the swimming pool for fear that he would see girls in bikinis and banning him from watching certain TV programmes.[41]

In fact, rather than social alienation preceding radicalisation, it is actually in many cases a consequence of it. Part of the radicalisation process was to draw the individual away from non-Muslims and the Western lifestyle, and many of the dataset went though a process of separating from non-Muslim friends and society. At the age of 14, Asif Hanif grew a beard, distanced himself from friends of other faiths, spoke in Urdu and began praying five times a day. One former pupil reported that 'he used to hang around a group of deeply faithful Muslims and would hardly talk to anyone else'.[42] A schoolfriend of Germaine Lindsay reported that his demeanour changed after he converted to Islam and started hanging around with a group of Asian lads. He was a bit of a joker and very good at sports, but 'he became really distant. He changed. He was talking about *al Qaeda* and preaching. He used to wear a Walkman all the time and not speak.'[43]

Another former schoolfriend remembers Lindsay as a 'normal lad' at school before his sudden conversion to Islam:

> All of a sudden he became very quiet and withdrawn. He would talk to other pupils about being a Muslim. Before that, he was like the rest of us and a good student. He was very good at sport and German. After we came back from the summer holidays and started our final year Germaine had become very strict. He used to talk about doing the right thing and did not like other pupils drinking or smoking. He would tell them not to drink or smoke, because it was bad for them. Soon he was praying in empty classrooms three times a day. But nobody would say anything to him. Germaine was a big lad and nobody messed with him.[44]

This analysis suggests that, while some members of the dataset, particularly the devout ones, were clearly separated from wider society and non-Muslim influences from a relatively early age, a significant proportion of the dataset tried to forge a new Western social identity for themselves and, to a certain extent, did integrate with wider society in the years prior to their involvement in terrorism. For some reason, however, they went on to renounce this Western social identity and adopt a new one based on Fundamentalism or Islamism, and, in doing so, they shunned non-Muslim friends, the Western lifestyle and society outside of their radicalised networks. For this sub-set, social marginalisation occurred as a *result* of their radicalisation rather than vice versa.[45]

RACISM AND ISLAMOPHOBIA

The rejection of a Westernised social identity and the separatism that is prevalent among some sections of the Muslim population links in with a strong sense among many Muslims that British society and politics is Islamophobic, and has become more so since 9/11 and subsequent terrorist incidents in the UK. This was confirmed by the

Director of Public Prosecutions, Ken MacDonald QC, when he reported to the House of Commons Home Affairs Select Committee that:

> terrorism is creating divisions between communities, which of course is one of its purposes; it is intended to do that. We have evidence from our point of view of an increase in ... low-level tensions ... One is talking about racially and religiously aggravated crimes involving racist and religiously motivated abuse of cab drivers at night, shop owners, people in the street, that sort of low-level aggressive criminal conduct which we find has increasingly been accompanied by that sort of abuse, so it was a feeling which my front line prosecutors have that there are increasing tensions at that sort of low level which are probably inspired or contextualised by the threat of international terrorism.[46]

Mainstream Muslim representative groups, spokespeople and media regularly denounce incidents of alleged Islamophobia within society and claim that Islam is under threat. For many Muslims, these allegations have been confirmed by high-profile issues such as the police's use of 'stop and search' powers which have disproportionately targeted Asians and Muslims. There have also been a number of highly publicised controversies over female Muslim clothing, which have been seen as a further assault on Islam and Muslim culture. These have included Shabina Begum's fight to be allowed to wear the *jilbab* to school, the controversy generated when former Foreign Secretary Jack Straw stated that he asked female Muslim constituents to remove their veils when they came to meet him,[47] and the sacking of Muslim teacher Aishah Azmi for refusing to remove her veil in class, which later prompted the former Prime Minister Tony Blair to claim that the veil was a visible symbol of separation.[48]

These views are naturally reflected in Muslim newspapers. The *Muslim Weekly* publishes a significant number of reports about

Islamophobia, both within the UK and abroad. One such editorial referred to 'the ceaseless antagonisation of Muslims',[49] while another, responding to a speech made by the Pope in which he quoted a Byzantine Emperor who had claimed that Islam was a religion of violence, declared:

> last week's Pope comments didn't surprise any of us. Any opportunity to downgrade Muslims or their idol Mohammed is a good opportunity. It is part of ingraining Christians, Westerns and others with the idea that Islam is evil, Muslims are bad and anything that came after Christianity is wicked and corrupted.[50]

The reaction of community spokespeople in Gloucester after the arrest of Saajid Badat was fairly typical. There were demands for the resignation of the then Home Secretary David Blunkett, who had spoken out in support of the police action. Blunkett was accused of showing Gloucester's Muslims enormous disrespect. They felt that their community had been unfairly tainted, and one spokesperson declared: 'You have not arrested an individual but an entire community ... Saajid is innocent and so is this community.' Another said, 'We are always expected to apologise for something that we have not done ... Everyone in this community has condemned 9/11 time and time again. But we are being demonised and castigated despite being British through and through ... Well a lot of us feel that we should not have to do it any more – and it's time we made a stand.'[51]

Radical political and religious groups have often sought to capitalise on these controversies, with *Hizb ut-Tahrir* being linked with Shabina Begum's campaign to be allowed to wear the *jilbab* to school.[52] Polls suggest that the sense of Muslim identity is strengthened by a feeling of being a community under siege.[53] This is confirmed by research which has shown that, in the aftermath of 9/11, when many Muslims felt that Islam and Muslims were being blamed for what had happened, many young people began practising their religion far more rigorously than their parents' generation, finding strength in their faith, and a sense of international solidarity through the *ummah*.[54]

In other respects, low-level non-political racist or Islamophobic violence is another of the factors which serve to drive a wedge between some young Muslims and wider society. Maajid Nawaz suggests that experience of violent racism is one of the key precursors to becoming involved in militant political groups. As an Asian teenager growing up in Essex, he had a sense of being different due to the actions of a minority of organised racists who made his life exceptionally difficult. By the age of 15, he was having to flee unprovoked knife attacks and witnessed friends being stabbed. His alienation was compounded by the fact that he felt the police were institutionally racist because no one was ever charged over these attacks. It was even rumoured that the perpetrators had 'friends' in the police.[55]

There is no reliable central collection of data on the incidence of Islamophobia in the UK, although anecdotal evidence suggests that there has been a significant rise in Islamophobia since 9/11. However, there has been a recorded rise in racist incidents, and it is possible that an increase in attacks on Asians is actually a consequence of Islamophobia. The total number of racist incidents in London during 2002/03 was 47 per cent above the 1998/99 level and, in 2003/04, the actual or perceived religion of the victim in 22 of the 44 religiously aggravated cases was Muslim.[56] It is of course impossible to accurately determine the extent of low-level harassment which never gets reported, but occasionally there have been spontaneous outbreaks of inter-communal violence between Asian and white youths. The most serious of these occurred in a number of Northern cities, including Oldham, in 2001.[57]

However, it is not just official statistics which are important; equally significant are perceptions among the Muslim population. Opinion polls indicate that Muslims perceive society to be more Islamophobic than it was before 9/11, with one poll in March 2004 showing that 55 per cent of respondents believed that community relations had worsened since the start of the war in Iraq.[58] Opinion polls for the *Guardian* found that, in November 2004, 38 per cent of respondents had experienced hostility or abuse to themselves or their family because of their religion.[59] Immediately after the 7 July bombings, that percentage fell to 20 per cent,[60] but by June 2006 it had risen again to 30 per cent, with 52 per cent of respondents also reporting that other people were more suspicious of them.[61] The Home Office citizenship survey in 2001 found that a significant minority of especially young Muslims (37 per cent) were not satisfied with government and employers' protection of their rights.[62] However, witnesses to the House of Commons Home Affairs select committee were divided on whether community relations had deteriorated since September 2001: some felt that they had not got significantly worse, particularly when set against the racist violence of the 1970s and 1980s, while others argued that the situation varied by location and community.[63]

Yet there is some evidence of a difference between the perception and the reality of Islamophobia in British society. A poll for Channel 4 television found that more than half of the respondents thought that hostility to Muslims had increased since the 7 July bombings, and a third thought that it had increased significantly. Yet more than three-quarters of respondents had not themselves been subject to hostility, and, of those that had, the vast majority had suffered from verbal rather than physical abuse. This indicates a gap between the perception and reality of Islamophobia in Britain, but the consequences are the creation of a siege mentality within Muslim communities, generating anger and resentment, and making Muslims more inward looking.[64]

There is evidence concerning some members of the dataset's direct experience of Islamophobia or racism. Abu Mansha was convicted of affray after a fight provoked by a racial insult,[65] and Hasib Hussain was involved in a brief period of racial tension at his school.[66] Richard Reid was encouraged to become a Muslim by his father as a reaction to the racism that he suffered,[67] and he also encountered racism and violence during his time in prison. Tanweer was involved in fights between white and Asian youths in Beeston,[68] and Shahid Butt led a street gang in Birmingham during the early 1990s which fought with racist gangs. It is reasonable to assume that other members of the dataset may also have experienced similar discrimination and perhaps physical violence.

The fact that the 7 July bombings occurred on the fifth anniversary of the 2001 Oldham riots suggests that there may have been an undeclared link to the wider Muslim experience of living in the UK, yet it was not referred to in the 'martyrdom' videos of the 7/7 cell. Nevertheless, all of the dataset would have been aware of the perception of Islamophobia within the Muslim population, and it is reasonable to assume that they may have shared it.

POLITICAL MARGINALISATION

Kenan Malik, a prominent Muslim writer, has suggested that the social alienation of Muslims is compounded by their political marginalisation. Some young Muslims are disillusioned with mainstream Muslim organisations that are perceived to be pedestrian, ineffective and, in many cases, 'sell-outs' to the government.[69] This may well be a consequence of generational conflict within Muslim communities, and socially conservative elders who disenfranchise the young. However, it is also probably a reflection of the disillusionment with the political system felt by similarly disadvantaged youth from all racial and religious backgrounds.

This is supported by evidence that Muslim community leaders are out of touch with ordinary Muslims. In 2006, a poll for Channel 4 television found that less than four per cent of respondents thought that the Muslim Council of Britain represented British Muslims, and just 12 per cent thought it represented their political views. Most surprisingly, a quarter of Muslims had never even heard of Sir Iqbal Sacranie, the organisation's General Secretary at that time, and the most prominent Muslim leader in the country. Other Muslim organisations were viewed as even less representative. Even mosques did not fare well, with just one in thirty considering that the mosque represented Muslim views, and less than one in five that it represented their political views. The most worrying figure was that almost nine out of ten Muslims seemed unsure who actually represented Muslim views in Britain and four out of five did not know who represented their political views.[70] The implication is that the lack of representative and effective political leadership creates a vacuum in which individuals become alienated and disillusioned, and this can be exploited by militant recruiters.

Yet the overall picture in respect of political marginalisation is mixed. Muslims vote in elections and mosques are instrumental in encouraging their congregations to vote. An opinion poll of Muslims in February 2006 showed that only 13 per cent were certain not to vote in a general election.[71] In 2008, there were only four Muslim Members of Parliament, but there is much greater representation at local government level, where mainstream parties tend to select candidates that reflect the ethnic and religious make-up of particular constituencies. For instance, in 2008, 23 per cent of Bradford City Council councillors were Muslim, which is actually slightly higher than the proportion of Muslims who live in the city. And, despite the under-representation of Muslims in national politics, mainstream politics can prove capable of meeting the aspirations of the Muslim population, such as the law against incitement to religious hatred and policy on faith schools. What is most noteworthy, however, is the extent of political alienation among young Muslims, but there is no data on this.

The significant issue is how effective this level of Muslim political representation is in meeting the aspirations of their communities. The Cantle Report highlighted a lack of leadership and readiness to confront issues and find solutions among agencies and community leaders at local level, noting that:

In some areas, the Asian community have drawn our attention to a situation where some local political activities, including the selection of candidates, owe more to familial and other inappropriate connections, than to the legitimate and pressing concerns of the local electorate. The 'politics from back home' was often cited, not only as a distraction, but also as a factor in priorities and decision making, overriding the merits of the local circumstances.[72]

This analysis indicates that the picture of political alienation among Muslims is mixed. Involvement in mainstream politics has delivered many things that Muslims want, but equally it has failed to deliver what the majority of Muslims demand on some big issues, particularly foreign policy, which will be examined in more detail in the next chapter. What remains unclear is the extent of the engagement of young Muslims with mainstream politics.

ALIENATION FROM THE CRIMINAL JUSTICE SYSTEM

The extent to which people receive justice is one of the key variables which gives them a stake in society. However, relations between the Muslim population and the police and criminal justice system are poor. There is mixed evidence of the Muslim population receiving justice under the criminal justice system. The Crown Prosecution Service reports high prosecution rates for racially and religiously aggravated offences,[73] but, on the other side of the equation, the number of Muslims in prison increased by over 190 per cent between March 1993 and June 2003, when 8.3 per cent of prisoners in England and Wales were Muslim (which contrasts with Muslims only constituting approximately 2.8 per cent of the population as a whole).[74]

One of the issues identified by the inquiry into the murder of Stephen Lawrence was the gap between the police's own view of their activities and perceptions of those activities by minority communities. Commenting on a series of public hearings in London and around the country, the report noted:

Wherever we went we were met with inescapable evidence which highlighted the lack of trust which exists between the police and the minority ethnic communities. At every location there was a striking difference between the positive descriptions of policy initiatives by senior police officers, and the negative expressions of the minority communities, who clearly felt themselves to be discriminated against by the police and others. We were left in no doubt that the contrast between these views and expressions reflected a central problem which needs to be addressed.[75]

Since the 9/11 attacks, the strengthening of counter-terrorism legislation and its use against Muslim suspects has become a touchstone of relations between Muslim communities and the state, with relations between the Muslim population and the police and criminal justice system strained even further by the increased emphasis on counter-terrorism. The application of domestic counter-terrorism policy has increasingly impacted upon the lives and consciousness of ordinary British Muslims, and further alienated some of them. Muslim communities in the UK are increasingly concerned that anti-terrorism legislation is being strengthened and then used punitively against them. They feel that they are being disproportionately targeted by the police, and many argue that their communities are being stigmatised with the suspicion of terrorism as a result.[76]

The extent of this alienation from the criminal justice system was evident in an opinion poll of Muslims in November 2004, which found that only 25 per cent of the respondents agreed that Muslims should inform on people who are involved or connected with terrorist activities.[77] This was evident in reactions to the police raid on the Finsbury Park mosque in 2003 in which Abu Hamza was arrested. Ghayasuddin Siddiqui, leader of the Muslim Parliament of Great Britain, said that he was 'appalled', claiming that it would increase Islamophobia and racism. Sir Iqbal Sacranie said that he was saddened, and felt that the way the raid had been carried out had been unprofessional.[78] These feelings of distrust were reflected in

83

opinion polls which suggested that only 52 per cent of Muslims believed that the prosecution of Abu Hamza was fair, and a significant minority of 25–30 per cent believed that his prosecution, conviction and sentence were unfair.[79]

However, the bombing of the London transport system on 7 July 2005 appears to have provoked a sea-change in Muslim attitudes towards the police and criminal justice system. In the immediate aftermath of the bombings, 88 per cent of Muslim respondents to another poll indicated that Muslims should work with the police to root out extremism, with just eight per cent disagreeing.[80]

One of the most high-profile aspects of police counter-terrorism strategy has been the use of 'stop and search' powers under the Police and Criminal Evidence Act (1984), the Criminal Justice and Public Order Act (1994) and Section 44 of the Terrorism Act (2000). 'Stop and searches' are not recorded by religion, on the grounds that the religion of a suspect is not relevant to the offence for which an individual might have been stopped, but figures are available by ethnicity for England and Wales. These data show that, in 2001/02, 8.7 per cent of all those who were stopped and searched were Asian. That proportion rose to 13.8 per cent in 2002/03, before falling back to 12.4 per cent in 2003/04.[81] In 2007, Asians were still 2.1 times more likely to be stopped than any other ethnic group. The police confirmed that 'stop and search' powers were being used to complement covert methods of fighting terrorism by having a more visible presence to deter and disrupt terrorist activity.[82]

The impact on community relations is difficult to ascertain. Muslim spokespeople have been quick to point out that these figures constitute evidence of Islamophobia, and an opinion poll for Channel 4 television showed that nearly half of the respondents believed that police disproportionately 'stop and search' Muslims. But just three per cent of respondents knew of anyone who had actually been stopped and searched,[83] thus indicating once more a gap between the perception and reality of Islamophobia in Britain.

Anecdotally, Muslim leaders suggest that young men with Islamic-style beards are being stopped more than other groups, but it is not just those with a 'religious' look who are being targeted. Imams and other Muslim spokespeople have reported police officers conducting 'fishing expeditions', simply stopping people without due cause in the hope of finding something incriminating. Perhaps the most high-profile person to have been stopped is Lord Nazir Ahmed, who said that his objection was not that he had been stopped:

> I don't mind that ... But on the second occasion, I was with the Mayor of Lahore in a queue of 65 people who were all white. We were selected to come forward for searching. When we asked why, the officer said it was random – but how random is it when the only two Asian people in the queue are stopped? ... I think he was stereotyping and had, in his own mind, taken Asians or Muslims and equated them with terrorism.[84]

Lord Ahmed said many of the cases that had come to his attention appeared to be nothing more than harassment of an individual because of their religious dress. Massoud Shadjareh of the Islamic Human Rights Commission says this sense of being publicly embarrassed is one of the most damaging aspects of the use of 'stop and search' powers, not least because it can also create prejudice in the eyes of those who witness the individuals being stopped and searched. Lord Ahmed argues that this sense of public embarrassment travels quickly through Muslim communities, generating anger, building up resistance to co-operating with the police and generally alienating communities.[85] As we discussed in the previous chapter, the social status of the British Muslim community is central to their collective social identity, and the issue of 'stop and search' may therefore have far-reaching psychological consequences that exceed the more obvious immediate impact of perceived harassment by the police.

However, the police argue that the 'stop and search' figures for Asians are not unreasonable given that 80 per cent of 'stop and searches' were in London, where the Asian population is 13 per cent, and were mainly carried out in areas of London containing large Asian populations. The House of Commons report on Terrorism and Community Relations in 2005 noted that the proportion of Asians that are stopped and searched is very close to their proportion in the population of London, and concluded that it did not believe that the Asian community is being unreasonably targeted by the police.[86]

But, regardless of whether 'stop and search' powers are being used appropriately by the police, again it is the perception of Muslim communities that is the most important variable in our analysis of the psychological impact. The perception that counter-terrorism legislation is being used to harass Muslims is further heightened by the fact that 'stop and search' results in very few arrests and no terrorist incident is known to have been prevented by the use of these powers. Data from 2003/04 showed that fewer than 1.5 per cent of 'stop and searches' of pedestrians under the Terrorism Act (2000) resulted in an arrest. Sir Iqbal Sacranie said that 'it seems a very clear message that certainly prejudice does play a part, and the community can perceive that this can be part of Islamophobia'.[87] The disparity in the number of 'stop and searches' that result in arrests between those carried out under Section 44 and those carried out under other legislation is primarily due to the power being used for the disruption and deterrence of terrorism, rather than for detection. In evidence to the House of Commons, the police admitted that it was used in 'a pretty random way', but that there were very strong safeguards against indiscriminate use of the power.[88] Superficially, this confirms one of the main criticisms of the power, that it is used for 'fishing expeditions' without due cause, which results in the stigmatisation of the Muslim population.

Equally damaging is the discrepancy between the total number of arrests made under the Terrorism Act (2000) and the number of those who were subsequently charged. Between 11 September 2001 and December 2004, there were 701 arrests under the Terrorism Act (2000), but only 119 of those arrested were actually charged under the Act (although a further 135 were charged under other legislation, including terrorist offences that are covered in general criminal law, such as murder, grievous bodily harm and use of firearms and/or explosives). Of those, only 17 were convicted under the Terrorism Act (2000).[89]

These allegations of 'fishing expeditions' and unfair targeting of the Muslim population are further fuelled by the number of failed prosecutions under the Terrorism Act (2000). While at one level this indicates that Muslims are treated fairly by the criminal justice system and are found innocent when the evidence is lacking, it nevertheless reinforces the perception that Muslims are being targeted by the police. This criticism has been exacerbated by a number of catastrophic mistakes, such as the shooting dead of Jean Charles de Menezes shortly after the failed 21/7 bombings, when he was incorrectly identified as a suicide bomber by police surveillance officers. Almost as damaging was the raid on a family home in Forest Gate in 2006, following a tip-off from Abu Mansha. Two brothers were arrested during the raid, one of whom was shot and injured by the police, yet no evidence of terrorist activity was uncovered at the house and no charges were brought against the men.

These feelings of injustice have led to a backlash from mainstream Muslim leaders and groups, who have become increasingly vocal in their criticism of government counter-terrorism policy. Massoud Shadjareh, chair of the Islamic Human Rights Commission, said that 'the problem is that these raids are continually creating an image which equates Islam with terrorism and acts of violence ... The Muslim community is extremely law abiding ... There is a limit to how much they will be the target of Islamophobia.'[90]

Following police raids in 2004, Yasin Rehman, of the Luton Council of Mosques, said the town's Muslim community were feeling persecuted: 'Muslims have been targeted and their lives have been tarnished.'[91] Similarly, following the arrest of Parviz Khan and five others in 2007, Dr Mohammed Naseem, a community leader in Birmingham, claimed that British Muslims were being treated like

Jews in Nazi Germany. He told a 2,000-strong congregation outside the Birmingham central mosque that 'there is a political objective behind these arrests. It is something that has been magicked up.'[92]

Yet the reactions of community spokespeople to counter-terrorism activities are not always negative. Many Muslims recognise that there are violent extremists living within their communities, and are prepared to work with the police to root them out. Many community leaders have also worked hard to minimise the impact of counter-terrorism raids in their communities and ensure that community relations do not suffer as a consequence. This indicates that there is an acknowledgement among ordinary Muslims that the violent extremists who live within their Muslim communities pose as much of a threat to the lives and beliefs of other Muslims as they do to the rest of society.

THE MEDIA

The media is one of the key actors informing and influencing public opinion on the 'war on terror' and the domestic terrorist threat. Since 9/11, the media has increasingly been accused of having an anti-Muslim bias by British Muslims. These allegations were supported by research in 2007 that found that 91 per cent of one week's media reports represented Islam and Muslims negatively, and portrayed Islam as a threat to the West.[93] This criticism of the media falls into four broad categories: sensationalism; insensitive use of terminology; lack of publicity given to the releases of terrorist suspects; and outright errors in reporting. The principal question for our analysis is to what extent media reporting contributes to the radicalisation of UK Muslims.

Muslim communities feel that the reporting of constant government warnings about the domestic terrorist threat or of impending terrorist attacks which never materialise fuels Islamophobia, and creates a climate of fear for Muslims. Given the relatively small number of Muslims who have actually been convicted of terrorist offences, these official warnings are viewed with considerable suspicion by British Muslims, fuelling the perception that the media is working with the government in pursuing an anti-Islamic agenda for the 'war on terror'.

The media has also been rightly criticised for a number of major errors in reporting alleged and actual terrorist incidents, mistakes which in some cases seem to have been fuelled by unofficial leaks of information or an unwillingness on the part of the authorities to correct the reports. In 2003, for instance, there was widespread reporting of the arrest of nine men for an alleged plot to use the biological poison ricin to attack the London Underground system. It was not until the trial in 2005 that it emerged that no ricin had been discovered, and only one of the defendants, Kemal Bourgass, was subsequently convicted. Similarly, in April 2004, 10 Kurdish men were arrested on suspicion of plotting a terrorist attack on Old Trafford during a football match. All of the men were subsequently released without charge after only ticket stubs for old matches were found.[94]

Another complaint from Muslim spokespeople is that terrorism arrests are often sensationalised. After Saajid Badat was arrested, local leaders branded the national tabloids as being 'filthy and racist' and the local paper, *The Citizen*, was condemned for sensationalist headlines referring to suicide bombers.[95] The other side of the coin is that, when terrorist suspects are released without charge, it is generally not reported or given only low prominence. Massoud Shadjareh argued that this 'is creating a deception in the minds of ordinary people that we have a bigger problem than we really have'.[96] Despite this, when a terrorism trial does not result in a conviction, it is reported, as are high-profile police failures, such as the shooting of de Menezes and the Forest Gate raid.

Equally offensive to many Muslims is the terminology that the media has frequently used, the major issue being the linking of Islam and terrorism, through the use of terms such as 'Muslim terrorist' and 'Islamic terrorism'. Muslims argue that the religion of Islam has nothing to do with terrorism, and that the ideology of terrorist groups is a perversion of Islam. They therefore see such an association as a deliberate and gratuitous attack on Islam. The Muslim Council of Britain particularly argued that some media coverage of the arrest of the Ammonium Nitrate cell was unfair. Inayat Bunglawala picked out one headline which described the police operation as 'Islamic bomb attack foiled' on the grounds that at that time it was not known whether it was a bomb attack and to describe it as Islamic was offensive to ordinary Muslims.[97]

The result is that many Muslims believe that the media is demonising both them and their religion, and as a result is generating Islamophobia within the wider population of the UK. The record of the media in reporting on the domestic terrorism threat is open to criticism on a number of points, but, irrespective of whether or not it is really Islamophobic, again it is the perception within the Muslim population that is crucial, and they largely perceive the media to be hostile. The extent to which the media might contribute to the isolation and politicisation of young Muslims through this reporting is unclear; however, it all adds to the climate of alienation that has built up in some communities.

THE PAKISTAN CONNECTION

It is common for young Britons of Pakistani descent to visit Pakistan for extended periods of time. In 2004, there were nearly 400,000 visits to Pakistan by UK residents, for an average length of 41 days.[98] The reasons are generally to visit family, attend marriages, study at schools for Islamic studies or simply to sightsee, but a small minority have also engaged in extremist activity in Pakistan and Afghanistan. Attention tends to focus on the Pakistan connection, but there is also evidence of some British Muslims being radicalised by influences in Bosnia, Egypt, Yemen and Syria.

Over half of the members of the dataset are of Pakistani descent, and many of them are known to have visited Pakistan, both before and after 9/11. Pakistani politics has always been turbulent, with powerful Islamist influences competing with the secular traditions of the larger, more established political parties. Pakistan's position as a frontline state in the *jihads* against the Soviet Union in Afghanistan and in Indian-controlled Kashmir has meant that *jihadi* influences are firmly embedded in grassroots Pakistani society, which is reflected in the number of Pakistani citizens who continue to travel to fight in Afghanistan and Kashmir. There are roughly 45 Islamist groups committed to violent *jihad* based in Pakistan, the most well known of which are *Harkat-e-Jihad-e-Islami* (Movement for Islamic Jihad), *Jaish-e-Mohammed* (Army of Mohammed) and *Jundullah* (Army of God), but, with constantly changing names, splits and overlapping ideologies, it is often difficult to differentiate one from another.[99] Some of these groups also have strong links to South Asian communities in the UK.

When Britons visit Pakistan, they will be surrounded by these attitudes and influences. A small number of the dataset claim to have been influenced by incidents they experienced overseas, and there are a few others for whom there is a strong suspicion that such experiences contributed towards their radicalisation.

Omar Khyam spoke at his trial of the impact of a chance meeting with a group of Kashmiri *mujahideen*, while he was on a family holiday in Pakistan. He approached them to find out more, and that discussion seems to have affected him. Unknown to his parents, he subsequently travelled to Pakistan in January 2000 to attend a military training camp. In 2001, he returned and travelled to Afghanistan to meet members of the Taliban. He told the Old Bailey that 'they were amazing people. People who loved Allah. They were soft, kind and humble to the Muslims, harsh against their enemies. This is how an Islamic state should be.'[100]

Similarly, Salahuddin Amin used to go to Pakistan for an extended summer holiday every year. On a visit to the town of Murree, a resort in the hills above Rawalpindi in 1999, he heard a speech about the plight of Muslims in Indian-controlled Kashmir. He recalled,

There were a lot of stalls on the main road – on the Mall Road ...
The stalls were set up by the *mujahideen*, the fighters fighting in

Kashmir. I was walking up and down, at one point I heard a lady making an emotional speech about the atrocities that were happening in Kashmir that was under Indian rule – how women were raped and kidnapped all the time and they had to move from there to Pakistani Kashmir and were in difficulties. She made a very emotional speech and that affected me.

Captivated by what he had heard about the suffering of Muslims, he decided on his return to Luton that he would donate part of his wages towards the 'cause'.[101] This appears to have been his first step into political activism.

In contrast to Khyam and Amin, Hasib Hussain was sent to Pakistan by his family in 2003 in an effort to straighten him out after he started to get into trouble. It is not known what he did in Pakistan, but it appears to have had a profound effect on him; he returned from Pakistan a devout Muslim, and had developed self-discipline.[102] It therefore seems likely that his experiences in Pakistan were at least a precursor to his becoming involved with extremist individuals in the UK. However, the Official Narrative of the 7 July bombings identified the seminal moment in his radicalisation as being his undertaking of the *Hajj* in 2002. Afterwards, he began wearing traditional clothing and a prayer cap and would wear white on Fridays. He later told his teacher that he wanted to become a cleric when he left school, and would regularly sit up until the early hours reading religious texts and praying. At the same time, he became open about his support for *al Qaeda* in school and told people that he regarded the 9/11 attackers as martyrs.[103]

Mohammed Kamel is slightly different from the other members of the dataset, as it seems that he may have been deliberately taken abroad to be radicalised. He was taken to Egypt by his father, Abu Hamza, when he was three, and did not see his mother again until he was convicted of terrorism in Yemen, aged 17.[104] Nothing is known about Kamel's time in Egypt, but it is evident that he was radicalised during his time living there. Hamza was linked to a number of Egyptian Islamist groups and he may well have introduced Kamel into those circles.

Asif Hanif and Omar Sharif had both been involved in radical Islamist political groups in London, but there is a strong suspicion that they both decided to make the step change into committing an act of political violence by influences that they were exposed to overseas. Both had travelled to Syria in the years immediately prior to their involvement in terrorism, ostensibly to study Islam, and it is believed that their experiences in Damascus provided the key to their decision to commit themselves to the use of violence. Syria has become a magnet for young British Muslims wanting to improve their Arabic, but Damascus is also a city in which it is possible to come into contact with every shade of Islamic thought, including the international *jihad*. A number of groups, such as *Hamas*, the *Al-Aqsa* Martyrs Brigade, *Hezbollah* and various insurgent groups fighting in Iraq, have representatives in Syria. In addition, public opinion in Syria is strongly opposed to the war in Iraq and is passionate about the Palestinian cause. Because Syria is a geographical neighbour of both Israel and Iraq, the public debate about the conflicts in those states has an immediacy that is lacking in those taking place in the living rooms of England.[105] However, other reports suggest that Hanif had also visited Saudi Arabia, Afghanistan and the United Arab Emirates,[106] which are also places where he could have come into contact with militants.

Unlike Hanif and Sharif, there is no indication that Omar Sheikh had been politically radicalised when he first joined an aid convoy to Bosnia, run by Asad Khan, a veteran of the war in Chechnya, but through the convoy he met more radical individuals who proved to be a powerful influence on him. When Sheikh reached Bosnia, he became associated with a fighter called Abdul Rauf, a member of *Harkat ul-Mujahideen* (Movement of Holy Warriors), who seems to have been the mentor who persuaded him to become involved in violent *jihad* and encouraged him to attend a training camp in Afghanistan. When he returned to the UK in 1993, he appears to have been completely radicalised and spoke of kidnapping in order to stimulate international action to help the Bosnian Muslims. When Sheikh went to Afghanistan for training, he joined *Harkat ul-Ansar*, the most extreme and violent militant group fighting in Kashmir.[107]

An indication of how *jihadi* groups might draw Westerners into their activities was provided by Moazzem Begg, a former detainee at Camp Delta in Guantanamo Bay. On a visit to Pakistan in 1993, he and his friends met members of *Jamaat-e-Islami* who invited them to their centre in Lahore, which was walled off from the rest of the city and contained mosques, *madrassas*, a university and a hospital. In the hospital, Begg met wounded veterans of the conflicts in Bosnia, Kashmir and Afghanistan, and they invited him to visit their training camp in Afghanistan. Begg accepted the invitation, and found the visit to be a life-changing experience. He claimed, 'I had met men who seemed to me exemplary in their faith and self sacrifice, and seen a world that awed and inspired me.' From then on, he became a practising Muslim.[108] While Begg himself did not join a *jihadi* group as a result of his experience, it is possible to imagine how others who might be similarly moved might commit themselves to violent *jihad*.

Although these overseas influences played a role in the radicalisation of a number of the dataset, they should not be seen in isolation from the other factors to which they were subjected in their everyday lives in the UK. Significantly, these influences are primarily related to the *jihads* in Afghanistan, Kashmir and the occupied Palestinian territories, causes which have considerable support within Muslim communities in the UK, but they are not about *al Qaeda's* ideology of international *jihad*.

SOCIAL MARGINALISATION AND INVOLVEMENT IN STREET GANGS

The response to the threats and pressures identified above has varied, and some young Muslims have sought a new identity outside of that of their traditional communities and of wider society, in the street gangs which exist within a number of Muslim communities across the UK. To a certain extent, the existence of these gangs is a reflection of young Muslims' disillusionment with the way that their elders handle issues affecting the younger generation, but it is also an indication of their marginalisation from society in general. While some are purely criminal or anti-social in nature, others have a more political dimension in rejecting mainstream society, defending their communities from racism and outsiders, and enforcing separatism.

Much of this violence occurs below the public radar, but since 9/11 there has been an increasing number of reports of gang activity in the national media. Shortly after 9/11, a group in Derby called the Youth Muslims Organisation began stirring up trouble, with gangs roaming the streets chanting bin Laden's name. Following a scuffle between Sikh and Muslim girls who had been arguing over 9/11, a mob of young Muslims stormed a local school assaulting staff and pupils.[109] Tension simmered for weeks afterwards and resulted in further assaults.[110] While this outbreak of violence resulted from a specific incident, some violence in other cities has been more systematic and sustained.

In 2001, the police expressed concern that disaffected young Asians might try to establish 'no-go' areas in districts that they regarded as their strongholds. This was supported by data released by Greater Manchester Police which showed that 62 per cent of the 572 racial attacks reported in Oldham in 2000 were committed by Asians on white victims. Chief Superintendent Eric Hewitt claimed, 'Sometimes the motive is robbery, but often it is just violence. The attackers are gangs of Asian youths, aged between eight and 18, who have carried weapons including knives, bricks and sticks'.[111]

This same situation was replicated in Walsall in the West Midlands. By 2003, Pakistani youths had threatened and assaulted dozens of Afro-Caribbean teenagers, in what community leaders defined as racially motivated attacks. One black youth who had been attacked by a Pakistani gang claimed, 'They call us niggers and say they want to drive us off what they say is their turf.' One local voluntary worker claimed that the problem increased after 9/11, possibly because they felt that the world had become anti-Muslim since then.[112]

The links between this violence and the activities of militant groups is unclear, but it is known that militant groups do operate in these communities and this inter-communal violence is in their ideological interests, particularly where it is directed at establishing 'no-go' areas for the authorities in Muslim communities. But, while members of militant groups may have been involved, there is no evidence that they were controlling and directing it.

Nevertheless, members of gangs have provided useful foot soldiers for terrorist cells. Mohammed Siddique Khan and Tanweer were both members of a gang in Beeston known as the Mullah Crew. The group met at the Iqra Islamic bookshop and a gym beneath the Hardy Street mosque, which became known as the 'al Qaeda gym'.[113] The other members of the dataset who have been linked to street gangs are Shahid Butt, Richard Reid and Muktar Said Ibrahim. Butt was the leader of a notorious Birmingham gang called The Lynx, which he founded to protect the community and themselves against racist attacks. The gang had no ideology and its members led Western lifestyles, drinking, nightclubbing and taking drugs,[114] but, nevertheless, the theme of protecting the community from attack, and the kudos that the gang acquired within the community for doing so, was something that Butt would take with him into his future life as a *jihadi*. Reid and Ibrahim were both members of violent criminal gangs, during which time they were both involved in mugging people, before they converted to Islam.[115]

Muslim street gangs are not necessarily a breeding ground for terrorists, and individuals who engage in street violence will not necessarily go on to become involved in terrorism, but membership of a gang reflects alienation from their own community leaders as well as from wider society, and these are among the kind of individuals that militant Islamist groups try to recruit. It also displays a willingness to engage in violent behaviour and, as we shall discuss in later chapters, this may facilitate the journey into violent extremism.

This analysis illustrates how many members of the dataset tried to embrace a more Western form of identity in urban youth culture, or else a counter-culture identity such as involvement in street gangs. For some reason, those new identities proved to be transient. The dataset were undoubtedly exposed to some or all of the social, economic and political influences identified above, which may have alienated them from their new Westernised identities. However, these are the same influences to which many other young Muslims who have not become involved in terrorism are also subjected, and this indicates that there must also be other factors which have influenced them.

Notes and references

1 'Orphans of Islam, The history of Britain's Mirpur population may help to explain why some became suicide bombers', *Guardian*, 18 July 2005, http://www.guardian.co.uk/attackonlondon/comment/story/0,,1530640,00.html.

2 'Terrorism and Community Relations', House of Commons, Home Affairs Select Committee, 6th Report, 5 April 2005, pp 23–24, http://www.publications.parliament.uk/pa/cm200405/cmselect/cmhaff/cmhaff.htm.

3 'Young Muslims and Extremism', Home Office-FCO Paper, 10 May 2004, p 6, http://www.timesonline.co.uk/article/0,,22989-1688872,00.html.

4 For instance, reports suggested that the Yemen 8 were from poor families, but exactly how poor is uncertain. Thamesmead, where Abu Mansha lived, is a deprived area of London with high crime rates, and his flat on a housing estate was described as being 'near derelict', which suggests that Mansha was not well-off, yet his father owned a travel agency which points to his coming from a reasonably affluent background. 'Terrorists or tourists', *Guardian*, 26 June 1999, http://www.al-bab.com/yemen/artic/gdn42.htm; 'Terror suspect "had personal details about British soldier"', *The Times*, 30 March 2005, http://www.timesonline.co.uk/article/0,,2-1546787,00.html.

5 Report of the Official Account of the Bombings in London on 7 July 2005, HC1087 (London: The Stationery Office), 11 May 2006.

6 Malik S, 'My brother the bomber', *Prospect*, June 2007, http://www.prospect-magazine.co.uk/article_details.php?&id=9635.

7 Report of the Official Account of the Bombings in London on 7 July 2005, HC1087 (London: The Stationery Office), 11 May 2006.

8 'Muslim was planning dirty bomb attack in UK', *Daily Telegraph*, 13 October 2006,
http://www.telegraph.co.uk/news/main.jhtml?xml=/news/2006/10/13/nterr13.xml.

9 'The London bombers', *The Times*, 15 July 2005,
http://www.timesonline.co.uk/article/0,,22989-1693739,00.html.

10 Taseer A, 'A British jihadist', *Prospect*, August 2005, http://www.prospect-magazine.co.uk/article_details.php?id=6992.

11 'Terrorism and Community Relations', House of Commons, Home Affairs Select Committee, 6th Report, 5 April 2005, p 24,
http://www.publications.parliament.uk/pa/cm200405/cmselect/cmhaff/cmhaff.htm.

12 In 1999, only 37 per cent of Pakistani and Bangladeshi girls and 22 per cent of Pakistani and Bangladeshi boys achieved five or more GCSEs at grades A*–C (or equivalent). Between 1997 and 1999, all ethnic groups, with the exception of Pakistanis and Bangladeshis, saw a rise in educational achievement by 16-year-olds. As a result, the gap between the lowest- and highest-achieving ethnic groups widened over this period. 'Young Muslims and Extremism', Home Office-FCO Paper, 10 May 2004, http://www.timesonline.co.uk/article/0,,22989-1688872,00.html.

13 Maher S, 'Campus radicals', *Prospect*, September 2006, http://www.prospect-magazine.co.uk/article_details.php?id=7742.

14 Salahuddin Amin was educated at a private school in Pakistan between the ages of 4 and 16, although this did not equip him particularly well for life in Britain, because he only spoke Urdu when he arrived back in the UK. Germaine Lindsay was also academically successful at school, while Dhiren Barot obtained GCSEs followed by a City and Guilds qualification in tourism. Omar Abdur Rehman had a good education in Christian schools, and, even though Richard Reid did not achieve academically, the schools in the area that he lived in were not too bad. Report of the Official Account of the Bombings in London on 7 July 2005, HC1087 (London: The Stationery Office), 11 May 2006; 'Muslim convert who plotted terror', BBC NewsOnline, 6 November 2006, http://news.bbc.co.uk/1/hi/uk/6121084.stm; 'The plotters uncovered', *Sun*, 15 June 2007, http://www.thesun.co.uk/article/0,,2-2007270793,00.html.

15 The following members of the dataset are known to have accessed further or higher education:
Mohammed Siddique Khan, a graduate of business studies from Leeds Metropolitan University.
Hasib Hussain went to college to study for an Advanced Business Programme.
Asif Hanif studied business at Cranford Community College in Hounslow and

Arabic at Damascus University.
Malik Nasser Harhara obtained a BSc in information systems from Westminster University.
Ayaz Hussain was a computer studies graduate.
Mohsin Ghalain was an engineering student.
Ghulam Hussein completed a one-year engineering course at Dunstable College before enrolling on a business studies course at Luton University.
Shahid Butt: some reports suggest he went to Birmingham University, others that he went to Birmingham Polytechnic; some suggest he has a degree in finance, others in business studies.
Saajid Badat enrolled at the College of Islamic Knowledge and Guidance in Blackburn.
Jawad Akbar attended Brunel University.
Nabeel Hussain was a student at Brunel University at the time of his arrest.
Sarmad Ahmed was on a computing course at Kingston University; other reports indicate that it was an accountancy course.
Salahuddin Amin attended the University of Hertfordshire.
Anthony Garcia failed his GCSEs but went on to further education.
Dhiren Barot completed a City and Guilds qualification in tourism at Newham College.
Omar Sheikh studied maths at the London School of Economics.
Omar Sharif studied at King's College London.
Shehzad Tanweer studied sports science at Leeds Metropolitan University and obtained an HND.
Naveed Bhatti had a first degree and an MSc in engineering and was studying for a PhD at Brunel University at the time of his arrest.
Zia Ul Haq had a degree in construction management.
Omar Rehman was studying for a degree in graphic design at Westminster University at the time of his arrest.
Qaisir Shaffi went to college but no details are available.
Aadel Yahya was studying for a degree in computer networking at London Metropolitan University.
Yassin Omar enrolled on a science course at Enfield College, but dropped out.
Assad Sarwar enrolled on an earth sciences course at Brunel University, but dropped out.
Abdulla Ahmed Ali was an engineering graduate from City University.
Arafat Khan attended Middlesex University but dropped out.
Waheed Zaman studied biomedical sciences at London Metropolitan University.

16 'Exclusive: Was M15 trigger for bungled terror swoop a prisoner with I.Q. of 69?', *Sunday Mirror*, 18 June 2006.

17 'Terror accused "ran away" to join jihad', *The Times*, 14 September 2006, http://www.timesonline.co.uk/article/0,,2-2357829.html. Omar Sharif attended King's College London before dropping out, and Omar Sheikh was a student at the LSE before dropping out and going to Bosnia. Shehzad Tanweer studied

sports science at Leeds Metropolitan University and obtained an HND but left before completing the follow-on BSc course.

18 'Young Muslims and Extremism', Home Office-FCO Paper, 10 May 2004, http://www.timesonline.co.uk/article/0,,22989-1688872,00.html.

19 Moinul Abedin was a waiter; Abu Mansha was a market-stall holder; Ghulam Hussein was a security guard; Shazad Nabi was a bus driver; Shahid Butt was a clerical worker; Asif Hanif had worked at Heathrow Airport for more than two years before returning to education; Waheed Mahmood was a gas fitter; Omar Rehman worked in a hotel. The only members of the dataset who seem to have been comfortably off were Junade Feroze, who worked in the family firm buying and selling cars; Zia ul Haq, who worked for a firm of chartered surveyors in London; Ramzi Mohammed, the only member of the 21/7 cell to have had a regular job, who worked for a marketing and merchandising company; and Kazi Rahman, who was a plumber.

20 Omar Sharif was not in regular employment after dropping out of university. Malik Nasser Harhara, of the Yemen 8 cell was unemployed. Richard Reid did not have stable employment after leaving school.

21 Report of the Official Account of the Bombings in London on 7 July 2005, HC1087 (London: The Stationery Office), 11 May 2006.

22 Report of the Official Account of the Bombings in London on 7 July 2005, HC1087 (London: The Stationery Office), 11 May 2006.

23 'Muslim convert who plotted terror', BBC NewsOnline, 6 November 2006, http://news.bbc.co.uk/1/hi/uk/6121084.stm.

24 'Study rejects claim that Muslim areas harbour terrorists', Guardian, 20 November 2006, http://www.guardian.co.uk/terrorism/story/0,,1952281,00.html.

25 Community Cohesion: A Report of the Independent Review Team Chaired by Ted Cantle, para 2.1.

26 Alam MY & Husband C, 'British-Pakistani men from Bradford: Linking narratives to policy', Joseph Rowntree Foundation, November 2006, http://www.jrf.org.uk/knowledge/findings/socialpolicy/1960.asp.

27 'ICM poll for the Guardian', ICM, March 2004, http://www.icmresearch.co.uk/reviews/2004/guardian-muslims-march-2004.asp.

28 'ICM poll for the Guardian', ICM, July 2005,

http://www.icmresearch.co.uk/reviews/2005/Guardian%20-%20muslims%
20july05/ Guardian%20Muslims%20jul05.asp.

29 'ICM poll for the *Sunday Telegraph*', ICM, February 2006,
http://www.icmresearch.co.uk/reviews/2006/Sunday%20Telegraph%20-
%20Mulims%20Feb/Sunday%20Telegraph%20Muslims%20feb06.asp.

30 'ICM poll for the *Sunday Telegraph*', ICM, February 2006,
http://www.icmresearch.co.uk/reviews/2006/Sunday%20Telegraph%20-
%20Mulims%20Feb/Sunday%20Telegraph%20Muslims%20feb06.asp.

31 Report of the Official Account of the Bombings in London on 7 July 2005,
HC1087 (London: The Stationery Office), 11 May 2006.

32 Malik S, 'My brother the bomber', *Prospect*, June 2007, http://www.prospect-
magazine.co.uk/article_details.php?&id=9635.

33 'How bombers' town is turning into an enclave for Muslims', *The Times*, 21
October 2006, http://www.timesonline.co.uk/article/0,,2-2414708.html.

34 Richard Reid grew up in Bromley, South London; Dhiren Barot in Kingsbury,
North London; Germaine Lindsey was born in Huddersfield.

35 'The London bombers', *The Times*, 15 July 2005,
http://www.timesonline.co.uk/article/0,,22989-1693739,00.html.

36 'Terrorists or tourists', *Guardian*, 26 June 1999, http://www.al-bab.com/
yemen/artic/gdn42.htm; also Caged Prisoners website.

37 BBC News Online, 'Who is Richard Reid?', 28 December 2001,
http://news.bbc.co.uk/1/hi/uk/1731568.stm.

38 These are: Mohammed Siddique Khan, Lindsay, Asif Hanif, Akbar, Abedin,
Ghulam Hussein, Waheed Mahmood and Shahid Butt.

39 'How an introverted boy fell under the spell of a militant', *Independent*, 16
June 2007, http://news.independent.co.uk/uk/crime/article2663173.ece.

40 Omar Sharif only began the process of radicalisation when he left the family
home at the age of 18, while Sheikh's teachers described him as being well
adjusted, very intelligent, helpful to others, kind, never violent and never
unruly; he had non-Muslim friends and frequented pubs when he went to
university. Khyam went to a predominantly white school in Crawley where he
was captain of the cricket team. Mohammed Siddique Khan's first school had
mainly white pupils and he seemed to integrate well. Later, he attended
another school, which was more Pakistani, but he still had many white friends.

One of them, who remembered Khan as a young teenager in the late 1980s, recalled that 'Sid wasn't in your face or outspoken, but ... he wasn't completely strait-laced either. He was friends with the in-crowd. He had white mates as well as Asian, and he would quite often be round the back of the gym at break time smoking a fag with the rest of us. He didn't have any girlfriends that I know of, but he'd talk to girls. He was friendly.' As he grew older, he would frequent nightclubs, drink alcohol and take drugs. Similarly, Qaisir Shaffi went to raves and smoked cannabis before starting on crack: 'Cocaine, women, hotels, I got a taste for it,' he declared. The Yemen 8 were all described by their families as being 'party animals' who drank beer. A key element of their defence at their trial was that they had gone to Yemen to party, although some reports suggest that, by the time they went to Yemen, some of them had turned their back on that lifestyle. Anthony Garcia grew up with mainly white friends; he wanted to become a model and was obsessed with rap music, girls and playing basketball. As a teenager, Islam played no part in his life, and he drifted through a variety of jobs and spent his money on trendy clothes, drink and cigarettes. Salahuddin Amin grew up in Pakistan between the ages of four and 16, but when he returned to the UK he quickly started to date women and drink alcohol. When Barot was growing up, he was known for his interest in fashion and music, and planned to travel the world. Parviz Khan used to drink, smoke, go clubbing and play football in his twenties. Germaine Lindsay, Hussain Osman and Ramzi Mohammed of the 21/7 cell worshipped American culture, hip-hop music, women and dancing. 'Papers focus on bomb suspects', BBC NewsOnline, 2 May, 2003, http://news.bbc.co.uk/1/hi/uk/2994485.stm; Lévy B, *Who Killed Daniel Pearl?* (New York: Melville House, 2003), p 73. However, other reports suggest that he may not have been quite so well integrated. One contemporary described him as 'always a bit odd, poor social skills and the tendency to bully people rather than mix with them, which doesn't make for a well-balanced individual'. Josie Appleton, 'The Fundamentalist question', 14 February 2002, http://www.spiked-online.com/Printable/00000002D40F.htm; 'Profile: Omar Khyam', BBC NewsOnline, 30 April 2007, http://news.bbc.co.uk/1/hi/uk/6149794.stm; Malik S, 'My brother the bomber', *Prospect*, June 2007, http://www.prospect-magazine.co.uk/article_details.php?&id=9635; Report of the Official Account of the Bombings in London on 7 July 2005, HC1087 (London: The Stationery Office), 11 May 2006; 'The plotters uncovered', *Sun*, 15 June 2007, http://www.thesun.co.uk/article/0,,2-2007270793,00.html; 'Terror suspect says he did buy fertiliser', *The Times*, 26 September 2006, http://www.timesonline.co.uk/article/0,,2-2374710.html; 'Profile: Anthony Garcia', BBC NewsOnline, 30 April 2007, http://news.bbc.co.uk/1/hi/uk/6149798.stm; 'Profile: Salahuddin Amin', BBC News Online, 30 April 2007, http://news.bbc.co.uk/1/hi/uk/6149790.stm; 'Muslim was planning dirty bomb attack in UK', *Daily Telegraph*, 13 October 2006, http://www.telegraph.co.uk/news/main.jhtml?xml=/news/2006/10/13/nterr13.xml; 'Profile: Parviz Khan', *Guardian*, 18 February 2008, http://www.guardian.co.uk/uk/2008/feb/18/uksecurity3.

[41] 'Profile: Omar Khyam', BBC NewsOnline, 30 April 2007, http://news.bbc.co.uk/1/hi/uk/6149794.stm.

[42] 'Brit bomber worked at Heathrow', *Sun*, 20 September 2003, http://www.thesun.co.uk/article/0,,2-2003200959,00.html.

[43] 'Brainwash campaign by Lindsay', *Huddersfield Daily Examiner*, 19 July 2005, http://ichuddersfield.icnetwork.co.uk/0100news/0100localnews/tm_headline=brainwash-campaign-by-lindsay%26method=full%26objectid=15754099%26page=3%26siteid=50060-name_page.html.

[44] 'Brainwash campaign by Lindsay', *Huddersfield Daily Examiner*, 19 July 2005, http://ichuddersfield.icnetwork.co.uk/0100news/0100localnews/tm_headline=brainwash-campaign-by-lindsay%26method=full%26objectid=15754099%26page=3%26siteid=50060-name_page.html.

[45] 'Study rejects claim that Muslim areas harbour terrorists', *Guardian*, 20 November 2006, http://www.guardian.co.uk/terrorism/story/0,,1952281,00.html.

[46] 'Terrorism and Community Relations', House of Commons, Home Affairs Select Committee, 6th Report, 5 April 2005, p 25, http://www.publications.parliament.uk/pa/cm200405/cmselect/cmhaff/cmhaff.htm.

[47] 'Straw veil remarks demo cancelled', BBC NewsOnline, 12 October 2006, http://news.bbc.co.uk/1/hi/england/lancashire/6045644.stm.

[48] 'Blair's concerns over face veils', BBC NewsOnline, 17 October 2006, http://news.bbc.co.uk/1/hi/uk_politics/6058672.stm.

[49] 'Unabated antagonization', *Muslim Weekly*, undated, http://www.themuslimweekly.com/fullstoryview.aspx?NewsID=EF92FF24B1230263D0754E17&MENUID=EDITORIAL&DESCRIPTION=Archives. (Accessed March 2008.)

[50] 'Muslims' reaction to pope', *Muslim Weekly*, undated, http://www.themuslimweekly.com/fullstoryview.aspx?NewsID=9BC70B38BD271E77FC793AFB&MENUID=EDITORIAL&DESCRIPTION=Archives. (Accessed March 2008.)

[51] 'Gloucester Muslims tell Blunkett to resign', BBC NewsOnline, 2 December 2003, http://news.bbc.co.uk/1/hi/england/3253314.stm.

[52] 'The Shabina Begum case never had anything to do with modesty', *Daily Telegraph*, 23 March 2006, http://www.telegraph.co.uk/opinion/main.jhtml?xml=/opinion/2006/03/23/do2303.xml.

[53] Malik K, 'What Muslims Want', *Dispatches*, Channel 4 TV, http://www.channel4.com/news/microsites/D/dispatches2006/muslim_survey/muslims.html.

[54] 'Strangers in the family', BBC NewsOnline, 12 July 2004, http://news.bbc.co.uk/1/hi/magazine/3826983.stm.

[55] 'Why I joined the British jihad – and why I rejected it', *Sunday Times*, 16 September 2007, http://www.timesonline.co.uk/tol/news/uk/article2459969.ece.

[56] 'Terrorism and Community Relations', House of Commons, Home Affairs Select Committee, 6th Report, 5 April 2005, p 20, http://www.publications.parliament.uk/pa/cm200405/cmselect/cmhaff/cmhaff.htm.

[57] 'Young Muslims and Extremism', Home Office-FCO Paper, 10 May 2004, http://www.timesonline.co.uk/article/0,,22989-1688872,00.html.

[58] 'ICM poll for the *Guardian*', ICM, March 2004, http://www.icmresearch.co.uk/reviews/2004/guardian-muslims-march-2004.asp.

[59] 'ICM poll for the *Guardian*', ICM, November 2004, http://www.icmresearch.co.uk/reviews/2004/Guardian%20Muslims%20Poll%20Nov%2004/Guardian%20Muslims%20Nov04.asp.

[60] 'ICM poll for the *Guardian*', ICM, July 2005, http://www.icmresearch.co.uk/reviews/2005/Guardian%20-%20muslims%20july05/Guardian%20Muslims%20jul05.asp.

[61] 'ICM poll for the *Guardian*', ICM, June 2006, http://www.icmresearch.co.uk/reviews/2006/Guardian%20-%20muslims%20-%20june06/Guardian%20Muslim%20june06.asp.

[62] 'Young Muslims and Extremism', Home Office-FCO Paper, 10 May 2004, p 8, http://www.timesonline.co.uk/article/0,,22989-1688872,00.html.

[63] 'Terrorism and Community Relations', House of Commons, Home Affairs Select Committee, 6th Report, 5 April 2005, p 24, http://www.publications.parliament.uk/pa/cm200405/cmselect/cmhaff/cmhaff.htm.

[64] Malik K, 'What Muslims Want', *Dispatches*, Channel 4 TV, http://www.channel4.com/news/microsites/D/dispatches2006/muslim_survey/muslims.html.

[65] Report of the Official Account of the Bombings in London on 7 July 2005, HC1087 (London: The Stationery Office), 11 May 2006.

[66] Report of the Official Account of the Bombings in London on 7 July 2005, HC1087 (London: The Stationery Office), 11 May 2006.

[67] 'My son the fanatic', *Guardian*, 2 January 2002, http://www.guardian.co.uk/ukresponse/story/0,11017,626641,00.html.

[68] '"Khaka" and "Sid", the committed jihadists who turned to murder', *Independent*, 20 May 2007, http://news.independent.co.uk/uk/crime/article333650.ece.

[69] 'Young Muslims and Extremism', Home Office-FCO Paper, 10 May 2004, http://www.timesonline.co.uk/article/0,,22989-1688872,00.html.

[70] Malik K, 'What Muslims Want', *Dispatches*, Channel 4 TV, http://www.channel4.com/news/microsites/D/dispatches2006/muslim_survey/muslims.html.

[71] 'ICM poll for the *Daily Telegraph*', ICM, February 2006.

[72] Community Cohesion: A Report of the Independent Review Team Chaired by Ted Cantle, p 23.

[73] In 2003–04, there were 3,616 prosecutions for racially aggravated offences, with an 86 per cent conviction rate, and 44 prosecutions for religiously aggravated offences with a 77 per cent conviction rate.

[74] 'Terrorism and Community Relations', House of Commons, Home Affairs Select Committee, 6th Report, 5 April 2005, p 24, http://www.publications.parliament.uk/pa/cm200405/cmselect/cmhaff/cmhaff.htm.

[75] 'Terrorism and Community Relations', House of Commons, Home Affairs Select Committee, 6th Report, 5 April 2005, p 12, http://www.publications.parliament.uk/pa/cm200405/cmselect/cmhaff/cmhaff.htm.

[76] An opinion poll of British Muslims in March 2004 found that 64 per cent of respondents believed that anti-terrorism laws were being unfairly used against

the Muslim community. 'ICM poll for the *Guardian*', ICM, March 2004, http://www.icmresearch.co.uk/reviews/2004/guardian-muslims-march-2004.asp.

[77] 'ICM poll for the *Guardian*', ICM, November 2004, http://www.icmresearch.co.uk/reviews/2004/Guardian%20Muslims%20Poll%20 Nov%2004/Guardian%20Muslims%20Nov04.asp.

[78] 'Muslims concerned about mosque raid', BBC NewsOnline, 20 January 2003, http://news.bbc.co.uk/1/hi/uk/2675769.stm.

[79] 'ICM poll for the *Sunday Telegraph*', ICM, February 2006, http://www.icmresearch.co.uk/reviews/2006/Sunday%20Telegraph%20- %20Mulims%20Feb/Sunday%20Telegraph%20Muslims%20feb06.asp.

[80] 'ICM poll for the *Guardian*', ICM, July 2005, http://www.icmresearch.co.uk/reviews/2005/Guardian%20-%20muslims% 20july05/Guardian%20Muslims%20jul05.asp.

[81]

Ethnic Group	2001–02	2002–03	2003–04
White	6,629	14,429	20,637
Black	529	1,745	2,704
Asian	744	2,989	3,668
Other/Not recorded	618	2,414	2398
TOTAL	8,550	21,577	29,407

Source: House of Commons Debates, 1 November 2004, cols 55-60W and *Statistics on Race and the Criminal Justice System 2004*

[82] 'More whites than Asians stopped by antisuicide bomber police', *The Times*, 26 September 2007, http://www.timesonline.co.uk/tol/news/uk/crime/article2531840.ece?token=null &offset=12.

[83] Malik K, 'What Muslims Want', *Dispatches*, Channel 4 TV, http://www.channel4.com/news/microsites/D/dispatches2006/muslim_survey/m uslims.html.

[84] 'Muslim anger over stop and search', BBC NewsOnline, 2 July 2004, http://news.bbc.co.uk/1/hi/uk/3860505.stm.

[85] 'Muslim anger over stop and search', BBC NewsOnline, 2 July 2004, http://news.bbc.co.uk/1/hi/uk/3860505.stm.

[86] 'Terrorism and Community Relations', House of Commons, Home Affairs Select Committee, 6th Report, 5 April 2005, p 41, http://www.publications.parliament.uk/pa/cm200405/cmselect/cmhaff/cmhaff.htm.

[87] 'Rise in police searches of Asians', BBC NewsOnline, 2 July 2004, http://news.bbc.co.uk/1/hi/uk/3859023.stm.

[88] 'Terrorism and Community Relations', House of Commons, Home Affairs Select Committee, 6th Report, 5 April 2005, p 18, http://www.publications.parliament.uk/pa/cm200405/cmselect/cmhaff/cmhaff.htm.

[89] 'Terrorism and Community Relations', House of Commons, Home Affairs Select Committee, 6th Report, 5 April 2005, p 44, http://www.publications.parliament.uk/pa/cm200405/cmselect/cmhaff/cmhaff.htm.

[90] 'UK Muslims react to terror raids', BBC NewsOnline, 4 August 2004, http://news.bbc.co.uk/1/hi/uk/3536638.stm.

[91] 'UK Muslims react to terror raids', BBC NewsOnline, 4 August 2004, http://news.bbc.co.uk/1/hi/uk/3536638.stm.

[92] 'Preacher calls for death to all Muslim soldiers', *Sunday Times*, 4 February 2007, http://www.timesonline.co.uk/article/0,,2087-2583243_2,00.html.

[93] 'Muslims "demonised" by UK media', BBC NewsOnline, 13 November 2007, http://news.bbc.co.uk/1/hi/england/london/7093390.stm.

[94] 'Man U bomb plot probe ends in farce', *Guardian*, 2 May 2004.

[95] 'Gloucester Muslims tell Blunkett to resign', BBC NewsOnline, 2 December 2003, http://news.bbc.co.uk/1/hi/england/3253314.stm.

[96] 'Terror raid coverage "offensive"', BBC NewsOnline, 31 March 2004, http://news.bbc.co.uk/1/hi/england/3585085.stm.

[97] 'Terror raid coverage "offensive"', BBC NewsOnline, 31 March 2004, http://news.bbc.co.uk/1/hi/england/3585085.stm.

[98] Report of the Official Account of the Bombings in London on 7 July 2005, HC1087 (London: The Stationery Office), 11 May 2006.

[99] 'Pakistan: the incubator for al-Qaeda's attacks on London', Toby Harnden and Massoud Ansari, *Daily Telegraph*, 23 July 2005, http://www.telegraph.co.uk/news/main.jhtml?xml=/news/2005/07/24/nterr224.xml&page=3.

[100] 'Profile: Omar Khyam', BBC NewsOnline, 30 April 2007, http://news.bbc.co.uk/1/hi/uk/6149794.stm.

[101] 'Profile: Salahuddin Amin', BBC News Online, 30 April 2007, http://news.bbc.co.uk/1/hi/uk/6149790.stm.

[102] 'The boy who didn't stand out', Ian Cobain, 14 July 2005, *Guardian*, http://www.guardian.co.uk/attackonlondon/story/0,,1528199,00.html; 'The London bombers', *The Times*, 15 July 2005, http://www.timesonline.co.uk/article/0,,22989-1693739,00.html.

[103] Report of the Official Account of the Bombings in London on 7 July 2005, HC1087 (London: The Stationery Office), 11 May 2006.

[104] Wikipedia, http://en.wikipedia.org/wiki/Abu_Hamza_al-Masri.

[105] 'Making of a martyr: From pacifism to jihad', *Observer*, 4 May 2003, http://www.guardian.co.uk/terrorism/story/0,12780,949104,00.html.

[106] 'What turned two happy teenagers into hate-driven suicide bombers?' Nick Britten, Rosie Waterhouse, Sean O'Neill, 2 May 2003, http://www.telegraph.co.uk/news/main.jhtml?xml=/news/2003/05/02/wbomb102.xml.

[107] Lévy B, *Who Killed Daniel Pearl?* (New York: Melville House, 2003), pp 90–96.

[108] Begg M, *Enemy Combatant: A British Muslim's Journey to Guantanamo and Back* (London: The Free Press, 2006), pp 48–57.

[109] 'Race hate fear over attacks on Sikhs', *Daily Telegraph*, 30 October 2001, http://www.telegraph.co.uk/news/main.jhtml?xml=/news/2001/10/31/nsikh31.xml.

[110] 'Children injured in school rampage', *Daily Telegraph*, 16 October 2001, http://www.telegraph.co.uk/news/main.jhtml?xml=/news/2001/10/17/nramp17.xml.

[111] 'Police fear Asian gangs may set up "no go" areas', *Daily Telegraph*, 20 July 2001, http://www.telegraph.co.uk/news/main.jhtml?xml=/news/2001/04/20/nogo20.xml.

[112] 'Pakistani gangs are targeting us, say fearful black youths', *Daily Telegraph*, 7 December 2003, http://www.telegraph.co.uk/news/main.jhtml?xml=/news/2003/12/07/nrace07.xml.

[113] 'The jihadist who needed no brainwashing to blow up Aldgate train', Ian

Herbert and Kim Sengupta, *Independent*, 10 September 2005, http://news.independent.co.uk/uk/crime/article311539.ece.

114 Begg M, *Enemy Combatant: A British Muslim's Journey to Guantanamo and Back* (London: The Free Press, 2006), p 37.

115 'At school with the shoe bomber', *Guardian*, 28 February 2002, http://www.guardian.co.uk/g2/story/0,3604,659184,00.html.

Chapter 4

Afghanistan, Iraq and the 'war on Terror'

BRITISH MUSLIMS AND VIOLENT *JIHAD*

In 2001, the UK joined the US in invading Afghanistan and ousting the Taliban regime that had been sheltering *al Qaeda*. Two years later, they joined the US again to invade Iraq and overthrow the regime of Saddam Hussein. Both invasions were successful in achieving their immediate objectives, but the political fallout from these conflicts would be felt on the streets of UK cities in the following years. Since 2003, there has been a dramatic increase in terrorist activity in the UK by individuals and groups based within the Muslim population. Prior to the invasion of Afghanistan, violent militant activity among the Muslim population of the UK was primarily manifested as involvement in *jihad* overseas, particularly in Bosnia, Kosovo, Chechnya and Kashmir. But following the invasions of Afghanistan and Iraq this activity has become much more inwardly directed, against the UK itself. To appreciate the significance of the UK's involvement in the 'war on terror' as one of the catalysts to the upsurge of terrorist violence in the UK since 9/11, it is necessary to understand the ideology of Islamist terrorism, how it has evolved since the 1990s and how it has engaged British Muslims.

Traditional Islamic jurisprudence sees violent *jihad* as an obligation

111

in a world divided between the land of Islam (*dar al-Islam*) and the land of conflict (*dar al-Harb*). Further distinction is made in the *Qur'an* between offensive and defensive *jihad*. When non-Muslims invade *dar al-Islam*, it is possible to issue a *fatwa* to sanction a state of *jihad*. In these situations, it is an individual obligation for all Muslims to take part, either through fighting, providing funding or praying. An offensive *jihad* to attack non-Muslim countries (*dar al-Kuffar*) to subject them to *Sha'ria* law is a collective obligation. The 'sword verses' in the *Qur'an* direct Muslims to 'fight and slay the pagans wherever ye find them and seize them, beleaguer them and lie in wait for them'.[1] In history, the 'sword verses' were used as the religious justification for armed expansion, and contemporary militants claim that these more aggressive verses abrogate the earlier verses in the *Qur'an* which enjoin a non-violent form of *jihad*.[2] The ideology of contemporary Islamist terrorists defines their struggle as a defensive *jihad* against apostate regimes in the Muslim world and the more powerful Crusader-Zionist alliance which is repressing the Muslim *ummah*. For the Islamist ideologues, the medieval Crusades never ended and they are effectively still fighting them.

When the Soviet Union invaded Afghanistan in 1979, the Saudi cleric Sheikh Abdullah Azzam and other religious leaders issued *fatwas* declaring a defensive *jihad* to free Afghanistan.[3] This call to arms was answered by many young Muslims, including Osama bin Laden, determined to free Afghanistan from foreign invaders and establish an Islamist regime that would govern according to *Sha'ria* law. Following the defeat of the Soviet Union in 1989, the foreign *jihadis* in Afghanistan were at an impasse: some returned to their countries of origin, while others remained in Afghanistan intent upon continuing the *jihad*. But, with the unifying force of the war against the Soviet Union gone, they quickly divided into rival factions which advocated different visions of the future direction of the *jihad*. One group, inspired by the ideas of Azzam, advocated the use of *jihad* to reclaim lands that were once Muslim, such as the Philippines, Palestine and Andalucía (southern Spain). The other group, mainly consisting of Egyptians, inspired by the ideas of Sayyid Qutb, focused on the short-term goal of overthrowing the Egyptian government and replacing it with an Islamist regime.[4]

While British Muslims supported the fight of the Afghan *mujahideen* against the Soviet Union, there is little evidence of British-born Muslims actually fighting in the war. It was not until the 1991 Gulf War that international affairs and British foreign policy appear to have begun to play a significant role in the radicalisation of young British Muslims. The conflict was sparked by the Iraqi invasion of Kuwait, which gave Iraq control of Kuwaiti oil reserves. Acting under the authority of UN resolutions demanding that Iraq withdraw from Kuwait, the US led an international coalition of states which used military force to drive out the Iraqi army. Despite the fact that the US coalition was responding to flagrant aggression against the state of Kuwait, and that the Saddam regime was one of the most brutal dictatorships in the world, many British Muslims opposed the war and Britain's involvement in it. For them, the war was nothing more than a demonstration of Western hypocrisy based on blatant self-interest. Western use of military force to implement the UN resolutions demanding that Iraq pull its armed forces out of Kuwait contrasted sharply with the failure of the West to enforce various other UN resolutions related to the Middle East, particularly those which called for Israel to withdraw from the lands it has occupied since the 1967 Arab–Israeli war, and a just settlement to the Palestinian refugee problem. Western policy *vis a vis* the invasion of Kuwait was considered to be driven by greed for oil, and the failure to compel Israel to implement UN resolutions was seen as bias in favour of Israel and anti-Islamic in nature.

Despite this opposition to US and British foreign policy in the Middle East, the only evidence of British-born Muslims leaving the country to fight in *jihad* was of Britons of Pakistani descent travelling to Pakistan to join the insurgency in Indian-controlled Kashmir, where a number of groups were fighting to achieve independence from India for the predominantly Muslim state. The involvement of

British Muslims in this conflict seems to have been more as a result of community and nationalist sentiments among Britons of Pakistani descent than it was about the spread of Islamist ideology within the UK.

Following the 1991 Gulf War, the presence of US troops in Saudi Arabia and Somalia provided the catalyst for renewed calls among Islamist ideologues for a defensive *jihad* to drive US forces from the Gulf region. However, a more global vision of Islam's problems began to take shape at that time: the leaders of Muslim states were seen as pawns of global US power, and the US was identified as the main obstacle to the re-establishment of the *caliphate*, the Islamic super-state which would reintroduce God's law into the world. They argued that, once the US had been forced to withdraw their support for non-Islamist regimes in the Muslim world, those regimes would be vulnerable to being overthrown and replaced by Islamist alternatives. This group coalesced around Azzam's deputy, Osama bin Laden, and his *al Qaeda* network. *Al Qaeda* believes that Western commerce with Muslim and Arab countries has resulted in Western military support for corrupt and 'apostate' regimes, specifically Saudi Arabia, Egypt, Jordan and Morocco, and has contributed to the corruption of Muslim societies through imported Western values and the 'theft' of Muslim natural resources, particularly oil. It believes that, once these regimes lose Western economic, political and military support, they will be vulnerable to being overthrown by the people and replaced by Islamist regimes imposing *Sha'ria* law.[5]

But, despite the emergence of this ideology, which sought to mobilise Muslims to fight against US foreign policy, the US military presence in Saudi Arabia failed to galvanise any significant mobilisation of British Muslims. Instead, it was only where Muslims were in direct military conflict with non-Muslims that any such mobilisation occurred. The first evidence of young British Muslims becoming indoctrinated with an Islamist ideology and mobilising to fight in *jihad* overseas began to emerge during the war in Bosnia in the mid-1990s. In an age before widespread internet access, young

Muslims became aware of the realities of the war in Bosnia through the mainstream media, discussions in community forums and among community networks, as well as from alternative media such as videotapes that were circulating in the community. The mainstream media reported extensively on the atrocities perpetrated by the Serbian military against Bosnian Muslim civilians and the systematic campaign to drive Bosnian Muslims from land which the Serbs claimed for themselves. This ensured that the brutal reality of 'ethnic cleansing' was brought into the living rooms of everyone in the UK. At the same time, the media reported the failures and weaknesses of the response from the international community, including British foreign policy. In particular, it highlighted the imposition of an arms embargo, which was seen to deprive Muslims of the weapons they needed to defend themselves, and the failure of the UN forces to protect the designated safe haven of Srebrenica, which led to the massacre of thousands of Bosnian Muslim men and boys by the Serb army. Although the British government committed troops to the UN peacekeeping force, it was considered by many to be insufficient. Alongside this reporting in the mainstream media, propaganda videos produced by terrorist and insurgent groups were also circulating in the Muslim communities of the UK. Omar Sheikh was just one British Muslim who was motivated by a film produced by a mainstream documentary maker to join a humanitarian aid convoy to Bosnia, and he then subsequently fought in the war.

The impact of the war in Bosnia on radicalising British Muslims was enormous. Maajid Nawaz argues that 'the Bosnian genocide, however, struck a chord like no other. Up until that point I had mainly been concerned with racism at home. Bosnia was strikingly different. Here were white European Muslims being identified solely as Muslims and being slaughtered for it.'[6]

Angry at what they saw as the failure of NATO and British foreign policy to protect the Bosnian Muslims, unknown numbers of British Muslims made their way to Bosnia to join the Bosnian army. Several were killed in the fighting, such as Sayyad al Falastini, who died loading explosives on to a truck in 1995, apparently in preparation for becoming a suicide bomber. *Al Qaeda* announced that al Falastini was the sixth British Islamic volunteer to be killed in Bosnia.[7] Among the dataset, Sheikh, Shahid Butt and Andrew Rowe all fought in the Bosnian war. When the war ended in 1995, the issue of British *jihadis* dropped off the public radar. Below the radar, however, Islamist propagandists, recruiters and facilitators were busy building networks in the UK to enable recruits to join overseas *jihads*.

The motivations of these early *jihadis* seem to have been varied, and some may simply have been seeking adventure, in the same way as some non-Muslims fought with the Bosnian army. However, empathy or sympathy for the suffering of Muslims in conflicts in other countries is a key driver for British Muslims to fight in *jihad* overseas. At a superficial level, their motivation was their desire to support the *ummah* in conflicts where Muslims are fighting non-Muslims, particularly if it also reflects their own ethno-nationalist background (for example, individuals of Pakistani descent fighting in Kashmir). Shahid Butt describes the *ummah* as an integral part of Islam as 'telling Muslims to take the *ummah* out is like asking me to cut my heart out of my body ... Defending another Muslim is a compulsory act in Islam. You have to do it ... if somebody came to my house and kicked the door down and tried to attack my family I'm gonna go in the kitchen and get the knife and I'm gonna defend them.'[8]

Justice and injustice are powerful motivating forces in Islam. Tyranny or *zulm*, as the opposite of justice, has to be resisted, just as it was by the Prophet Mohammed and his followers, as well as by others over the centuries.[9] For some, this could be driven by a simple sense of idealism generated by their social identification of themselves as Muslims and heightened by their radicalisation over these conflicts. This basic sense of injustice about the weak being oppressed by the strong can be a very powerful motivation and justification for violent action. For others, however, there could be other political or ideological motivations. Some may have been fighting for narrow objectives, such as liberating Kashmir from Indian rule or protecting Bosnian Muslims against the Serb army, while others may have had wider agendas in seeking to establish Islamist regimes. Therefore, although these individuals clearly believed in the concept of violent *jihad*, it does not necessarily mean that they adhered to the ideology of *al Qaeda*, and none of them returned to perpetrate acts of terrorism in the UK.

In Afghanistan, the advocates of a global *jihad*, using the continuing presence of US troops in Saudi Arabia as a rallying cry, began to grow in strength after the war in Bosnia ended. The beginnings of the global *jihad* emerged in August 1996, when bin Laden issued his declaration 'War against the Americans Occupying the Land of the Two Holy Places (Expel the Infidels from the Arab Peninsula)', in which he declared that there is no more important duty than to push US military forces out of the Holy Land. The declaration stated that 'to fight in defence of religion and belief is a collective duty, there is no other duty after belief than fighting the enemy who is corrupting the life and religion'.[10] Just over a year later, in February 1998, bin Laden issued the *fatwa* of the World Islamic Front declaring '*jihad* against Jews and Crusaders', which became the manifesto of the fully fledged global *jihad*. The justification for the *jihad* was given as the US occupation of Saudi Arabia, its support for Israel and the killing of Iraqi children through the maintenance of tough economic sanctions on Iraq long after the 1991 Gulf War had ended, which were considered to be 'a clear attack on Allah, his messenger, and Muslims'. It stated:

> The ruling to kill Americans and their allies – civilians and military – is an individual duty for every Muslim who can do it in any country in which it is possible to do it … We – with Allah's help – call on every Muslim who believes in Allah and wishes to be rewarded to comply with Allah's order to kill the Americans and plunder their money wherever and whenever they find it. We also call on Muslim *Ulema*, leaders, youths, and soldiers to

launch the raid on Satan's troops and the devil's supporters allying with them, and to displace those who are behind them so that they may learn a lesson.[11]

The declaration of war and the *fatwa* unleashed a wave of attacks that have been attributed to *al Qaeda*, including the 1996 bombing of the Khobar Towers in Saudi Arabia, the 1998 suicide bombing of the US embassies in Kenya and Tanzania, the 2000 suicide bombing of the USS *Cole* in Yemen, and 9/11, as well as a number of unsuccessful attacks. The objective of attacking US targets around the world and inside the US itself was to coerce the US government into withdrawing their economic, military and political support for what *al Qaeda* defined as the 'apostate' regimes in the region, but the attacks had no impact on US foreign policy. Britain and British targets were spared *al Qaeda*'s attentions in the 1990s. However, as the US's principal ally in Europe, and a key supporter of policies such as the economic sanctions on Iraq, the *fatwa* implicitly identified the UK as a target and its message was directed at Muslims in the UK, as well as those in many other countries. It was therefore simply a matter of time before aspiring *jihadis* chose to bring the global *jihad* to the UK.

In the meantime, increasing numbers of Britons travelled to fight *jihad* abroad in the late 1990s. The first terrorist plot involving British Muslims following bin Laden's *fatwa* occurred in 1998, when the Yemen 8 cell travelled to Yemen to join the Islamic Army of Aden in trying to overthrow the government and replace it with an Islamist regime. The alleged targets of the cell were the UK consulate in Sa'na, an Anglican church, a Swiss-owned hotel and a gay nightclub.[12] The plot was uncovered by chance when members of the cell were stopped by a traffic policeman for a driving violation. It reflects the views of the *jihadis* who were inspired by the ideas of Qutb, to overthrow individual Muslim governments and replace them with Islamist regimes. Yemen was chosen as the target for the cell because of its close resemblance to Afghanistan, but the cell had also been encouraged to support *jihad* in Kosovo and Egypt, because 'they do not follow the Islamic way', meaning they were not governed according to *Sha'ria* law.[13]

Other Britons continued to be drawn into the conflict in Kashmir, where the objective more closely reflected Azzam's ideals to liberate Muslim land from non-Muslim rule. Among the dataset, Omar Sheikh, Dhiren Barot and Omar Khyam all travelled to Kashmir to fight in the late 1990s. Sheikh was put in touch with militant groups in Pakistan by contacts that he had made in Bosnia, and subsequently flew out to join *Harkat ul-Ansar*, a group that was leading the fight against the Indian army in Kashmir.[14] Barot claims that he travelled to Pakistani-controlled Kashmir in 1995 to 'investigate the duty of *jihad*'. He trained with one of the groups fighting Indian troops in Indian-controlled Kashmir, and it was there that he 'witnessed a side of Islam which cannot be found in classrooms', before going on to fight.[15] Barot would become one of the key *al Qaeda* operatives in the UK and was in direct contact with *al Qaeda* planners in Pakistan, which suggests that he started out as a national *jihadi*, but became an international *jihadi* through further indoctrination in Pakistan and Afghanistan. Also among this wave of *jihadis* was Mohammed Bilal from Birmingham, who became the first British suicide bomber when he was killed during the bombing of an Indian army post in Kashmir, in 2000.

Others made their way to Afghanistan to support the Taliban regime, which they deemed to be the only truly Islamic regime in the world. After receiving training in Kashmir, Mohammed Siddique Khan travelled to Afghanistan in July 2001 to fight against the Northern Alliance, which comprised Afghan nationals opposed to the Taliban. The fact that Khan fought against fellow Muslims in Afghanistan indicates that he was driven by a belief in an Islamist ideology, rather than any sense of outrage against Muslims being oppressed. Others, including Andrew Rowe, made their way to Chechnya to support the Chechen separatists in their struggle for independence from Russia. However, while these individuals had been radicalised by events in other countries and had decided to act due to the inaction or perceived failures of British foreign policy, there was no political drive to turn their violence towards the UK itself.

Although the focus of British *jihadi* activity in the late 1990s was on supporting oppressed Muslims overseas, British Muslims were quietly being drawn into the global *jihad*. Ideological texts were circulating in the UK, and the ideologies of Azzam and Qutb were spreading among the young. Abdulla Ahmed Ali, one of the leaders of the Airline cell, possessed copies of *The Lofty Mountain* by Azzam and *Milestones* by Qutb, as well as books about the experiences of *mujahideen* in Afghanistan.[16] At this time, young Britons began travelling to Islamist training camps in Afghanistan, from where some of them were talent-spotted and recruited into *al Qaeda*. Prior to 9/11, MI5 estimated that 600–800 Britons had trained in camps run by *al Qaeda* in Afghanistan,[17] and evidence uncovered in *al Qaeda* camps at Tora Bora after the invasion of Afghanistan suggests the number was as high as 1,200.[18] Among these early recruits were Reid and Badat. The influence of bin Laden was acknowledged by Umar Islam of the Airline cell, when he declared in his 'martyrdom' video that bin Laden had inspired him personally to follow the 'true path of the prophet'.[19]

THE 'WAR ON TERROR'

The presence of US troops in Afghanistan and Iraq has provided new opportunities for the global *jihadis* to fight the US armed forces, and new conflicts on which to declare a *jihad*. *Al Qaeda* and other Islamist terrorist groups have used the conflicts in Afghanistan and Iraq as a rallying call for the *ummah* to join the international *jihad*. Since 9/11, bin Laden and his deputy, Ayman al Zawahiri, have issued numerous video- and audio-tape messages declaring the US-led 'war on terror' to be a war on Islam, and urging Muslims to join the *jihad* against the West. Muslims from across the world, including Britain, have heeded these calls and have made their way to fight in Afghanistan and Iraq. These messages have been widely reported in the Western media and spread across the internet. However, bin Laden's calls for a *jihad* are not only directed against the US and its Western allies, they have also urged Muslims in strategically important countries such as Pakistan and Saudi Arabia to rise up and oust their rulers.

As was the case during the war in Bosnia, British Muslims were first introduced to the realities of the wars in Afghanistan and Iraq by reporting in the mainstream media, as well as through community forums and networks. The media has played a major role in raising public awareness of a whole range of issues surrounding the 'war on terror'. This has included exposing the fallacies of the British government's case for invading Iraq, as well as reporting the killing and suffering of Afghan and Iraqi civilians, and the abuses of the US and UK military. Some of the most damaging reporting was of the Abu Ghraib prison scandal, in which Iraqi detainees were physically abused and tortured by their US guards. Much of this reporting has been highly critical of the British government.

Even in mainstream mosques, British Muslims can be exposed to highly emotive anti-Western rhetoric about conflicts overseas. In a speech entitled 'The globalised suffering of the Muslims', Riyadh al Huq argued that:

The truth is, whether it's Macedonia or whether it's Kosovo or whether it's Bosnia, Allah has told us in the *Qur'an* why they are being targeted, why their blood is being shed, why they are being massacred, why they are being butchered, tortured, why their women are being raped: Allah says: 'They do not take revenge against them, except because they have believed in Allah, the Almighty, the one full of praise.' That is their only crime, that they are Muslims. Europe has made it clear, they will not tolerate a Muslim force or power in Europe, and if it means massacring Muslims, if it means genocide, if it means a holocaust in Europe again, so be it. For this time, the target is Muslims ... The demonic powers of the west have joined together in a concerted, potentially genocidal mission to humiliate, murder, rape and pillage Muslim lands and people. Their target is Islam.[20]

These conflicts are also occurring in the internet age, which has led to an explosion in the amount of terrorist propaganda available online. *Al Qaeda* itself is known to have operated a number of websites, but they represent only a fraction of the militant websites that exist. The internet has had a significant impact on the dissemination of militant Islamist propaganda because of its ability to host enormous quantities of material, its global reach and its flexibility, which enables propagandists to post new material as soon as it is available and to switch between websites if one is closed down. Some of this propaganda is ideological in nature, comprising speeches, sermons and statements by terrorist leaders, ideologues and propagandists. But a lot of it is war footage from various *jihads* that has been shot on camcorders by the *jihadis* themselves. This propaganda celebrates the military success of the insurgents as well as eulogising their 'martyrs'. Most of the dataset either possessed or are known to have viewed a wide range of this propaganda. But not all of this propaganda material concerned the 'war on terror', Afghanistan or Iraq; considerable amounts of it related to the more longstanding conflicts in the Palestinian territories, Chechnya and Kashmir.

Opposition to the 'war on terror' is widespread within radical Muslim political groups and networks in the UK, such as *al Muhajiroun* and *Hizb ut-Tahrir*. These groups were active in facilitating and recruiting young British Muslims to fight in Afghanistan and Iraq, but they were not involved in violent terrorist activity in the UK itself. However, it is not just 'radical' or 'militant' Muslims who oppose British foreign policy in the 'war on terror'; it has also caused considerable resentment and anger throughout the Muslim population. British Muslims were overwhelmingly opposed to the invasions of Afghanistan and Iraq; an opinion poll in March 2004 showed that 80 per cent of the respondents felt that the war to remove Saddam Hussein was unjustified, and 61 per cent felt the UK should pull its troops out of Iraq immediately. The same poll also showed that 60 per cent agreed that the 'war on terror' was not a war against Islam,[21] but a later poll in November 2004 indicated that 80 per cent of respondents disagreed with the contention that the 'war on terror' was not a war on Islam.[22]

Underpinning the opposition of British Muslims to the 'war on terror' are a number of interlinked issues. Foremost among them is concern about the number of civilian casualties and the resulting humanitarian crises that both interventions caused. Second is a profound distrust of the US and Western motives in invading Iraq and Afghanistan. It is widely suspected that the US invaded Afghanistan to secure new oil pipeline routes and invaded Iraq in order to control its vast oil supplies. These views link into wider concerns that the US is seeking world domination, politically, economically and culturally. One of the main ways that Muslims believe the US is trying to achieve this is through exporting Western culture, ideas and values to the Middle East. Third, this fuels one of the main suspicions in the Muslim population about the 'war on terror', that it is actually a war on Islam. These views were reinforced by the belief that the US and UK did not have a just cause for either invasion because neither the Taliban nor Saddam Hussein was involved in the events of 9/11. These views were confirmed when the failure to find any weapons of mass destruction in Iraq exposed the fallacy of the US and UK governments' arguments that Iraq posed an imminent threat to peace in the Middle East. This is not to say that the majority of British Muslims had any particular sympathy for either the Taliban or Saddam regimes, but their disquiet about these regimes is outweighed by their opposition to the US and UK military intervention. The attitudes are particularly strong among young Muslims, with a study published in January 2007 finding evidence that 58 per cent of Muslims in the 16- to 24-year-old age group believed that many of the world's problems were the result of 'arrogant Western attitudes'.[23] Many members of our dataset fall within this age group.

This opposition to the 'war on terror', and its identification as a war against Islam, is often articulated and led by mainstream

Imams. In late 2001, Riyadh al Huq gave a lecture entitled 'Infinite Justice' in which he argued that:

> The question is: is this war against the Muslims of Afghanistan just? Is this campaign justified? Is justice with the coalition or not? And I'm sure most will say that it is offensive from the very outset to consider this war to be just. And if it is not just, then those who are perpetrating it are directly responsible for the tyranny and injustice that they are visiting upon the Muslims of Afghanistan. As such, they are tyrants and oppressors in the laws of Islam and in the sight of the Muslims. This is tyranny. What crime has the government of Afghanistan [the Taliban] committed? All they have done is they have refused to hand over a person [Osama bin Laden] whose guilt is yet to be proven. Because of that crime, the entire nation is being punished. And as a result, because they strive to represent Islam, the whole of Islam is being demonised. As a result, Muslims all over the globe are being discriminated against. We are being warned, hints are being dropped and a lot is happening. And worst of all, the religion of Islam itself is under attack … America and Britain, two countries, the most powerful combination of forces on earth, are on the warpath against a country that has suffered more than four years of drought and a number of years of famine, that has no civilian infrastructure, let alone a military infrastructure. And why is Afghanistan being bombed? We're doing it in self-defence. They call it self-defence. Isn't this tyranny, isn't this injustice, isn't this terror ? How can we as Muslims support such a war? Never.[24]

The inability to influence the government's decision making on the 'war on terror' has led to an increased alienation of many Muslims from the political mainstream. Opposition to the wars in Afghanistan and Iraq is one of the issues on which the views of militant political and religious groups dovetail with mainstream discourse in the

Muslim population. Militant Islamist and terror groups have exploited these sentiments with rhetoric about the Islamic duty to protect the *ummah*, and claims that the two wars are part of a wider war on Islam. This has added impetus to increased levels of activism and radicalisation among some sections of the Muslim population, particularly the young. For many, this has simply involved charity work to ease the suffering of the civilians caught up in the fighting; others have become politically active with radical political or religious groups, while others have provided material support to the fighters in what they perceive to be wars of national liberation.

While the majority of Muslims cannot support the 'war on terror' and the UK's role in it, they are faced with the dilemma of what they should do about it. Mainstream Muslim representative groups and Imams have no answer, and have failed to influence government policy. Street protests were equally ineffective. Muslims witnessed the overwhelming groundswell of popular opposition to the war in Iraq, but also its inability to influence the course of events. They also perceived the mainstream political process as failing to address their concerns. When the opportunity came for the British public to express its opposition to the Iraq war in the 2005 general election, the Labour government was returned to power. For politicised young Muslims, the most galling aspect of this was that significant numbers of Muslims continued to vote for the Labour Party. The former Foreign Secretary Jack Straw, in particular, was reliant on Muslim votes to be re-elected. Only George Galloway, leader of the Respect party in the Bethnal Green constituency in London, who campaigned on a left-wing anti-war agenda, succeeded in galvanising Muslims to break with their established political allegiances. But Galloway's success had little impact on a Labour government that was re-elected with a sizeable majority in Parliament.

For politicised and radicalised young Muslims, the lesson appeared to be that engagement in the mainstream political process had not delivered what they sought. Among the dataset, Abdulla Ahmed Ali in particular declared his anger at the failure of the mass public protest against the Iraq war in 2003.[25] For some, the people who are to blame for this are the British electorate. This was argued forcefully by Umar Islam of the Airline cell, in his 'martyrdom' video. When asked off-camera what he thought about 'so-called innocent people that might be killed in this operation', he stated:

> I say to you disbelievers that, as you bomb, you will be bombed and as you kill, you will be killed and if you want to kill our women and children, then the same thing will happen to you. I do not consider anyone innocent who while their sons and their daughters and their soldiers are pillaging the Muslim lands of its resources and dishonouring our Muslim brothers and sisters and you sit back and pay taxes which is funding this army to do what it was doing ... These are not innocents ... Even if you disagree you're just sitting there, and you're still funding the Army and you haven't put down your leader, you haven't pressured them enough. Most of you are too busy, you know, watching *Home and Away* and *EastEnders*, complaining about the World Cup and drinking your alcohol to even care about anything.[26]

This failure to influence government policy has provided a renewed impetus for British Muslims to engage in violent *jihad* overseas, with Islamist terror groups offering a practical solution for those who feel compelled to act. The exact numbers who have fought in overseas conflicts since 9/11 are unknown. The Pakistani intelligence services have confirmed that a number of British Pakistanis are known to have fought alongside the Taliban. A source close to the Taliban claimed that 'no more than 10' of its fighters were known to be British passport holders, although it could not vouch for exactly how many of its Pakistani volunteers also held British passports.[27] Seven British Muslims are known to have been killed in Afghanistan in 2001,[28] including Suragah al Andalusi, who was killed by an American airstrike in the mountains of Tora Bora in November 2001. In writings published after his death, al Andalusi urged Muslims to abandon the 'pessimism and despair' of the 'capitalist mindset'. He saw *jihad* and martyrdom as evidence of religious commitment, and declared that 'the victory will come from Allah, but upon us is to obey the commandments and join the path of *jihad*'. He called for the imposition of *Sha'ria* law in Muslim lands and labelled democracy 'the way of the Devil'. While it is not known whether Mohammed Siddique Khan ever met al Andalusi, although Khan was evidently inspired by him, because his last will and testament draws heavily on al Andalusi's writings.[29] Others continued to fight in more longstanding conflicts, and a number of Britons have been killed fighting for the insurgents in Chechnya.[30]

As the 'war on terror' has unfolded, new conflicts have emerged for would-be *jihadis*, the most prominent of which has been the war in Iraq. In 2006, one intelligence estimate put the number of British Muslims who had gone to fight in Iraq at 150.[31]

In 2006, another new front opened up in Somalia, where the Union of Islamic Courts achieved a remarkable success in defeating the warlords who had ravaged the country for almost two decades, and imposing *Sha'ria* law on large parts of the country. Its victory was short-lived, however, as concerns over the Union of Islamic Court's links to *al Qaeda* led Ethiopia to invade Somalia with US air support that same year, and oust it. In response, Ayman al Zawahiri declared a *jihad* against the new government of Somalia and its Ethiopian backers in January 2007. Among those who responded to the call to arms were some members of Britain's Somali community. In 2006, four Britons were arrested in Kenya after fleeing Somalia, although they denied any involvement in the fighting.[32] Only one of the dataset, Hassan Mutegombwa, has been linked to the conflict in Somalia; in 2008, he was convicted of receiving terrorist training and seeking money for terrorism, after being stopped by police at Heathrow airport as he tried to catch a flight to Nairobi allegedly en route to become a suicide bomber in Somalia.[33]

Since 2001, evidence has emerged of links between some of the groups fighting in these national *jihads* and international terrorism inspired by *al Qaeda*. This nexus has become increasingly evident with a number of the groups fighting in Indian-controlled Kashmir. *Lashkar-e-Taiba*, for instance, has been fighting to liberate Kashmir since the end of the war against the Soviet Union in Afghanistan, but it has also embraced the wider objective of establishing an Islamic *caliphate*.[34] The attack on Mumbai in 2008 by terrorists linked to *Lashkar-e-Taiba* can primarily be viewed as part of its campaign to liberate Kashmir, but the specific targeting of Jews, Americans and Britons during the attack also suggests that it was inspired by the ideology of the international *jihad*. Links between *al Qaeda* and certain of these *jihadi* groups indicate that the potential for individuals to become involved in international terrorism through those conflicts will remain strong.

It is also apparent that, for every British citizen who makes it to the front line in these conflicts, there are an unknown number of others who are prevented from doing so. In 2006, one police force alone reported that it had detained up to a dozen individuals suspected of being en route to fight against US and UK forces in Afghanistan or Iraq. They were described as men who had 'come to terms with death'.[35] This has led to a number of young British Muslims who want to fight the coalition forces in Iraq or Afghanistan either being prosecuted or placed under control orders to prevent them from joining the insurgents. This includes Lamine and Adam Garcia, the brothers of Anthony Garcia of the Ammonium Nitrate cell. However, many of them are simply prevented from travelling, and are released because the police cannot charge them with anything. The presence of these thwarted *jihadis* within the UK poses an immediate problem for domestic security. Therefore, there is good evidence that the wars in Afghanistan, Iraq and elsewhere have had a key role in catalysing *jihadi* violence among British Muslims. The important question is what links involvement in overseas *jihad* to terrorist violence in the UK.

THE DATASET AND THE 'WAR ON TERROR'

It is a reasonable assumption that all of the dataset were angry about the 'war on terror' and were opposed to the British government's policy, but it cannot be seen as the catalyst which triggered the start of their radicalisation because virtually all of them had either begun the process of radicalisation, or had joined terrorist cells, prior to 9/11.[36] Among the dataset, only Kazi Rahman is known to have fought in either Afghanistan or Iraq. In late 2001, he was fighting with the Taliban, when he confided to another British *jihadi* that he intended to return to the UK and attack civilian targets. Rahman escaped to Pakistan, and, instead of staying there to continue the fight in Afghanistan, he returned to East London where he became the alleged leader of a terrorist cell. It is also possible that Hanif and Sharif were catalysed into action by the 'war on terror', even though their attack was part of the decades-old conflict in the occupied Palestinian territories. In their 'martyrdom' video, they declared that they were acting 'for the sake of Allah and to get revenge against the Jews and Crusaders'.[37] Elsewhere on the tape, Sharif declared that 'Muslims are being killed every day. It is an honour to kill one of those people [Jews].'[38] The reference to Crusaders hints at ideological motivations beyond the Israel–Palestine conflict, reflecting the ideological belief of Abdullah Azzam and *al Qaeda* that Muslims are engaged in a continuing war with the Crusader nations of the West.

In addition, a number of others in the dataset attended training camps with the apparent intention of fighting in these conflicts but never actually did so, and instead were redirected to perpetrate terrorist attacks in the UK. This is particularly true of the Ammonium Nitrate cell. A key element of the cell's defence in court was that they were overseas *jihadis* rather than terrorists, and Garcia claimed that the ammonium nitrate itself was for use in Kashmir. However, there is no evidence that any of them actually fought in Kashmir. Similarly, Mohammed Siddique Khan wanted to return to fight in Afghanistan, and, when he met with Omar Khyam in February 2004, they discussed arrangements for getting to the 'front', which can be taken to mean the frontline in Afghanistan.[39] It is therefore likely that, when Khan visited Pakistan in November 2004, it was with the intention of going to fight in Afghanistan,[40] but there is no evidence that he actually did so. Similarly, Muktar Said Ibrahim, the leader of the 21/7 cell, spent four months in Pakistan in late 2004 and early 2005, apparently with the intention of waging *jihad* in Afghanistan, but returned to the UK in March 2005.[41]

Although the 'war on terror' was not the catalyst that started the radicalisation of the dataset, it can be viewed as a trigger for these individuals to either engage in terrorist violence or to redirect their violence towards terrorism in the UK. This is borne out by the case of Omar Khyam, who, prior to 9/11, was on the fringes of violent extremist activity, acting as a courier between militants in the UK and Pakistan. It was not until after the invasion of Iraq that a facilitator in the UK arranged for Khyam to meet Abdul Hadi, a senior *al Qaeda* figure based in Pakistan, to whom he offered his services as more than just a courier.[42] At his trial, Khyam stated that the war in Iraq was 'the final straw' for radical Muslims. He told the jurors that 'it was a war on Islam. I was in Pakistan at that time. A lot of people's attitudes changed. Whereas before, myself and others make excuses, now they believe the UK and America needed to be attacked.'[43] When asked about his reaction to the attacks on the World Trade Center, Khyam stated that he 'was happy. America was, and still is, the greatest enemy of Islam ... They put up puppet regimes in Muslim countries like Saudi Arabia, Jordan and Egypt ... I was happy that America had been hit because of what it represented against the Muslims, but obviously 3,000 people died so there were mixed feelings.'[44] This illustrates his transition from national to international *jihadi*, reflecting the ideology of Azzam and *al Qaeda*. There is no available evidence about Abu Mansha's ideological beliefs, but the 'war on terror' was the backdrop to his plan to murder a British soldier, after he read about the soldier's exploits in Iraq in a newspaper.[45]

Three of the 7/7 cell declared their grievance about the 'war on terror'. Khan had been radicalised prior to 9/11 but had no known involvement in violent terrorist activity prior to the 7 July bombings. He had first expressed a desire to fight in *jihad* in 1999 but it was not until after the 'war on terror' had started that he was persuaded to undertake terrorist attacks in the UK. He did not specifically mention Iraq or Afghanistan in his 'martyrdom' video, but declared that:

I and thousands like me are forsaking everything for what we believe. Our driving motivation doesn't come from tangible commodities that this world has to offer. Our religion is Islam, obedience to the one true God, Allah and follow in the footsteps of the final prophet and messenger Mohammed ... This is how our ethical stances are dictated. Your democratically elected governments continuously perpetuate atrocities against my people and your support of them makes you directly responsible, just as I am directly responsible for protecting and avenging my Muslim brothers and sisters. Until we feel security, you will be our target. Until you stop the bombing, gassing, imprisonment and torture of my people, we will not stop this fight. We are at war and I am a soldier. Now you too will taste the reality of this situation.[46]

Similarly, Tanweer declared in his 'martyrdom' video that his actions had been provoked by British foreign policy and the persecution of Muslims. He said that 'what you have witnessed now is only the beginning of a string of attacks that will continue and become stronger until you pull your forces out of Afghanistan and Iraq and until you stop your financial and military support to America and Israel'.[47]

Germaine Lindsay's widow claimed that towards the end of 2004 he had became increasingly angry as he saw reports of Muslim civilians being killed in Iraq, Bosnia, Palestine and Israel.[48]

Six members of the Airline cell made 'martyrdom' videos in which they declared that their actions were in revenge for US interference in Muslim countries, and the wars in Iraq and Afghanistan, as well as for Britain and America's support for Israel. Umar Islam stated:

> This is to the people of the world to let you know the reasons for the action which, *inshallah*, I am going to undertake. This is revenge for the actions of the USA in the Muslim lands and their accomplices such as the British and the Jews. This is a warning to the non-believers that if they do not leave our lands there are many more like us and many more like me ready to strike until the law of Allah is established on this earth. Know that without doubt your dead are in the hellfire whilst the Muslims who died due to your attacks will be in paradise. Martyrdom operations upon martyrdom operations will keep on raining on these *kuffar* until they release you and leave our lands ... We love to die in the path of Allah. We love to die like you love life, so you cannot win.[49]

He called on other Muslims to attack military, economic and government targets in revenge for the Muslims suffering in Palestine, Afghanistan, Chechnya, Abu Ghraib, Iraq and Guantanamo Bay.[50]

Tanvir Hussain declared, 'I only wish I could come back and do it again and again until people come to their senses and realise – don't mess with the Muslims ... People say we target innocents but we are targeting economic, government and military targets. Collateral damage will be involved, people are going to die but it's worth the price.'

Abdulla Ahmed Ali said:

> We've warned you so many times to get out of our lands, leave us alone, but you have persisted in trying to humiliate us, kill us and destroy us and Sheikh Osama warned you many times to leave our lands or you will be destroyed, and now the time has come for you to be destroyed. You have nothing but to expect that floods of martyr operations, volcanoes of anger and revenge

and raping among your capital and yet, taste that what you have made us taste for a long time and now you have to bear the fruits that you have sown ... Stop meddling in our affairs and we will leave you alone, otherwise expect floods of martyr operations against you and we will take our revenge and anger, ripping amongst your people and scattering the people and your body parts and the people's body parts responsible for these wars and oppression decorating the streets.[51]

Waheed Zaman said, 'America and England have no cause for complaint ... I am warning these two nations and any other country who seeks a bad end, death and destruction will pass upon you like a tornado and you will not feel it, you will not feel any security or peace in your lands until you stop interfering in the affairs of Muslims completely.'[52]

These statements indicate that it is not specifically the 'war on terror', Afghanistan or even Iraq which is the fundamental issue; it is British foreign policy in respect of Muslims and Muslim countries which is crucial. While this might currently coalesce around the issues of Iraq and Afghanistan, it also encompasses issues such as the perceived double standard that the UK applies in the Middle East by acquiescing in Israel's breach of UN resolutions regarding the Palestinian territories. This was confirmed by a joint Home Office and FCO paper entitled 'Young Muslims and Extremism' in May 2004, which suggested that:

It seems that a particularly strong cause of disillusionment amongst Muslims, including young Muslims, is a perceived 'double standard' in the foreign policy of western governments (and often those of Muslim governments), in particular Britain and the US ... This seems to have gained a significant prominence in how some Muslims view HMG's policies towards Muslim countries. Perceived Western bias in Israel's favour over the Israel/Palestinian conflict is a key long-term grievance of the international Muslim community which probably influences British Muslims. This perception seems to have become more acute post 9/11. The perception is that passive 'oppression', as demonstrated in British foreign policy, e.g. non-action on Kashmir and Chechnya, has given way to 'active oppression' – the war on terror and in Iraq and Afghanistan are all seen by a section of British Muslims as having been acts against Islam. This disillusionment may contribute to a sense of helplessness with regard to the situation of Muslims in the world, with a lack of tangible pressure valves, in order to vent frustrations, anger or dissent.[53]

Britain's support for the US in not demanding an early ceasefire during the Israeli invasion of Lebanon in 2006, which resulted in additional civilian casualties and the destruction of homes and infrastructure in Lebanon, was seen as further evidence of an anti-Islamic pro-Israel bias in British foreign policy.

The way that 'war on terror' issues are bound up with wider foreign policy issues and traditional *jihads* for the dataset was emphasised at the trial of Parviz Khan. According to his co-defendant, Zahoor Iqbal, Khan had been watching a lot of propaganda and anti-war material, and he began blaming Britain for the Israel–Palestine issue and Kashmir, as well as for the civilians dying in Iraq and Afghanistan.[54] But the objectives of the dataset were also consistent with the global *jihadi* ideology. Arafat Waheed Khan of the Airline cell urged people to look at historic events including the Crusades to see the 'big war going on from east to west'.[55] This indicates that it is not just the wars in Afghanistan and Iraq which motivated the dataset to perpetrate acts of terrorism within the UK, but also wider foreign policy issues.

FROM OVERSEAS *JIHAD* TO TERRORISM IN THE UK

Fighting in overseas *jihad* represents a number of significant steps in the radicalisation process. At one level, it creates opportunities for further ideological indoctrination by Islamists. Those that fight in these conflicts meet other *jihadis*, and they can become indoctrinated, and ultimately get recruited into international terrorist networks (see Chapter 6). At another, much more significant level, fighting for Muslim causes in foreign wars represents the step change into violent activity, which is just one step removed from engaging in terrorism. Acts of terrorism were also a common element of the wars in Bosnia, Kashmir, Chechnya and Iraq, which might make it psychologically easier to make the transition from fighting in *jihad* to becoming a terrorist. The ease with which *jihadis* can make the transition into terrorism is evident from the case of Omar Sheikh, who initially engaged in terrorist activity in order to secure the release of *Harkat ul-Ansar* members from Pakistani jails. Nevertheless, not all individuals who engage in *jihad* overseas have returned to commit acts of terrorism in the UK.

There is strong evidence that terrorist recruiters overseas, possibly with links to *al Qaeda*, are persuading would-be *jihadis* to redirect their violence towards terrorism in the UK. This comes out strongly in the cases of the Ammonium Nitrate cell and the 7/7 cell. While he was still living in the UK, Waheed Mahmood advocated a violent response to the problems he saw Muslims suffering around the world, but it was not until 2003, when he headed for a paramilitary training camp in the Northwest of Pakistan, with Akbar and Khyam, that they agreed that they should attack the UK because they could not get into Afghanistan to fight.[56] It is unknown what role *al Qaeda* figures played in redirecting their violence in this way, but it is possible that they had some influence, given that the cell were linked to *al Qaeda* figures in Pakistan.[57] As was the case with the Ammonium Nitrate cell, it seems that once Mohammed Siddique Khan was in Pakistan he was persuaded by members of *al Qaeda* to perform a terrorist attack in the UK, rather than go to fight in Afghanistan.

If the activities of the dataset were driven by the 'war on terror', one might have expected them to have attacked US or Israeli targets in the UK. However, attacking British population and economic targets is consistent with *al Qaeda's* broader strategy, to isolate the US from its allies. This was the rationale for the Madrid train bombings in 2004, which killed 190 people. In December 2003, the Norwegian intelligence services found an *al Qaeda* planning document on an Islamist website which outlined a strategy for forcing the US and its allies out of Iraq. This document argued that more 9/11-type attacks on the US would be ineffective, and instead it would be more effective to attack America's European allies to force them to withdraw their forces from Iraq, which would increase the economic and military burden on the US, thereby increasing the pressure on it to withdraw. Spain, the UK and Poland were identified as potential targets. Spain was top of the list because of its upcoming elections and Spanish public opinion was opposed to the war in Iraq.[58] The Madrid train bombings occurred three days before the 2004 Spanish elections. The opposition Socialist party won the election and subsequently withdrew Spanish troops from Iraq. The Madrid bombings and their perceived impact on the Spanish election were heralded as a major success by *al Qaeda*. It is a reasonable assumption that the 7 July bombings and attempted 21 July bombings in London were attempts to replicate the perceived success of the Madrid attack. Therefore, certain terrorist attacks in the UK can be argued to be consistent with *al Qaeda*'s strategy for Iraq, and thus can be argued to have been a direct consequence of the British government's support for the US in Iraq and Afghanistan.

While an analysis of the lives of the dataset indicates that the majority had at least begun the process of becoming radicalised before 9/11 and the 'war on terror', for new generations of British terrorists these issues might play a much more central role in the initial stages of their radicalisation. For our dataset, however, it is apparent that foreign policy issues, and the 'war on terror' in particular, were a significant influence in catalysing their engagement in terrorist violence. There also seems to be a clear stepping stone from fighting in overseas *jihad* to engaging in terrorist attacks inside the UK. For these individuals, the ideological legitimisation of the former can be seen to legitimise the latter. Some of them were believers in the global *jihadi* ideology before they went abroad, while others seem to have been indoctrinated on the battlefield.

However, not all of those who fight in *jihad* overseas return to commit acts of terrorist violence in the UK; therefore fighting in *jihad* overseas is not an automatic indicator that an individual believes in the global *jihadi* ideology, or that he has been radicalised to commit acts of terrorist violence.

Notes and references

[1] *Qur'an*, 9:5.

[2] Burke J, *Al-Qaeda: The True Story of Radical Islam* (London: Penguin, 2004), pp 29–30.

[3] Sageman M, *Understanding Terror Networks* (University of Pennsylvania Press, 16 April 2004), p 2.

[4] Sageman M, *Understanding Terror Networks* (University of Pennsylvania Press, 16 April 2004), p 18.

[5] Sageman M, *Understanding Terror Networks* (University of Pennsylvania Press, 16 April 2004), p 19.

[6] 'The causes of alienation', *The Times*, 16 September 2007.

[7] Clutterbuck L, 'Violent Jihad and the UK: Suicide Terrorism in Context', Presentation to the Royal United Services Institute (RUSI), 3 November 2006, Research Leader, RAND Europe.

[8] 'Britain Under Attack', *Dispatches*, Channel 4 TV, http://www.channel4.com/news/articles/dispatches/britain+under+attack/656252.

[9] Burke J, *Al-Qaeda: The True Story of Radical Islam* (London: Penguin, 2004), pp 29–30.

[10] Sageman M, *Understanding Terror Networks* (University of Pennsylvania Press, 16 April 2004), p 19.

[11] Sageman M, *Understanding Terror Networks* (University of Pennsylvania Press, 16 April 2004), p 19.

[12] 'On Yemen's death row', *Guardian*, 17 January 1999, http://www.guardian.co.uk/yemen/Story/0,2763,209259,00; 'Terrorists or tourists', *Guardian*, 26 June 1999, http://www.al-bab.com/yemen/artic/ gdn42.htm.

13 '"Confession" statements attributed to the defendants', 14 June 2002, http://www.al-bab.com/yemen/hamza/statemts.htm.

14 'Manhunt for public school kidnapper', *Guardian*, 9 February 2002, http://www.guardian.co.uk/pakistan/Story/0,2763,647495,00.html; Lévy B, *Who Killed Daniel Pearl?* (New York: Melville House, 2003), p 89.

15 'Muslim was planning dirty bomb attack in UK', *Daily Telegraph*, 13 October 2006, http://www.telegraph.co.uk/news/main.jhtml?xml=/news/2006/10/13/nterr13.xml; 'Profile of Dhiren Barot', *Channel 4 News*, 7 November 2006, http://www.channel4.com/news/special-reports/special-reports-storypage.jsp?id=3838.

16 'Airline plot leader "considered taking own children"', *Daily Telegraph*, 24 April 2008, http://www.telegraph.co.uk/news/main.jhtml?xml=/news/2008/04/23/nterror423.xml.

17 'Police investigation: How many more are out there?', *Independent*, 27 February 2007, http://news.independent.co.uk/uk/crime/article301236.ece.

18 'Hunt for 1,200 Britons who trained with al-Qa'eda', *Daily Telegraph*, 25 January 2003, http://www.telegraph.co.uk/news/main.jhtml?xml=/news/2003/01/26/nalq26.xml&sSheet=/news/2003/01/26/ixnewstop.html&secureRefresh=true&_requestid=52048.

19 '"Suicide" video shown to airline terror trial', *Daily Telegraph*, 10 April 2008.

20 Riyadh al Huq, 'Speech: The globalised suffering of the Muslims', *The Times*, 6 September 2007, http://www.timesonline.co.uk/tol/comment/faith/article2401855.ece?token=null&offset=48.

21 'ICM Muslims poll', ICM, March 2004, http://www.icmresearch.co.uk/reviews/2004/guardian-muslims-march-2004.asp.

22 'ICM Muslims poll', ICM, November 2004, http://www.icmresearch.co.uk/reviews/2004/Guardian%20Muslims%20Poll%20Nov%2004/Guardian%20Muslims%20Nov04.asp.

23 'Young, British Muslims "getting more radical"', *Daily Telegraph*, 29 January, 2007, http://www.telegraph.co.uk/news/main.jhtml;jsessionid=tzvh0nw5nia3pqfiqmgsff4avcbqwiv0?xml=/news/2007/01/29/nmuslims29.xml.

24 'Speech: Infinite Justice', *The Times*, 6 September 2007, http://www.timesonline.co.uk/tol/comment/faith/article2402218.ece?token=null&offset=12.

25 '"Astonishment" at terror verdicts', BBC NewsOnline, 9 September 2008, http://news.bbc.co.uk/1/hi/uk/7605583.stm.

26 'Alleged bomb plotters made suicide videos', BBC NewsOnline, 4 April 2008, http://www.telegraph.co.uk/news/main.jhtml?xml=/news/2008/04/04/nterror504.xml.

27 'UK Muslims join Taliban to fight against British troops', *Sunday Times*, 3 September 2006, http://www.timesonline.co.uk/article/0,,2087-2340571.html.

28 The other six are: Afzal Munir, Aftab Manzoor and Muhamed Omar from Luton; Yasir Khan from Crawley, and Afrasiab Ilyas and Arshad Miaz from Burnley. 'Fundamentalist: Muslim militants may have used the town as a training base', *Crawley Today*, 7 November 2001, http://www.crawleytoday.co.uk/ViewArticle2.aspx?SectionID=496&ArticleID=264044; 'Britons fall victim to an Islamic dream', *Daily Telegraph*, 5 October 2001, http://www.telegraph.co.uk/news/main.jhtml?xml=/news/2001/10/05/ntal05.xml.

29 'Khan inspired by British role model', *Daily Telegraph*, 7 July 2006, http://www.telegraph.co.uk/news/main.jhtml?xml=/news/2006/07/07/njuly407.xml.

30 'Russians kill Briton in Chechnya', *Daily Telegraph*, 16 July 2002, http://www.telegraph.co.uk/news/main.jhtml?xml=/news/2002/07/17/wchech17.xml; 'Russians kill British citizen in Chechnya', *Evening Standard*, 10 March 2004; 'Briton among Chechen dead', *Evening Standard*, 26 September 2002.

31 'Al-Qaeda "planning big British attack"', *Sunday Times*, 22 April 2007, http://www.timesonline.co.uk/tol/news/uk/article1687360.ece.

32 'Britons held in Somali clash', *The Times*, 10 January 2007, http://www.timesonline.co.uk/article/0,,2-2539564,00.html.

33 'How the terror camp gang were bugged and caught', *The Times*, 26 February 2008, http://www.timesonline.co.uk/tol/news/uk/crime/article3437865.ece?token=null&offset=12.

34 'The "charity" that plotted the Mumbai attacks', *The Times*, 8 December 2008.

35 'PM shelves Islamic group ban', *Observer*, 24 December 2006.

36 Sheikh, Barot and possibly Butt and Harhara were radicalised in the early 1990s; Khan, Khyam, Sharif, Badat, Reid and the other members of the Yemen 8 cell in the mid- to late 1990s; Abedin was arrested in 2000. Hanif was radicalised in the late 1990s or early 2000s, and Salahuddin Amin, of the Ammonium Nitrate cell, said that he had been radicalised by the time he went to Pakistan, just before 9/11. 'Accused "influenced by Abu Hamza"', BBC NewsOnline, 25 July 2006, http://news.bbc.co.uk/1/hi/uk/5214174.stm.

37 'Plot to attack civilians', *Evening Standard*, 31 March 2008.

38 Malik S, 'Society NS Profile – Omar Sharif', *New Statesman*, 24 April 2006.

39 Prepared text of Tuesday's portion of the Crown's opening statement in the trial of seven men alleged to have plotted to bomb London. The rest of the statement was to be delivered on Wednesday: Regina v Omar Khyam, Anthony Garcia, Nabeel Hussain, Jawad Akbar, Waheed Mahmood, Shujah-ud-din-Mahmood, Salahuddin Amin, 21 March 2006, *Ottawa Citizen*, http://www.canada.com/ottawacitizen/news/story.html?id=408dc2ed-d950-4ee5-a4b7-392eb5faaf34&k=75162.

40 'Revealed: Bomber transcript', BBC NewsOnline, 1 May 2007, http://news.bbc.co.uk/1/hi/uk/6611803.stm.

41 Report of the Official Account of the Bombings in London on 7 July 2005, HC1087 (London: The Stationery Office), 11 May 2006.

42 'Muktar Said Ibrahim: From robbery and indecent assault to bomb plot leader', *The Times*, 10 July 2007, http://www.timesonline.co.uk/tol/news/uk/crime/article2051428.ece.

43 'Profile: Omar Khyam', BBC NewsOnline, 30 April 2007, http://news.bbc.co.uk/1/hi/uk/6149794.stm.

44 'Suspect happy about 9/11 attacks', *Crawley Today*, 15 September 2006, http://www.crawleytoday.co.uk/ViewArticle2.aspx?SectionID=496&ArticleID=1771407.

45 'Bomb-plot suspect halts evidence', BBC NewsOnline, 18 September 2006, http://news.bbc.co.uk/1/hi/uk/5355976.stm.

46 'Man jailed for Iraq revenge plot', BBC NewsOnline, 26 January 2006, http://news.bbc.co.uk/1/hi/england/london/4650000.stm.

47 'London bomber video: full statement', *The Times*, 2 September 2005, http://www.timesonline.co.uk/article/0,,22989-1762124,00.html.

48 'I blame war in Iraq and Afghanistan, 7/7 bomber says in video', *The Times*, 7 July 2006, http://www.timesonline.co.uk/article/0,,22989-2259892,00.html.

49 'Nightmare', *Huddersfield Daily Examiner*, 6 July 2006, http://ichuddersfield.icnetwork.co.uk/0100news/0100localnews/tm_method=full%26objectid=17340559%26siteid=50060-name_page.html.

50 'Alleged bomb plotters made suicide videos', BBC NewsOnline, 4 April 2008, http://www.telegraph.co.uk/news/main.jhtml?xml=/news/2008/04/04/nterror504.xml.

51 'Martyrdom video man thanked Osama bin Laden for plane bomb inspiration', *The Times*, 11 April 2008.

52 'Alleged bomb plotters made suicide videos', BBC NewsOnline, 4 April 2008, http://www.telegraph.co.uk/news/main.jhtml?xml=/news/2008/04/04/nterror504.xml.

53 'Young Muslims and Extremism', Home Office-FCO Paper, 10 May 2004, http://www.timesonline.co.uk/article/0,,22989-1688872,00.html.

54 'Parviz Khan: Promising footballer to terrorist', *Daily Telegraph*, 18 February 2008, http://www.telegraph.co.uk/news/main.jhtml?xml=/news/2008/02/18/nkidnap718.xml; 'Profile: Parviz Khan', *Guardian*, 18 February 2008, http://www.guardian.co.uk/uk/2008/feb/18/uksecurity3.

55 'Martyrdom video man thanked Osama bin Laden for plane bomb inspiration', *The Times*, 11 April 2008.

56 'Profile: Jawad Akbar', BBC NewsOnline, 30 April 2007, http://news.bbc.co.uk/1/hi/uk/6149788.stm; 'Profile: Omar Khyam', BBC NewsOnline, 30 April 2007, http://news.bbc.co.uk/1/hi/uk/6149794.stm.

57 'Profile: Jawad Akbar', BBC NewsOnline, 30 April 2007, http://news.bbc.co.uk/1/hi/uk/6149788.stm.

58 Pape R, *Dying to Win: Why Suicide Bombers Do It* (New York: Random House, 2005), pp 254–55.

Chapter 5

Fellow Travellers

One of the key moments in the journey of our dataset was their involvement with 'fellow travellers' in the Islamist community. Humans are social beings and most of us need company. Within society, there are a large number of different social groups that are defined in numerous different ways, for example, by race, religion or income. Evolutionary psychologists refer to this subdivision of society as 'tribalism', where the smaller groups act as 'tribes'. The basis of this idea is that, when social groups grow so large that individuals cannot recognise each other easily, they feel the need to join smaller groups in which they believe they can belong and identify with other members. This system creates what are known as in-groups and out-groups, which is the evolutionary basis of ethnocentrism and xenophobia. This need for social contact is best described as affiliation and our understanding of this process focuses on the motives for, and consequences of, seeking out the company of our peers. The desire to affiliate with others is higher when people are feeling either happy or threatened, and lower when they are feeling tense/nervous or need to concentrate. There are four basic reasons for affiliation: to reduce uncertainty by comparing yourself to others; to obtain positive stimulation through contact; to gain attention and praise; and to obtain emotional support.[1] Based on our analysis so far, the members of our dataset's logical reasons for affiliation would appear to be that they had become alienated from their families and/or traditional communities and felt threatened by a hostile Islamophobic environment.

Rather than passively acquiring recruits, radical Islamist groups such as *Hizb ut-Tahrir* and *al Muhajiroun* aggressively seek to recruit new members. Recruiters for these groups and networks commit a considerable amount of time and effort to identifying and indoctrinating potential recruits by first discerning those individuals from within larger groups who may be susceptible to radicalisation. Hassan Butt recalled that recruiters would identify individuals with strong Islamic tendencies and then pursue them relentlessly, but, unlike Traditionalist groups, they would not judge a potential recruit by his actions. 'If the network see a drug dealer or someone from a gang, they will not condemn him like the Traditionalists and say "oh brother *haram*, *haram* [i.e. religiously forbidden]". What they'll try to do is to utilise his energy.'[2] However, government reports have indicated that a significant number of radicalised individuals had been identified and recruited through a single contact, often by chance. For instance, Butt's first contact with members of *Hizb ut-Tahrir* was outside his local mosque because it was full and he was unable to get in. Similarly, Shiraz Maher, a former regional leader of *Hizb ut-Tahrir*, happened to have a conversation with a member of the group at a mosque and within weeks he had been recruited.[3]

JOINING 'RADICAL' GROUPS

One of the simplest psychological findings is that physical proximity and exposure are strong determinants in friendship formation. Whether this will change with the increasing use of the internet is difficult to gauge, but it is reasonable to infer that virtual relationships will replicate physical ones, and that, therefore, the factors that operate in close physical proximity will also operate in cyberspace. Numerous psychological studies have found that friendships develop between strangers living together in communal

he 1983 suicide truck bombing of the US Marine Corps and French Paratrooper rracks in Beirut, by Islamic Jihad/Hezbollah, clearly demonstrated the effectiveness 'martyrdom' operations. This event is probably the genesis of the tactical decision by ilitant Islamists to use suicide bombs.

As with other members of our dataset, Mohammed Siddique Khan led a double life that appears contradictory. We need to understand why essentially 'normal' people make such 'abnormal' decisions. The key to preventing future attacks is to influence that decision-making.

The suffering of Bosnian Muslims, such as those at the Omarska concentration camp, was perceived as a clear indication that the UK was not prepared to intervene on their behalf. 'Ethnic cleansing' was seen by the Islamists as a part of the global attack on Islam that has not stopped since the Crusades.

The ongoing conflict in Indian-occupied Kashmir provides a common cause for both mainstream Muslim discourse and militant ideology. Support for Mujahideen groups fighting in Kashmir provides a route for some into Islamism.

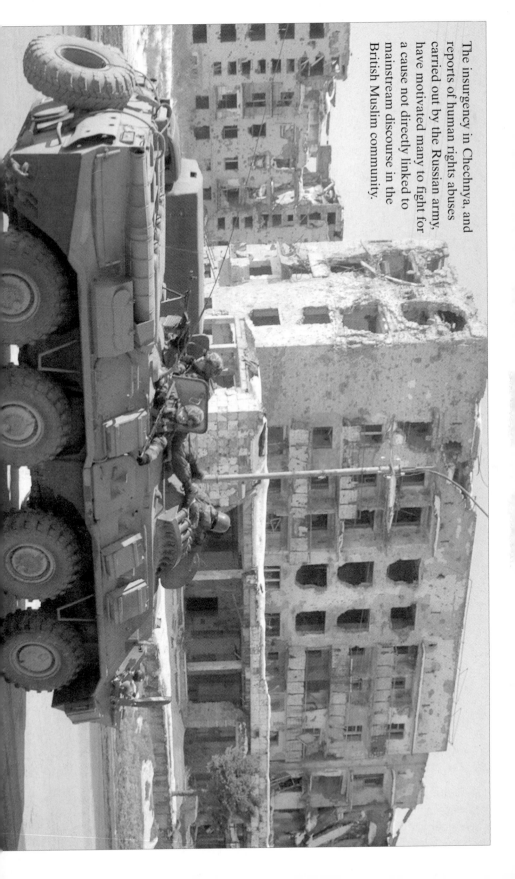

The insurgency in Chechnya, and reports of human rights abuses carried out by the Russian army, have motivated many to fight for a cause not directly linked to mainstream discourse in the British Muslim community.

The Arab-Israeli conflict and occupation of Palestinian land were at the heart of international terrorism for most of the twentieth century, and persist into the twenty-first. The inability of the West to diplomatically resolve these issues provides an ongoing rationale for violent extremism.

كما تقصفون نا ستقصفرن

ليار دولار لشراء حصة في شركة الاتصالات الباكستانية

bove: The failure of
aceful demonstrations to
er British foreign policy
d prevent the war in Iraq –
llowed by the re-election
the Labour government –
dicated to some that
ainstream politics was not
e solution to their real and
rceived grievances.

ght: Militant Islamist
opaganda, such as these
leos, offers an extreme
lution to real and perceived
ievances that attracts those
ho are pro-violence in their
titudes and behaviour.

Above left: Veneration of martyrs is central to cultures around the world, and the lure of martyrdom is therefore common to those cultures. As long as martyrs are venerated people will believe that they can achieve more in death than they ever would in life.

Above right: Richard Reid was vulnerable to becoming a violent extremist during his time in Feltham Young Offenders Institution. If these vulnerabilities were known at the time, it may have been possible to prevent him becoming a suicide bomber.

Below: The fighting between Hamas and the Israeli Defence Force (IDF) in Gaza, durin 2009, is likely to provide another justification for young Britons to engage in violent extremism. The inability of the West to prevent the destruction and the corresponding humanitarian crisis will doubtless be perceived as tacit support for the IDF.`

housing on the basis of their location. Similarly, they may form between those who live close together, possibly through simple expediency, because people are more likely to be exposed to, and interact with, others who are close by. Through regular contact, shared interests and attitudes may be identified. However, if there are no grounds for affiliation, it is likely that negative interactions may occur, as the differences between people may become more pronounced. For the purposes of our analysis, the most important finding on proximity is that a shared adverse environment can enhance affiliation through the perception of a collective experience.

As we discussed earlier, there were many real and perceived grievances among the dataset about what was going on around them. Psychologists have found that individuals who feel threatened in stressful situations want to be in the company of others, as it is often useful to see how others are responding to such circumstances. A prime example can be found in student Islamic societies which may attract individuals who are away from home for the first time, when it may also be their first experience of mixing with significant numbers of non-Muslims, and who are generally learning to adapt to their changed environment. It is therefore natural that they should seek out fellow Muslims, many of whom will have come from similar backgrounds. It is no coincidence that radical political groups such as *Hizb ut-Tahrir* have targeted university Islamic societies as a rich source of potential recruits. Indeed, a number of members of the dataset became involved in radical politics at college and university.

Social Comparison theory suggests that comparing our response to a social situation with that of others allows us to assess whether our response is appropriate. Affiliation is therefore an adaptive response to uncertainty and stress. More importantly, though, we seek to affiliate with people who are in the same position as we are, rather than with any random individual. This suggests that individuals who feel threatened and are uncertain how to respond will congregate together and form social groups. If within these groups there are individuals who are coping better than others, the others will seek to affiliate with them so that their own anxiety is reduced. This anxiety reduction will be magnified if the group is able to provide information about the threat that they face and how to deal with it. The reassurance and social support offered by the group certainly provides a powerful pull on individuals to join groups of people in similar situations. For young British Muslims who feel threatened by the factors that we have discussed in the previous chapters, affiliating with others who feel the same way creates groups that then may become vulnerable to other psychological influences.

Once formed, groups are able to offer ongoing social support to their members even if the group's immediate reason for forming is no longer present. The availability of a social support network is one of the major moderators of stress. Social support provides a sense of belonging and the feeling that others care for your wellbeing; this in turn enhances self-esteem and feelings of self-worth. One young Birmingham man who became involved in a radical group in the 1990s recalled that, 'from being very confused and ashamed of my colour and my religion, I was told that I was a lion – a warrior, with an identity of my own that I could claim if I only accept Allah into my heart.'[4] As social support is reciprocal, there is also a sense of mutual dependence and obligations that reinforce social bonds within groups. Social support is able to help people cope with the stress of daily life by shielding them from its negative impact. This is an indirect effect and is best described as a buffer, but it does little to reduce or eliminate stress. Group action can also overcome stress by facilitating and supporting positive coping activities. For our dataset, the formation of street gangs to protect against racist attacks and provocation offers one example of using social support to eliminate stress.

Social support networks can be described as either informal, such as family or friends, or formal, such as the mosque or social services. These networks serve to provide the necessary support and information that we need to solve our day-to-day problems. It is not the size of these networks that is important, but the quality of the support that they provide. The most obvious groups to offer social support are the immediate family and the wider community in which the family is embedded. However, everyone's sources of social support change in line with altered circumstances, for example many teenagers see their peers as their source of support and not their families. As our earlier analysis found, family and community tensions may have pushed some members of our dataset away from such sources and towards groups that could provide alternative social support. Similarly, students, who tend to be geographically distanced from their parents and old friends for the first time have to form new social support networks. The lack of social support drives the search for affiliation through loneliness. A deficit in the nature and number of social relationships is believed to result in depression, impatient boredom, desperation and self-deprecation.

Relationships are mostly formed on the basis of similarities and, for the purpose of our analysis, the beliefs of the dataset are one of the most important similarities given their sometimes diverse social backgrounds. Broadly speaking, the larger the discrepancy between two people's attitudes and beliefs the less likely it is that they will become friends. This discrepancy is amplified by the importance of the attitude or belief to the individuals, the reason being that we all like to think that we are right and to have our friends support our worldview is reinforcing. This positive endorsement of our attitudes and beliefs creates positive emotional responses towards the endorser and so promotes friendship. The importance of similarity can be undermined during periods of crisis where the individual is uncertain and confused. In such situations, psychologists have found that someone who holds dissimilar attitudes and beliefs may be attractive because of the different perspective and new information that they provide. For our analysis, this process may explain the move away from one form of social support and towards another. That is, the family and the traditional mosque may be unable to offer solutions to the problems facing the individual so they seek answers from the Islamist community. If the Islamists are able to provide those answers, then the individual may adopt Islamist attitudes and beliefs as their own.

THE IDEOLOGY AND POLITICAL GOALS OF RADICAL ISLAMIST GROUPS AND NETWORKS IN THE UK

Overt radical activity in the Muslim population of the UK has been linked to a number of Islamist groups, particularly *Hizb ut-Tahrir, al Muhajiroun* and Supporters of *Sha'ria*. These are not terrorist groups but they do share similar ideologies, beliefs and goals. However, although the ideologies of these groups share many common elements, they are not a homogeneous movement, and there have been reports of conflicts and rivalries between them and their leaders. Joining such groups, and the radicalised networks of which they form part, represents a significant act for an individual in moving from passive to active support for a radical cause or ideology, demonstrating both a heightened level of commitment and also a willingness to act on one's beliefs. For a number of individuals in the dataset, involvement with these groups was a significant milestone in their political radicalisation. It is unknown how many Britons might be members of such groups, but the numbers appear to be relatively small.

The ideologies of these groups are a synthesis of politics and Islam. The groups regard Islam as an entire system for life, so they justify their goals and actions by reference to the *Qur'an*, the *Hadith* and Islamic concepts, such as the *ummah*. For all of these groups, divisions between people based on class, nationality or race are irrelevant, since all Muslims are members of the global *ummah*. These ideologies therefore characterise a communal social identity that is not constrained by localised traditions or national boundaries. Consequently, the members of these groups feel a sense of shared identity with oppressed Muslims in other countries, and are deeply opposed to what they consider to be 'apostate regimes' in the Muslim world which are not governed by *Sha'ria* law, as well as the foreign policy of Western states, both in terms of the 'war on terror' and in supporting these 'apostate regimes'.

The way these groups use the *Qur'an* is partial, with selected passages taken out of historical context, thereby enabling their meaning to be adapted to suit the purposes of the political objectives of the group. Consequently, it is impossible to separate the political from the religious aspects of their ideology, hence it is commonly defined as 'political Islam'. Maajid Nawaz described the synthesis of politics and Islam in this way:

> This was an ideology like no other. Religion had been merged with politics in such a way that we worshipped God through our political activities. Where our minds could not grasp a certain idea, we were coaxed through scripture. Where scripture did not bolster a certain notion, we were convinced through rational argumentation. The result was a potent mix of political and philosophical stances seemingly justified by religious scripture with the aim of liberating the Muslim nation, or *ummah*, whose minds had been colonised. The result was producing young men and women who were prepared to give up everything for the sake of a political ideology and go to a religious paradise.[5]

Given that the *Qur'an* is incontestable to the letter in being handed down directly from God to man, this gives these ideologies a powerful theological underpinning. These groups reject manmade laws, which they feel oppress mankind, and advocate replacing them with *Sha'ria* law, which they believe will bring freedom, purity and justice to mankind.[6] Whereas *Hizb ut-Tahrir* seeks the establishment of Islamist states only in Muslim countries, *al Muhajiroun* sought also to establish an Islamist republic in the UK. While these groups work for the creation of Islamist states, they believe that Muslims in Britain should live separately from the rest of society. Indeed, they declare it to be *haram* to vote in elections or befriend non-Muslims.

A central tenet of *Hizb ut-Tahrir*'s ideology is that it is a religious duty for all Muslims to work for the re-establishment of the Islamic *caliphate*, which it argues was abolished in 1924 with the dissolution of the Ottoman Empire. The *caliphate* is an Islamic super-state which would unite existing Muslim countries, and, according to some Islamist ideologues, should also encompass lands such as Andalusia in southern Spain, which were once Muslim. The original *caliphate*, or *Khilafah* in Arabic, emerged 1,400 years ago, and was government according to Allah's law (the *Sha'ria*), rather than laws designed by man. In the view of *Hizb ut-Tahrir*, 'slavery' to the manmade laws, which oppress mankind, would be replaced with submission to Allah's law, which is a source of liberation and human rights. *Hizb ut-Tahrir* advocates that the allegiance of British Muslims should not lie with Queen and country, but with a coming *caliph* in the Middle East, who is the head of state in a *caliphate*, and the leader of the *ummah*.[7] It argues that Muslims can work towards the re-establishment of the *caliphate* either physically, by involving themselves in revolutionary coups, or through political means.[8]

These groups promote ideological hatred of the West, by arguing that it is corrupt, decadent and Islamophobic, and that it is engaged in a war against Islam. They promote religious hatred between their supporters and non-Muslims, whom they consider to be inferior to Muslims. The *Qur'an* refers to non-believers as *kafir* (plural *kuffar*), but culturally it is used as a derogatory term, and routinely used by members of these groups to refer to non-Muslims. It appears they also share a particular hatred of Jews; in 2003, documents discovered on *Hizb ut-Tahrir's* website promoted racism and anti-Semitic hatred, and urged Muslims to kill Jewish people.[9]

These groups exploit a specific interpretation of Islamic history but root it in contemporary social, political and economic problems, which gives their ideology an immediacy for young Muslims who are trying to deal with life in modern secular Britain. However, as noted in Chapter 2, many of these views are similar to those being expressed in some mainstream mosques, particularly some of those that are run by *Salafis*, *Deobandis* and *Wahhabis*. This intersection between mainstream mosques and these radical politico-religious groups was noted by Ed Husain, whose first introduction to politicised Islam was at the East London mosque, which was run by *Jamaat-e-Islami*.[10]

Supporters of *Sha'ria* and *al Muhajiroun* have promoted the pursuit of violent *jihad* for British Muslims in conflicts overseas, to establish 'Islamic states' which are governed by *Sha'ria* law.[11] In contrast, *Hizb ut-Tahrir*, which is avowedly non-violent, prescribes violent *jihad* as the primary duty only for Muslims living in the occupied Palestinian territories, who directly face Israeli military occupation. It argues that Israel was formed by taking other people's land by force, and that Islam is 'in conflict with Israelis – not in their capacity as Jews who historically lived alongside Muslims in peace and security for centuries – but in their capacity as occupiers and aggressors'.[12]

While some of these groups have supported violent *jihad* abroad, they have never promoted the use of terrorist violence in the UK. Prior to the 7 July bombings, Omar Bakri Mohammed, the leader of *al Muhajiroun*, declared that Muslims lived under a 'covenant of security' in the UK, a *Qur'anic* concept which stipulates that Muslims should not attack the country that gives them shelter. Bakri argued that this covenant meant that British Muslims were forbidden from undertaking any type of military activity within the UK. He declared that, if British Muslims wish to support the Iraqi insurgents fighting against US and UK troops, they should go to Iraq to do so.[13] Prior to 9/11, this covenant of security was widely accepted by radical and militant Muslims living in the UK, although it was challenged by some of the more extreme elements, who argued that only foreign-born Muslims who had sought refuge in Britain were bound by it. Consequently, there was some limited terrorist activity directed at the UK prior to Britain's involvement in the 'war on terror', including the plot by Moinul Abedin. But, following the UK's involvement in the invasions of Afghanistan and Iraq, many militant Muslims consider that the covenant has been broken. In March 2005, Omar Bakri Mohammed declared that the covenant of security in the UK was no longer in force. Four months later, the 7/7 cell attacked the London transport system.[14] However, there is no evidence linking the 7/7 cell to Bakri.

A significant number of the dataset are known to have been either linked to, or members of, these groups: the Yemen 8 cell were linked to Supporters of *Sha'ria* through their association with its leader, Abu Hamza; Kazi Rahman, Dhiren Barot and Omar Sharif were linked to *Hizb ut-Tahrir*;[15] while the Ammonium Nitrate cell, as well as Omar Sharif and Asif Hanif, were members of *al Muhajiroun*.[16]

Al Muhajiroun comprised a number of local groups in London and other towns and cities including Derby, Luton and Crawley. It also seems to have had a large number of affiliated groups, which specialised in different fields, such as the Society of Muslim Lawyers, the Society of Converts to Islam, the Society of Muslim Parents, the London School of *Sha'ria*, the *Sha'ria* Court of the UK, the Society of Muslim Students, the Islamic World League, the Muslim Cultural Society and the Party of the Future. The group was ostensibly disbanded in 2004, but there is a widespread belief that many of its members simply formed into two new groups: the Saved Sect and *al-Ghuraba*. There are also other remnants of the organisation, such as the followers of *Ahl Us Sunnah Wal Jammaa'ah*, the *Muballigh*, the Islamic Thinkers Society and the Society of Muslim Lawyers. The Saved Sect is probably the most direct line back to *al Muhajiroun*, and among those who were associated with the Saved Sect were Mizanur Rahman, who demanded the beheading of those who insult Islam at a demonstration outside the Danish embassy in London to protest about the publication of cartoons of the Prophet Mohammed in the Danish media, and Islam Uddin, who called the Jewish people 'the most disgusting and greedy people on earth'.[17]

Al-Ghuraba and the Saved Sect, both of whom were proscribed under Section 3 of the Terrorism Act (2000) in 2006, had very similar views based on an Islamist ideology and indirectly encouraged young Muslims to emulate previous terrorist acts. Both organisations use the internet as their main medium to attack the values of UK society and praise those who want to use violence for ideological aims. The *al-Ghuraba* website depicted the US and its allies oppressing Muslims, and asked supporters to co-operate in eradicating manmade laws.[18]

The website also declared 'kill those who insult Mohammed' and 'we do believe in *jihad*, we do believe in violence, we do believe in terrorizing the enemy of Allah', and described Osama bin Laden as a lion. The Saved Sect produces similar propaganda. A spokesman for *al-Ghuraba* explicitly refused to condemn the 7 July bombings, saying, 'I have no allegiance to the Queen whatsoever or to British society; in fact, if I see *mujahideen* attack the UK I am always standing with the Muslims, never against the Muslims.'[19]

American investigators allege that *al-Ghuraba* comprised 81 front organisations, support groups and affiliates in six different countries, the overwhelming majority of which are based in the UK in London, the Home Counties, the Midlands, Lancashire and West Yorkshire.[20] The New York Police Department estimates that the groups have between 600 and 1,500 members in the UK and a further 1,500 around the world. Most are aged 19–29 and are of Pakistani descent,[21] the predominant age and social background of the dataset.

The British intelligence services are also concerned about groups or networks that are not formally organised and which have no badge or label. MI5 has evidence that some of those who go on to become involved in terrorist activity may have been radicalised as a result of associating with loose networks that revolve around a respected key individual.[22] This was particularly true of the 7/7 cell. Mohammed Siddique Khan, Shehzad Tanweer and Hasib Hussain were members of an informal network of extremists that operated from a number of premises in Beeston.[23] Evidence from the lives of the 7/7 cell suggests that the members of these radical groups can become very insular, and the social lives of Khan, Tanweer and Hussain revolved around the local mosques, youth clubs, gyms and Islamic bookshop, which some sources have reported were well known locally as centres of extremism. The network operated primarily from the Leeds Community School, the Iqra Islamic bookshop next door to it and a gym that was known locally as the '*al Qaeda* gym' because of the views of those who frequented it. It has also been reported that extremist preachers had visited the bookshop.[24]

The Training cell also operated independently of any established group. Mohammed Hamid and Atilla Ahmet created their own network of radicalised individuals. They recruited individuals off the street, indoctrinated them at Hamid's house and at a bookshop he owned, organised physical training for them and, in some cases, facilitated their members joining overseas *jihad*. Their lives seemed to revolve around their Islamist political activities.

These types of groups and the individuals associated with them were part of their own networks, and they also intersected to form an amorphous nationwide network of politicised radicals. The same people are often linked to a number of different groups, which often tend to be loose associations rather than organisations in the traditional sense.[25] These loose networks comprise the groundswell of radicalised individuals that terrorist recruiters and facilitators tap into, and within which smaller terror cells and networks exist.

The loose interconnections of this wider system of networks are evident from the interactions of different members of the dataset. Mohammed Siddique Khan and Shehzad Tanweer were associated with a wider network of British-born *jihadis*, through which they made the contacts which facilitated their path into terrorism. They had contacts with Asif Hanif and Omar Sharif in 2001, and Khan was in contact with Omar Khyam in 2003. Khan met Khyam on at least five occasions, once in Pakistan and four times in the UK, and Khyam also met Tanweer three times.[26] However, there is no evidence of Khan and Tanweer being members of *al Muhajiroun* itself. Similarly, Kazi Rahman was associated with the Ammonium Nitrate cell through his friendship with Anthony Garcia, even though they were formerly members of *Hizb ut-Tahrir* and *al Muhajiroun*, respectively, and Abdulla Ahmed Ali, the *emir* (leader) of the Airline cell, was networked with Muktar Said Ibrahim. Nevertheless, some cells appear to have been more self-contained, such as the logistics network run by Parviz Khan which seems to have been directly linked to *jihadis* in Pakistan, rather than to networks in the UK.

The exact number of people who are, or have been, members of these groups is unclear, but the overall numbers appear to be small. Involvement with such organisations does not automatically lead to involvement in terrorist activity, and many people belong to and even leave these groups without ever engaging in violent extremism. Indeed, for many young British Muslims looking to rebel against the traditional values of their parents' generation, the wider community and/or the government, involvement in these groups can simply provide a cathartic and vocal 'pressure valve' for their anxieties, frustrations and sense of helplessness. But some highly committed individuals may view the activities of these groups as 'pointless pontification and debate' and may simply bypass them as they search for facilitators through whom they can access terrorist networks.[27] There were some reports that genuine *mujahideen* mocked Abu Hamza as a 'wannabe', even referring to him as a '*mediahedin*' because of his links to the media.[28] Nevertheless, participation in such groups can be a significant stepping stone in the process of violent radicalisation. These groups, and some of their members, did interface with terrorist networks, recruiters and facilitators, which is evident from the fact that several of the dataset were recruited into terrorist activity from, and sometimes through, these groups.

THE PSYCHOLOGICAL INFLUENCE OF THE GROUP

Groups that form for a purpose, such as a street gang or a terrorist cell, require structure in order to function. In the initial stages, when the number of members is small, there will be informal communication between the members. Every group, no matter how small, develops a collective understanding of how members should behave, which regulates interaction between the members and with outsiders. Sometimes this understanding is explicitly laid out as a set of rules or sometimes it is implicit and only becomes obvious when someone transgresses. As groups form, the members will tend to converge towards a collective understanding based on the most commonly held beliefs of the members.

A useful comparison for how our dataset formed into small groups is the formation of military units from raw recruits. These units are small groups of individuals who share a social identity and experiences while co-operating to achieve a common goal. Larger military structures are formed from the interdependence of these small military units, although there is little to no evidence in our dataset that any similar large organisational structures exist within the Islamist networks we have identified. There is, however, ample evidence that individuals came together to form small groups, the success of which depends on their cohesion, i.e. the identification of the individuals with the unit. It is widely recognised that, towards the end of the Second World War, the German army was able to effectively fight against much larger and better-equipped enemy forces due to their cohesion as military units. The German soldiers derived social support from their leaders and units, which provided them with everything they needed both physically and psychologically, and thus they were able to fight effectively, despite their chances of victory being small. There are three types of social bonding that occur within this type of unit: horizontal cohesion between the members of the unit/group; vertical cohesion between the unit/group and their leaders; and commitment to the values of the larger organisation.[29] This social bonding occurs through the development of friendships and social support networks.

However, it is important not to oversimplify the process of friendship formation as the processes outlined above do not automatically guarantee that lasting friendships are formed. Social Exchange theory argues that mutual attraction is required for friendship formation.[30] The reciprocity of knowing that people like each other is necessary at the beginning of a friendship as it reinforces that mutual attraction. As the friendship develops, mutual interdependence emerges as the friends take each other's interests into account in their interactions. Friendships are regulated by rules that are shared beliefs or opinions about how friends should behave, such as being there for each other and being trustworthy, particularly with personal information. Breaking these unwritten rules may lead to the end of the friendship. One of the most important factors in the break up of friendships is when one of the friends becomes critical or jealous of a friend's other relationships. For members of our dataset, this tended to occur as they started to immerse themselves in the Islamist community.

The key to understanding the behaviour of our dataset is the psychological influence of the group on the individual. As our social identity is linked to the groups that we join, the members of the most important and salient groups become the reference against which we compare our own behaviour. In order for this to occur, it is necessary for cognitive and emotional identification with this reference group to be high. Through the process of social learning (described more fully in Chapter 8), we learn from others how to think and behave, and our attitudes and behaviour are affected by the approval or disapproval of those around us. We then may alter our behaviour to fit what is expected of us so that we gain rewards and avoid punishment contingent on our behaviour. This process is termed compliance. Horizontal cohesion within a small group will occur when the members overtly reinforce the attitudes and behaviour that they expect of their members. In order to be a member of the group, the individual members must comply with the collective understanding of how to behave. However, when rewards and punishments are not provided for the individual, it is still possible for the group to influence them, and individuals may change their attitudes and beliefs in line with those of the majority of the other members in their group. This process is termed conformity.

The seminal studies on conformity were conducted by Solomon Asch in the early 1950s.[31] The basic Asch experiment involves a group of eight participants who are asked to decide on a simple visual experiment. The decision involves judging which of three lines is equivalent in length to a sample line placed next to them. Of the three lines one is actually identical, while the other two are longer or shorter. This is a fairly simple task and participants completing it on their own made virtually no errors. The Asch experiment involves replacing seven of the eight participants with actors so that there is only one real participant in the experiment. These actors followed a predetermined script for their answers to the comparisons so that on some trials they gave the correct answer and on others an obviously incorrect answer. The key finding was that the number of errors made by the participants increased dramatically when the actors gave unanimously wrong answers. The answers were obviously wrong but the participants chose, on some occasions, to agree with the majority. Afterwards, some of the participants underestimated the number of times that they had agreed with an obviously incorrect answer; therefore, they were either unaware of or chose to deny the influence of the group on their decisions. Some of the participants knew that the actors were wrong but chose to agree with them as they felt it would be easier. Others were convinced that the majority were right and they were obviously wrong. However, some of the participants remained independent throughout the experiment, so the effect of conformity in this experiment was not absolute.

Asch's experiment was an abstract laboratory task which was deliberately designed so that the errors made by the actors were obvious. In more complicated real-world decisions, the right answer is rarely so obvious and sometimes there just isn't one. When we make decisions, it is only natural that we want to be right, and, not only do we want to be right, but also we want others to approve of our decision. In order for us to evaluate whether our attitudes, beliefs and decisions are correct, we must interpret the world around us and the information provided by others. Informational influence occurs when we agree with others because we believe that they know more than we do and so we trust their judgement over our own. Normative influence occurs when we conform to the group because we do not wish to rock the boat. As we discussed above, being part of the in-group is important for us, and if we know that disagreeing with that group would lead to rejection and isolation then this is a powerful motivation for conforming. These two processes can occur simultaneously or one may be more relevant to one situation than another.

Group polarisation occurs when a group of people making a decision shift their original opinions so that they are more extreme. Most of us would assume that the outcome of a group discussion would be a consensus based on a compromise between the different viewpoints at the beginning. This assumption would predict that groups have a tendency towards moderate, less extreme decision making. However, the reality is that most groups tend to make decisions that are either too cautious or too risky, and the direction of the group's decision is usually based on the dominant position at the start of the decision-making process. If the social identity of an individual is important to them, they will act in a manner that is consistent with the stereotype of a typical group member. Therefore, we may infer that, within radical Islamist networks, there is a tendency for extreme views to be dominant.

The most extreme form of group polarisation is 'groupthink',[32] which occurs when a highly cohesive in-group of individuals becomes so concerned with finding consensus among the members that they lose touch with reality. The optimal conditions for groupthink to occur are a highly cohesive group that perceives a threat, an active leader who advocates a solution to that threat and insulation from independent judgements about that solution. Groups that form in this psychological environment develop an illusion of invulnerability which may predispose them to take risks due to excessive optimism. The optimism bias is a classic psychological problem for decision makers, who tend to discount the probability of negative outcomes from their decisions. In addition, there will be a collective rationalisation to reduce the impact of the potential negative outcomes that will occur, such as the killing of fellow Muslims. Part of this rationalisation will be the unquestioning belief in the moral superiority of the in-group, the shared illusion of unanimity and negative stereotypes of the out-group. It is likely that individuals in such situations will self-censor any potential deviations from the in-group consensus and may choose to protect the rest of the group from adverse information.

MARTYRDOM

One of the problems that we will encounter in understanding the social processes within groups will be the rationalisation of the members. It is unlikely that any of our dataset would acknowledge conformity to the group such as Asch found in his experiments. It is much more likely that alternative causal attributions will be found, particularly among those who are seeking to justify attitudes and behaviour that they have since renounced. Peer pressure is often cited as a rationale for the deviant behaviour of young people, as it provides a mechanism for explaining why young people act 'out of character'. The most common definition of peer pressure is that the peer group applies pressure to an individual to act in a way that they do not want to. This definition serves a useful purpose for everyone concerned. Young people are able to displace the blame for their behaviour on to others and thus protect themselves from censure. Parents are able to continue in the belief that their children are essentially 'good kids' that are influenced by the 'wrong crowd'. As we discussed above, the reality is that young people seek to affiliate with specific peer groups and their behaviour is a conscious effort to gain the approval of that peer group. Peer pressure is therefore best understood as pressure from the individual to the group rather than from the group to the individual. In this process the individual is not a passive recipient of instructions from outside actors but is an agent with free will who consciously chooses to behave as they see fit.

For many terrorist groups, status and personal reward are key drivers for individuals to become engaged in terrorism, which is one of the reasons why the nature of mainstream discourse in the Muslim population is so important. It can potentially create an environment in which individuals believe that engaging in militant activity can confer a heightened status on them within their communities. In particular, there is undoubted popular support among sections of the Muslim population of the UK for causes such as the liberation of Indian-controlled Kashmir, the Chechen insurgents fighting for independence from Russia and the Palestinian issue, which means that those who go to fight in such conflicts might achieve status in the eyes of their communities. For instance, Khyam told his trial that his whole family were interested in the cause of liberating Indian Kashmir from Indian rule and that all of them with the exception of his mother were pleased that he had gone to fight in Kashmir.[33] Among the dataset, Mohammed Siddique Khan in particular was noted for wanting kudos within his radicalised network, and among the Muslim community of Beeston.[34]

Opinion polls suggest that a small minority of the Muslim population support the use of violence for political or religious ends, and therefore engaging in terrorist acts does confer status on an individual within their own radicalised circles. In this context, successful operations will be admired by others. Therefore, radical groups and networks, no matter how small, represent constituencies among which would-be terrorists both seek and acquire status. Badat, however, actively sought status from the wider Muslim community in Gloucester by boasting that he was a member of al Qaeda. Ironically, those boasts were to prove his undoing, when one of his fellow worshippers at the mosque in Gloucester reported him to the police.[35]

It is also possible to argue that the status that these individuals achieved was about personal impression management and self-esteem. When Mohammed Siddique Khan declared 'I am a soldier' in his 'martyrdom' video, he was attempting to confer a status on himself that was beyond what he had in his everyday life as a teaching assistant. The majority of the dataset did not have good jobs or were unemployed and some could be considered to have failed in the workplace. Therefore, becoming a warrior in the international jihad can be considered to confer status and also counter the boredom of their day-to-day lives. Wilson and Daly have described a syndrome of competitiveness, violence and risk taking to explain murders that have occurred as a result of seemingly trivial altercations. This 'young male syndrome' focuses on the social status of the perpetrators as the prime cause of violence: many young men value their social standing more than their life and will react violently to any perceived insult or disrespect.[36]

LEADERS AND LEADERSHIP

As groups of individuals grow, they need a more formal structure, which is dependent on everybody adopting roles within it and co-ordinating their efforts in order to achieve success. Roles have rules attached, most of which revolve around standards of conduct that specify how to behave or what is expected of you. Role status is independent of the individual who occupies it: you acquire the status when you adopt the role. As groups develop an organisational structure, they maintain these roles through vertical cohesion, which is exerted through a chain of command or dominance hierarchy. The key here is communication; the hierarchy is established and maintained through communication within the group.

The most obvious role in any group or organisation is the leader. Psychologists have found that leaders will even emerge in groups of random people assigned a task. The role of the leader is to guide the group towards achieving its goals, and they will facilitate the behaviour of their followers who are likely to follow any suggestions made or orders given. Vertical cohesion occurs when the followers have confidence in their leader's abilities and believe that their leader respects and will care for them. Ultimately, followers identify with their leaders as role models, which fosters increased identification with the group. The emergence of explicit leaders within groups depends on the nature of the task at hand and the availability of someone to assume the role. Success is the key driver for the emergence of a leader, as the group must feel that success is achievable and of great value to them.

A logical basis for leadership is that an individual must exhibit the characteristics and abilities of a leader, as evidenced in the 'great-man' theory of leadership, which suggests that they will be more intelligent, educated and active and will have higher social status, but most importantly that they are motivated to take on the necessary responsibility. This approach is susceptible to the fundamental attribution error as it focuses on the disposition of the leader and ignores the situation in which they find themselves. These characteristics may describe many leaders but it is their behaviour as leaders that determines whether they are successful or not. Psychologists have identified two different types: the socio-emotional leader who focuses on creating a harmonious group and is subsequently the most popular person; and the task leader who focuses on getting the job done and is the person with the best ideas and skills. The socio-emotional leader will respond to their followers in a friendly fashion which involves a certain degree of openness, mutual trust and a willingness to explain decisions. The task leader will organise, direct and define the group, regulate their behaviour and ensure that the task is completed.

ISLAMIST IDEOLOGUES IN BRITAIN

Evidence from the dataset suggests that extremist spiritual leaders may play an important role in the radicalisation process, either through direct meetings and sermons or via video, DVD and written material.[37] During the early 1990s and early 21st century, there were a number of radical preachers and ideologues operating freely in Britain, including Abu Qatada, Abu Hamza, Omar Bakri Mohammed and Abdullah el Faisal. Hamza led Supporters of *Sha'ria* and Bakri initially founded the UK branch of *Hizb ut-Tahrir* in the 1980s before leaving the organisation to found *al Muhajiroun* in 1996. These individuals and other lesser-known ideologues may have played a role in radicalising an unknown number of Britons. Lord Carlile, the official reviewer of UK terrorism laws, estimated that there could be 20 such clerics in the country, but, because they could be working in places such as cities and custodial institutions, their activities could have a disproportionate effect.[38]

Abu Qatada was initially a central figure in the development of Algerian terrorist networks in the UK, publishing the newspaper of the Algerian Armed Islamic Group in London in the mid-1990s. He preached at Finsbury Park and at the Four Feathers social club, and as his influence grew it was claimed that he became the 'spiritual head of the *mujahideen* in Britain' and 'Osama bin Laden's European ambassador'.[39] Qatada is extremely charismatic and was adept at motivating his audiences. Reda Hussaine, who worked as an informant for the British – for MI6 and Scotland Yard – and for French security services, described hearing Qatada preach:

> it is hard for anyone who has not heard him speak to understand the power he exerts over young men. He tells them that the gates to paradise are sealed by two swords, and only by picking up the sword and striking down infidels can the gates be unsealed … His words have a way of eating your mind … To think of his words now, out of context, away from the hysteria he whipped up, it is hard to see how powerful they were. But he sent hundreds, possibly even thousands, to the training camps in Afghanistan. People were mesmerised by him. When you left his meetings you felt you could pick up a gun and kill, kill, kill.[40]

Videos of his speeches were found in the flat of Mohammed Atta, but the only member of our dataset who has been clearly linked to him is Richard Reid.[41]

The Special Immigration and Appeals Commission claimed that he was at the centre of terrorist activities associated with *al Qaeda*. He was considered to be the most significant of the spiritual leaders in Britain who provided terrorists with theological legitimacy for their attacks. His speeches and writings are known to have been an inspiration for a number of terrorists around the world, and it was claimed that he had been in direct contact with members and supporters of terrorist cells and networks across Europe. He is also said to have offered theological guidance in response to requests for authority to carry out attacks.[42] Between 1995 and 1999, Qatada issued a series of influential *fatwas* which supported the killing of non-believers,[43] as well as one which apparently justified the murder of the wives and children of apostates in Algeria. In September 1998, he is said to have told his followers that it was legitimate to break Western laws, steal and cheat *kuffar* and take their women for sex or sale.[44]

The groups who asked for his guidance are thought to include *al Qaeda*, Islamic *Jihad* in Egypt, the Armed Islamic Group and the Salafist Group for Preaching and Combat (now *al Qaeda* Organisation in the Islamic Maghreb) in Algeria, and other groups in Iraq, Indonesia, Libya, Tunisia and Morocco. It was also claimed that he was the 'spiritual leader' of the *al Tawhid* movement, led by Abu Musab al Zarqawi, which would later be rebranded as *al Qaeda* in Iraq. Omar Nasiri, a former *jihadi* who subsequently became an informant for the British security services, claimed that he passed messages to Qatada from Abu Zubayda, a senior aide to bin Laden who acted as a gatekeeper to several *al Qaeda* training camps in Afghanistan.[45] However, MI5 believe that Qatada avoided being drawn into the *al Qaeda* structure in order to maintain his independence and continue his activities in Britain, although he did have links to Ayman al Zawahiri, *al Qaeda*'s second in command, who he met in Afghanistan.[46] Qatada was subsequently detained without trial in Belmarsh Prison under the Terrorism Act in 2002, but was released in 2008.

The most infamous Islamist ideologue in Britain was Sheikh Abu Hamza al Masri, who operated from Finsbury Park mosque from 1997 to 2003. Hamza was convicted of incitement to murder and race-hate offences in 2006. The case against him was based on statements he made in his sermons, which were often circulated by video cassette. In one lecture he argued that 'killing a *kuffar* who is fighting you is OK. Killing a *kuffar* for any reason, you can say it is OK even if there is no reason for it.'[47] He also bitterly attacked Jews, claiming that 'they are enemies to one another and Allah has cursed them. This is why he sent Hitler for them', and urged his supporters to kill them. However, he advocated that his followers fight *jihad* overseas rather than inciting them to perpetrate violent attacks in the UK.[48]

Although Hamza primarily operated out of Finsbury Park mosque in North London, he also criss-crossed Britain on a Friday-afternoon prayer circuit, spreading his *jihadi* ideology and recruiting members.[49] Omar Nasiri observed that Hamza was very different to

Qatada: 'I was amazed when I heard him speak. He knew nothing at all about theology, which seemed odd for someone who had gone through the Afghan camps. He was loud and passionate but to me he also seemed ill-informed. He was nothing more than a demagogue ... Hamza knew nothing at all. He would just wave his hook wildly and shout. *Jihad, jihad, jihad.*'[50]

Nevertheless, Hamza was an influence on a number of the dataset. He personally encouraged the Yemen 8 cell to go to Yemen, and most of the 21/7 cell worshipped at Finsbury Park, as did Omar Sharif and Saajid Badat, while Richard Reid actually stayed at the mosque for a short period of time.[51] There are also unsubstantiated claims that three of the 7/7 cell had listened to sermons given by Hamza,[52] while Feroze encountered Hamza at a meeting in Blackburn about Chechnya.[53] However, the only member of the dataset who actually admitted that his radicalisation was due to the influence of Hamza is Salahuddin Amin, of the Ammonium Nitrate cell, who stated that he made up his mind to move to Afghanistan after hearing speeches made by Hamza at Finsbury Park mosque in 2001.[54]

Omar Bakri Mohammed was born in Syria, where he became involved in the work of the Muslim Brotherhood, and sought asylum in the UK in the 1980s. There are conflicting reports about why Bakri founded *al Muhajiroun* in 1996, with one account suggesting that Bakri fell out with other London-based ideologues, including Hamza, and another claiming he clashed with *Hizb ut-Tahrir*'s international leadership, based in Lebanon. Bakri claims the party told him that, since Britain was not part of the Islamic world, he could not work to establish *Sha'ria* here.[55]

Bakri was once glibly described by the media as the 'Tottenham Ayatollah' and dismissed as a fantasist with little real influence. However, that image completely understates the role he had in radicalising possibly thousands of young men. Seven days after the 9/11 attacks, he issued a *fatwa* containing a death threat against President Pervez Musharraf of Pakistan.[56] It is alleged that he preached hatred of 'non-believers' and incited followers of *Hizb ut-Tahrir* and *al Muhajiroun* to commit acts of violence.[57] Bakri declared that the only people he blamed for the 7 July bombings were the government and the British public. When he was asked whether he condemned those inspired by Osama bin Laden, he said, 'why [would] I condemn Osama bin Laden for? I condemn Tony Blair. I condemn George Bush. I would never condemn Osama bin Laden or any Muslims.'[58] Bakri was twice arrested for issuing a *fatwa*, one of them on the former Prime Minister John Major in 1991. He argued that, 'if somebody decided to land an aeroplane over 10 Downing Street, for example – this is a form of self-sacrifice.'[59]

Unlike other UK-based propagandists, Bakri did make reference to the use of terrorist violence in the UK. He told the journalist Jon Ronson, 'there is a time when a military struggle must take place in the UK ... The Muslims in Britain must not be naive. They must be ready to defend themselves militarily. The struggle, as I always say, is a struggle between two civilisations, the civilisation of man and the civilisation of God.'[60] Following the Madrid train bombings in 2004 which killed 191 people, he told an audience in East London that 'what happened in Madrid is all revenge. Eye for eye, tooth for tooth, life for life. Anybody [that] commits a crime should be punished – that's exactly what happened in relation to Spain. Objective number one – break the psychology of the occupier by hitting back in their homeland. To be worried about their own wives and loved ones. Prepare as much as you can from strength and from force to terrorise – because terrorism it is part of Islam.'[61]

Bakri was informally banned from mainstream mosques, but his preaching regularly found other outlets, principally the mainstream national media and the internet.[62] Under threat of detention and deportation, he left London for Lebanon in 2005 and was barred from re-entering the country. Bakri appears to have had a particularly strong personal influence over Omar Sharif who was initially a member of *Hizb ut-Tahrir* but followed Bakri into *al Muhajiroun*.[63] Bakri admitted that both Asif Hanif and Sharif had come to him for instruction, but that the relationship between him and them was that of teacher and student.[64] However, it is not known whether Bakri or *al Muhajiroun* facilitated their links with *Hamas*. He also admitted to having taught four of the Yemen 8 cell.[65]

Sheikh Abdullah el Faisal was different from Qatada, Bakri and Hamza. He did not lead any specific group and seemed to have no specific home base and no natural constituency. Instead, he operated as a freelance radical preacher. He travelled the UK preaching to different groups, and taped recordings of his lectures were sold at specialist Islamic bookshops around the country. He advocated racial hatred and urged his audiences to kill non-believers, specifically calling on teenage boys to learn how to use rifles, fly planes and use missiles to kill 'all unbelievers'. In his tape '*Jihad*', he told Muslim women to raise their children 'with the *jihad* mentality' by giving them toy guns. In another tape recorded after 9/11, he pronounced that 'the way forward is the bullet. Our motto is "might is right".' In another tape entitled 'Rules of *Jihad*', which is thought to have been recorded before 9/11, he claimed *jihad* had been declared against India.[66] In 2003, Faisal was convicted of soliciting the murder of Jews, Americans and Hindus and using threatening words to stir up racial hatred. When he completed his sentence, he was deported to Jamaica. Among the dataset, Barot, Reid, Hamid and Lindsay were all linked to el Faisal. A source close to Lindsay suggested that it was very likely that he was introduced to Mohammed Siddique Khan through his associations with el Faisal, who had twice preached in Beeston.[67]

These ideologues largely seemed to have their own groups and constituencies, but they also seem to have loosely co-operated with each other, because there is evidence that they appeared as guest speakers at each other's groups. In Crawley, for instance, Abu Hamza and el Faisal gave occasional lectures to meetings of *al Muhajiroun*.[68] It is therefore likely that the individuals in the various radicalised Islamist networks listened to a number of different ideologues.

This indicates that authority figures and mentors have had a significant role in the radicalisation of a number of the dataset. They are significant in inspiring not only the members of the radical groups that they lead, but also others who are not members of such groups. However, that seems to have changed. The Official Narrative of the 7 July bombings suggests that terrorist recruiters are changing their methods and encouraging their recruits to keep a lower profile. While the influence of an extreme spiritual leader may still be important, either through direct meetings and sermons or via video, DVD and written material, evidence suggests that radical recruiters are increasingly keeping potential recruits away from too strong an association with a public figure, and that their role is now beginning to diminish.[69]

ACTIVITIES

While these groups never pursued structured campaigns of violence in Britain, they were active in proselytising their ideology and political objectives. They ran stalls in the high streets of the towns and cities where they operated, handing out literature and seeking recruits. They also campaigned, often aggressively, for British Muslims not to vote in elections on the grounds that it is incompatible with establishing a Muslim state because it means voting for parties which do not subscribe to Sha'ria law. Al Muhajiroun also claimed all three main political parties have 'murdered Muslims' through their support of Israel and military action in Afghanistan and Iraq.[70]

Individuals within these groups have also been involved in acts of unstructured violence. In some respects, the members of these groups can be seen to have acted like gangs, particularly in 'defending' Muslim neighbourhoods against racist attacks, but also in responding to apparent indications of 'disrespect' with violence. In 1995, Saeed Nur and Umran Qadir, who were both members of Hizb ut-Tahrir, were convicted of murdering Ayotunde Obanubi, who was stabbed to death outside Newham College in East London. The murder was the culmination of rising tension between Muslim and non-Muslim students at the college. They had accused Obanubi of 'insulting Islam'.[71] Kazi Rahman was questioned by the police over this incident, but never charged. In other cases, violent acts by members of these groups had a more overt political rationale. Amer Mirza, a member of *al Muhajiroun*, was jailed for petrol bombing a Territorial Army base in London.[72] While these acts of violence might not necessarily be defined as terrorism, they are significant because they were driven by the perpetrators' Islamist ideology.

Mohammed Siddique Khan, Tanweer and other members of the informal network in Beeston were also members of a street gang called the Mullah Crew, which was a fluid group of 15 to 20 members that formed in the mid-1990s, initially with the aim of protecting the community from racist attacks and tackling the local drugs problem.[73] The Mullah Crew were known for sorting out young Muslim lads who had become heroin addicts. In some instances, they had even kidnapped young addicts, with their parents' consent, and locked them in a room to go cold turkey. The Mullah Crew's emphasis was on physically strengthening their recruits, through outdoor activities such as paintballing, climbing and canoeing, with Islam as an integral part of their creed of clean living. One source noted that a person had to be a part of their religious set in order to be invited on these outings, and they reportedly would not take lads who had become too Westernised.[74] When members of the Mullah Crew met, the conversation revolved around *jihad*, an imagined Jewish conspiracy, how the Holocaust was a fake, the 'Great Satan' America and Britain's alliance with the Satanic USA.[75] Members of the gang are believed to have murdered a young man in Beeston for allegedly insulting Islam, but no charges were ever brought.[76]

Besides acting as advocates for the creation of Islamist states, these groups were also heavily engaged in proselytising the ideology of violent *jihad* and materially supporting the activities of *jihadis* and *mujahideen* groups overseas. In 2000, for instance, *al Muhajiroun* organised a rally in Derby to support 'their brothers in Palestine',[77] and has also been heavily involved in fundraising for Kashmiri insurgents and other *mujahideen* groups.[78] Hassan Butt claimed to have raised $300,000, mainly from professional people but also from criminals and drug dealers. He told them that their activities would be 'cleansed' in return for 20 per cent of their earnings, which would legitimise them in Islamic eyes, leaving the rest of their income 'purified' as long as the drugs were being sold to non-Muslims. Butt saw this as a tactic of war, to undermine the non-Muslim community.[79]

It is not only these groups which are, or have been, active in materially supporting oppressed Muslims or *mujahideen* groups overseas. One of the easiest ways of making the transition from passive support for a cause to active involvement in it is by engaging in charity work. For Muslims, donating money to charity is one of the five pillars of Islam, and the giving of *zakat* (alms intended to relieve the poor and the sick) is even regularised as a kind of tax in some Muslim countries. However, for several members of the dataset, involvement in charity work can be argued to have been a key part of the deepening incremental process of political activism, and was an important first step in moving from passive to active support for Islamist causes. In many instances, this merely involves relief work for suffering Muslim civilians, but international terrorist and *mujahideen* groups have also raised funds in the UK under the guise of charity work.

Shahid Butt and Omar Sheikh both spent time working for the Convoy of Mercy. This charity has been linked to the Kashmiri militant group *Harkat ul-Mujahideen*, which is part of the United *Jihad* Council.[80] Butt joined the Convoy of Mercy as a projects co-ordinator and set up a second-hand-clothes project in Birmingham to raise funds. He also worked for Islamic Relief, a charity transporting clothes and money to Bosnia, and, like Sheikh, he also travelled to Bosnia.[81] Samad Ahmed was also involved in charity work with Butt in the late 1990s, while Ghalain and Kamel were part of an aid convoy to Albania during the war in Kosovo. Similarly, one of the steps in

Anthony Garcia's deepening involvement with radical political networks was his charity work for the cause of Kashmir.

Charity work also played a significant role in the formation of the Airline cell, all seven of whom worked for the Islamic Medical Association, which sent relief supplies to Afghan refugee camps in Pakistan. Abdulla Ahmed Ali travelled to Pakistan with the charity in 2003 as an ambulance driver. He introduced his former schoolfriends Arafat Khan, Ibrahim Savant and Tanvir Hussain to the charity, and met Umar Islam and Assad Sarwar through it.[82] Mohammed Hamid of the Training cell also worked for a time at the charity's shop in East London, although no formal links are known to have existed between the two cells.[83]

What is less clear is the extent to which these groups recruited British Muslims for overseas *jihad*. It is alleged that Omar Bakri Mohammed was involved in the commission and preparation of terrorist acts as well as recruiting for *jihad*, and that he had trained young men whom he sent to fight in Chechnya, Afghanistan and Jordan,[84] but he was never tried or convicted of any such offence. However, there is anecdotal and circumstantial evidence that *al Muhajiroun* recruited young Britons to fight in overseas *jihad*. Hassan Butt was active in recruiting people to fight against coalition forces in Afghanistan between 2001 and 2002, and, in Derbyshire, councillor Abdul Rehman claimed that *al Muhajiroun* had enlisted men from the area to fight in Afghanistan.[85] Russia also claims to have discovered some of the group's members fighting alongside insurgents in Chechnya.[86] More specifically, the group is alleged to have recruited three men from Luton, who were all killed in an American bombing raid in Afghanistan in 2001. This claim was not denied by a representative of the group in Luton who declared, 'They went to defend the Muslims and defend the security of Muslims ... We are not recruiting anyone specifically for violence but we do recruit for *jihad* ... There are three ways of waging *jihad* – physical, verbal, and financial. It is the duty of every Muslim to choose one of these three. Which one they choose is up to them ... We are not at war with the British people so we can't do anything here, but my belief obliges me to go and help the brothers in Afghanistan.'[87]

Similarly, the leader of *al Muhajiroun* in Crawley was reported as saying, 'We don't actually send people away to fight but we do encourage them to go if they want ... Every Muslim has an obligation to stand up against injustice – if you are killed for a noble cause it is something to be proud of.'[88]

Former *al Muhajiroun* websites promised to answer the prayers and questions of young Muslims who wished to 'travel abroad'. One such site advised potential recruits to train and then contact members of their own communities: 'you will know these people and they will know you ... you should only speak in confidence to those whom you trust ... We estimate that between 1,800 and 2,000 go abroad for military training every year. They either go for national service in Pakistan or to private camps in South Africa, Nigeria or Afghanistan where they learn of weapons and explosives.'[89]

A number of *al Muhajiroun* members have also been associated with terrorist groups abroad. One *al Muhajiroun* safe house in Lahore was run by Sajeel Shahid, known as Abu Ibrahim, who has a computer science degree from Manchester University. He was imprisoned and then expelled from Pakistan for his alleged support of *al Qaeda*. One of those who passed through the house was Mohammed Bilal from Birmingham, who died in 2001 during a 'martyrdom operation' on an Indian army barracks in Kashmir.[90]

Supporters of *Sha'ria* and *al Muhajiroun* also played a role in terrorist recruitment by running training camps. This training will be examined in more detail in Chapter 7. The available reports suggest that there was no weapons training or bomb making involved in this training, but that its primary purpose was to identify the recruits who were most committed and physically prepared for proper military training abroad. It was therefore significant as a conduit for members of these political groups to make the transition from being political activists to being terrorists. Therefore, the interface between the activities of these groups and individuals who recruit or facilitate terrorist activity can be seen as a key stepping stone from non-violent political activity to violent extremism.

RECRUITMENT AND INDOCTRINATION

There appear to be four interconnected strands to the indoctrination of new recruits to these types of groups:

(i) the promotion of clean living;
(ii) the exploitation of identity issues;
(iii) the exploitation of generational and cultural issues within Muslim communities; and
(iv) the channelling of idealism or rebelliousness though the ideology of the group.

In some cases, these groups politicise their recruits as part of the recruitment process. In other cases, they simply build on a politicisation that is already developing within the individual. Maajid Nawaz, for instance, joined *Hizb ut-Tahrir* as the end point of the process of his gradual politicisation that had started years earlier. He initially dealt with his identity issues and the racism he encountered by embracing a counter-culture inspired by American rap music, which, in the 1990s, seemed to provide a voice and identity to those who were not being seen or heard, and was inclined to be anti-establishment. As time passed, he became more aware of his own identity issues and of international affairs. The war in Bosnia and the ethnic cleansing of the Muslim population struck a deep chord with him. The war coincided with an emerging trend in rap music, in which American rappers began to identify themselves explicitly as Muslims and mixed samples of Malcolm X's speeches into their music. It was during this period that a member of *Hizb ut-Tahrir* explained the group's ideas to him. He recalled that his 'premature politicised mind was ripe to receive an ideology that advocated a black and white solution to the problems I had grown up with.'[91] Nawaz summed up the impact of this ideological indoctrination: 'I had finally discovered who I was. I was a sharp, ideological Muslim whose mission was to create a new world order. I took on board this ideology as my own, propagating it through campuses and across borders until it consumed my life.'[92]

Rebelliousness also appears to be a part of *Hizb ut-Tahrir*'s appeal to young Muslims. It has created an anti-establishment kudos for itself by advocating certain forms of law-breaking such as not purchasing car insurance on the grounds that it is inconsistent with Islam.[93] There have also been allegations that *Hizb ut-Tahrir* makes its recruits commit crimes in order to test their loyalty.[94] The case of Omar Sharif also indicates how a sense of approval from a significant other can potentially play a role in socialising an individual into more extreme behaviour.[95] Sharif met his wife Tahira Tabassum in *Hizb ut-Tahrir* circles at King's College. Her father recalled that their religious views strengthened as their relationship developed.[96] Sharif's brother and sister were also members of the group.

A key tactic in the recruitment and indoctrination process of these groups is to exploit the problems that many young Muslims are having with their identity. Hassan Butt would ascertain what his potential recruit identified with and then pick holes in it. If the potential recruit felt Pakistani, Butt would focus on the difficulty of being both British and Pakistani. He found this easy because he could identify with such feelings; being British but growing up in a strongly Pakistani household, he felt neither British nor Pakistani.[97] Islamism was a natural way of transcending this cultural dislocation because it offered a new social identity that transcended both nationality and ethnicity.[98]

In the early stages of the indoctrination of new recruits, there may be no hint of an extremist agenda. Instead, the group conversation might focus on being a good Muslim and staying away from drugs and crime. Hassan Butt's recruiter showed him how Islam could bring order to the chaos in his life. Like many of his friends, he was heading down a path towards drug addiction and crime. The recruiter was the first Muslim who talked to him about Islam in a manner that he could understand. He explained to Butt that, beyond the traditional recitation of the *Qur'an*, praying, fasting and the *Hajj*, Islam is a complete system and way of life, and showed him how he could direct his anger and frustration in a more productive direction.[99]

This was the same approach used by the informal network which Mohammed Siddique Khan, Tanweer and Hussain belonged to in Beeston. Khan used to give talks in the local youth clubs which focused on clean living, staying away from crime and drugs, and the value of sport and outdoor activity.[100] This was confirmed by Manchester businessman Kursheed Fiaz, who reported that Khan, Omar Sharif and Asif Hanif had visited his offices in the summer of 2001, trying to encourage the young Muslims who worked there in 'the new ways of Islam'. Fiaz recalled that the first few meetings were casual affairs and Khan simply talked about the importance of religious duties. Only at the fourth meeting did he get to the point. Fiaz recalled that 'what they tried to do is separate them from our side of it and perhaps give them different ideas. The youngsters that are involved with my organisation were told by Khan that to learn the new ways of Islam you may be asked to go to Pakistan ... But then the names such as Afghanistan and Syria were mentioned, so at that stage the lads asked what was going on.'[101]

Shiraz Maher, a former regional officer of *Hizb ut-Tahrir* in North East England, confirms this sense of 'in-group' love. He describes the group as being like a large family:

> a group offering social support, comradeship, a sense of purpose and validation. At 21, it was intoxicating to me. I embraced my new Islamist identity and family with eagerness. Islamism transcends cultural norms, so it not only prompted me to reject my British identity but also my ethnic South Asian background. I was neither eastern, nor western; I was a Muslim, a part of the global *ummah*, where identity is defined through the fraternity of faith. Islamists insist this identity is not racist because Islam

welcomes people of all colours, ethnicities and backgrounds. When I embraced *Hizb ut-Tahrir* and the Islamist way of life there was an established network offering social support and validation.[102]

Hassan Butt agreed: 'when you're cut off from your family, the *jihadi* network then becomes your family. It becomes your backbone and support.'

Under these circumstances it becomes very difficult for individuals to leave the network because there is nowhere else for them to go.[103]

However, as noted in Chapter 2, there are a number of other, more moderate, Islamist organisations operating in the UK from which these radical groups also try to recruit. For these potential recruits, the process seems to be slightly different, with the focus being more on channelling the idealism of the recruit through the ideology of the group. This process was described by Ed Husain, who was already a member of the Islamist group *Jamaat-e-Islami* when he met the person who recruited him into *Hizb ut-Tahrir*. His recruiter was able to convince him to join *Hizb ut-Tahrir*, by exposing *Jamaat-e-Islami*'s lack of intellectual rigour, as well as its lack of a practical programme of action for achieving the Islamic state, and contrasting it with *Hizb ut-Tahrir*'s practical and coherent strategy for achieving its goals.

After initially being bombarded with messages about being a good Muslim and clean living, recruits are gradually exposed to propaganda about the real and perceived injustices being committed against Muslims. At the domestic level, there are allegations of injustices against Islam and Muslims within the UK.[104] At the international level, this propaganda focuses on Muslims being persecuted in conflicts such as Iraq, Chechnya, the occupied Palestinian territories and Kashmir, while Muslims living in Muslim states are portrayed as being oppressed by leaders who are both corrupt and un-Islamic. Hassan Butt would follow up his initial contacts in the gym and in pool halls where they would talk about the suffering of the Muslims all over the world.[105] Omar Bakri Mohammed explained that 'we find young men in university campuses or mosques, invite them for a meal and discuss the situation for on-going attacks being suffered by Muslims in Chechnya, Palestine or Kashmir. We ... make them understand their duty to support the *jihad* struggle verbally, financially and, if they can, physically in order to liberate their homeland.'[106]

Islamist recruiters exploit perceived threats to their groups through propaganda. The internet, in conjunction with DVDs and videotapes, has had a significant impact in disseminating this propaganda because it enables access to a massive amount of extremist material. The network of extremists which Mohammed Siddique Khan and Tanweer belonged to in Beeston used to download videos and make DVDs in the backroom of the Iqra bookshop. Most of the dataset either possessed or viewed extremist videos and DVDs, some of which were ideological in nature, such as speeches by bin Laden or other Islamist ideologues, and the living wills of some of the 9/11 attackers. Others contained war footage from various *jihads* around the world.[107] Viewing these DVDs and videos was a common feature in the radicalisation of many members of the dataset. As we shall discuss in Chapter 8, this violent material also may have contributed to that radicalisation developing into violent extremism.

The potential impact of such videos and DVDs was explained by Anthony Garcia at his trial. Throughout 1998 and 1999, he attended Islamist political meetings and began discussing issues such as the treatment of Muslims in Indian-administered Kashmir. Garcia vividly recalled being shown a video about 'atrocities' allegedly perpetrated by the Indian armed forces against civilians in Kashmir. 'It was the worst thing anyone could have seen. Little children sexually abused and women ... and I still remember it quite clearly.' Garcia said he remembered crying as he watched the video and he decided to do something to help his fellow Muslims in Kashmir. He began by fundraising, but, by the beginning of 2002, he was determined to go to Pakistan and get military training.[108]

DEEPENING INDOCTRINATION OVERSEAS: *MADRASSAS*

The analysis above relates to recruitment and indoctrination inside the UK, but there are also suspicions that at least some of the dataset might have been indoctrinated overseas, in Islamic religious schools, or *madrassas*. Immediately prior to 9/11, attention had focused on the *Dar al-Hadith* School in Yemen, whose students came from a number of countries and included fighters from Afghanistan and Chechnya. The teachers and students denied claims that it was an ideological training ground for *jihadis*, insisting that it was simply a Fundamentalist school for the study of the *Qur'an*. However, the leader of the school, Sheikh Muqbel bin Hadie al-Wadie, a prominent cleric, was alleged to have had close links to *al Qaeda*. Western diplomatic sources claim that Sheikh Muqbel's ideas directly influenced bin Laden's aggressive stance towards the West, and the school is believed by some locals to be bankrolled by bin Laden. Several dozen Britons are believed to have attended the school,[109] but there is no evidence that any of them have subsequently become involved in terrorist violence. Evidence of other paramilitary training in Yemen emerged when young Briton Hosea Walker was shot and killed in 2000 in an accident at an apparent training camp being run by the *Salafi Islami* religious movement.[110]

In Pakistan, particularly, a number of *madrassas* are known to be run by or have close links with *jihadi* groups operating in Afghanistan and Indian-controlled Kashmir. For instance, the Muridke *madrassa*, which is legally registered with the Pakistani government, is well known to international investigators as a transit point for suicide bombers heading for Kashmir from the *jihadi* group *Lashkar-e-Taiba*. The group allegedly carried out 35 of the 42 suicide bombings targeting Indian security forces in Kashmir between 1999 and 2001. *Lashkar-e-Taiba* is also known to have handled Western fighters who volunteered to fight in Kashmir.[111] However, Professor Zafar Iqbal, the *madrassa's* director of education, condemned the 7 July bombings, claiming that 'this was not the work of a true *mujahideen* who can legitimately kill only those who are killing Muslims – as in Kashmir or Iraq'.[112]

Following the 7 July bombings, there was increased concern about the role that overseas *madrassas* were playing in radicalising young British Muslims after it was discovered that both Mohammed Siddique Khan and Tanweer had visited *madrassas* in Pakistan. In 2005, an estimated 1,400 foreign students were studying in Pakistan's 13,000–15,000 *madrassas*, and it is not unusual for British Pakistanis to study in *madrassas* for short periods.[113] The role that *madrassas* can play in indoctrinating individuals with a *jihadi* ideology is apparent from the stories of people such as Anwar Khan from Burnley, whose parents had sent him to a *madrassa* in Pakistan in an effort to cure him of his heroin addiction and criminal activities. As a result of his experience at the *madrassa*, he became a Taliban fighter, and was captured by the Northern Alliance in Afghanistan in 1998.[114]

The most high-profile mosque and *madrassa* involved in radical politics in Pakistan was the *Lal Masjid*, or Red Mosque, in Islamabad. The mosque and its associated seminary and *madrassa* mainly attracted students from the North West Frontier Province and the tribal areas bordering Afghanistan, where there is strong support for the Taliban and *al Qaeda*. Under the former leadership of Maulana Abdullah, who was renowned for his speeches promoting *jihad*, the mosque complex became the centre of a hard-line Islamist student movement which was strongly opposed to the government of President Musharraf. After Abdullah was assassinated in the 1990s, his two sons, who had previously admitted to having had contacts with *al Qaeda* leaders, including bin Laden himself, took over the running of the complex. In July 2005, the Pakistani security forces attempted to raid the mosque on the pretext of investigating a possible link between the seminary and one of the 7/7 cell, but were turned back by female students wielding sticks. Over the following years, the students increasingly challenged the government, and armed militants took refuge inside the mosque. In 2007, the government decided that it could no longer tolerate this challenge to its authority, and the Pakistani army stormed the complex, killing more than 100 people. The raid triggered a series of revenge suicide bombings and other attacks by militants across Pakistan, which killed hundreds of people.[115]

However, the role that overseas *madrassas* have had in indoctrinating the members of the dataset is very unclear. It is believed that Badat first crossed paths with Reid during a five-year period of studying in Pakistani *madrassas*,[116] yet it is clear that both Badat and Reid had at least begun the process of radicalisation while they were living in London. Therefore, it would seem that, for Badat, the role of the *madrassa* was to deepen his radicalisation.

Pakistani investigators believe that Shehzad Tanweer visited Pakistan five times between 2001 and 2005, staying for a total of seven months. The first of these visits is said to have been in 2001 when he was 18 years old. Accompanied by his father, he enrolled as a volunteer with *Tablighi Jamaat*, whose volunteers proselytise peacefully in the name of Islam. Tanweer returned in 2002, and again worked as a volunteer in the North West Frontier Province. It was during this trip that Pakistani intelligence sources believe that he might have come into contact with Sher Ali, a recruiter for *Jaish-e-Mohammed*, and taken his first steps towards involvement in *jihadi* activity.

Mohammed Siddique Khan and Tanweer visited Karachi together in late 2004 and returned to Britain in February 2005. Hasib Hussain travelled separately to Karachi in July 2004, and returned to Britain via a different route. Tanweer spent most of his time with relatives in Kottan, a village north of Faisalabad, where Khan visited him twice. Sources reported that Tanweer also visited several *madrassas* in Lahore, but never registered formally for tuition. It is believed that the *Jamia Manzoorul Islamia*, a *madrassa* linked with *Jaish-e-Mohammed*, might have been among them.

Tanweer then moved on to Faisalabad, but it is not known whether Khan accompanied him. Osama Nazir, a leader of *Jaish-e-Mohammed*, claimed that he met Tanweer at a *madrassa* in Faisalabad in December 2004, and Tanweer is also believed to have made contact with Sher Ali who was an associate of Nazir.[117] Other reports indicate that Tanweer stayed at the Markaz-e-Dawa *madrassa* for four or five days in early 2005. The mosque is run by *Dawa-ul-Arshad*, the political front for *Lashkar-e-Taiba*, which was set up in 1987 to fight against the Indian security forces in Kashmir. *Lashkar-e-Taiba* was banned by the Pakistani government in 2002 following the bombing of the Indian parliament in New Delhi, yet it is still active in Pakistan as *Tahrik al-Furquan*. There has also been speculation that Tanweer may have met a contact from *Lashkar-e-Taiba* at the Muridke *madrassa*.[118] These contacts are consistent with Khan and Tanweer attempting to make the necessary connections to fight in Afghanistan or Kashmir.

Despite Tanweer's connection to these *madrassas*, it is unlikely that he could have been fully radicalised by a three-month visit to Lahore. Arif Jamal, a Lahore-based journalist who has studied the role of *madrassas*, suggests that the fact that Tanweer had decided to go to Pakistan to pursue an Islamic education indicates that he had already decided on which path he would take.[119] In fact, Tanweer's links to *madrassas* suggest that, instead of being a forum in which foreigners are radicalised, some *madrassas* offer a space where *jihadi* facilitators and recruiters can operate, and perhaps where terrorist plans are formulated.

This analysis illustrates that the ideology of radical Islamist groups is firmly rooted in elements of the wider discourse within the Muslim population of the UK. The appeal of these groups is that they offer disaffected and rootless young Muslims an alternative social identity, which taps into the rebelliousness and the idealism that many young people exhibit. Many of the members of these groups simply remain as members without ever deciding to go further and join a terrorist network or cell. Equally, a growing number of members of these groups have become disillusioned, and left them. However, the experience of our dataset illustrates that some members of these groups do go on to engage in terrorist violence. Key links between these radical groups and terrorist cells are their ideologies and political objectives. The following chapters will explore the process of joining terrorist cells and why these individuals chose to kill for their cause.

Notes and references

1 Buunk BP, 'Affiliation, attraction and close relationships', in Hewstone M, Stroebe W & Stephenson GM (eds), *Introduction to Social Psychology* (Oxford: Blackwell Publishers, 1996).

2 Malik S, 'My brother the bomber', *Prospect*, June 2007, http://www.prospect-magazine.co.uk/article_details.php?&id=9635.

3 'How I became a Muslim extremist', BBC NewsOnline, 28 September 2007, http://news.bbc.co.uk/1/hi/programmes/panorama/7016299.stm.

4 'Background: Birmingham's holy warriors', *Daily Telegraph*, 17 January 1999, http://www.telegraph.co.uk/htmlContent.jhtml?html=/archive/1999/01/17/nholy117.html.

5 'Why I joined the British jihad – and why I rejected it', *Sunday Times*, 16 September 2007, http://www.timesonline.co.uk/tol/news/uk/article2459969.ece.

6 'Yemen: The British link', *Observer*, 19 January 1999, www.al-bab.com.

7 'I know how these terrorists are inspired', *Daily Telegraph*, 2 May 2007, http://www.telegraph.co.uk/opinion/main.jhtml?xml=/opinion/2007/05/02/do0203.xml.

8 'Prevention and Suppression of Terrorism', *Hansard*, Column 490, 20 July 2006; Taseer A, 'A British jihadist', *Prospect*, August 2005, http://www.prospect-magazine.co.uk/article_details.php?id=6992.
9 'Blair bid to ban group "opposed"', BBC NewsOnline, 19 November 2006, http://news.bbc.co.uk/1/hi/uk/6162690.stm.

10 'The Network', *Observer*, 6 May 2007, http://observer.guardian.co.uk/focus/story/0,,2073522,00.html.

11 Ansari H, 'Attitudes to Jihad, martyrdom and terrorism among British Muslims', in Abbas T, ed, *Muslim Britain: Communities under Pressure* (London: Zed Books, 2005), p 148.

12 'Q&A: Hizb ut-Tahrir', BBC NewsOnline, 10 August 2007, http://news.bbc.co.uk/1/hi/world/4127688.stm.

13 Taseer A, 'A British jihadist', *Prospect*, August 2005, http://www.prospect-magazine.co.uk/article_details.php?id=6992.

14 'Terror links of the Tottenham Ayatollah', *Sunday Times*, 24 July 2005, http://www.timesonline.co.uk/tol/news/uk/article547466.ece.

15 Shortly after going up to King's College, Sharif began attending *Hizb ut-Tahrir* meetings, and was known to have attended several which were addressed by guests such as Omar Bakri Mohammed and Mohammad al Massari, a radical who is said to have links to bin Laden. Sharif's former friend Zaheer Khan recalled that he never missed a meeting and subsequently began networking with its members outside the university as well. Malik S, 'Society NS Profile – Omar Sharif', *New Statesman*, 24 April 2006, http://www.newstatesman.com/200604240017.

16 'Cleric preaches that violence is part of Islam', *Daily Telegraph*, 1 May 2007, http://www.telegraph.co.uk/news/main.jhtml?xml=/news/2007/05/01/nplot901.xml.

17 'Prevention and Suppression of Terrorism', *Hansard*, Column 490, 20 July 2006.

18 'Profile: Omar Bakri Mohammad', BBC NewsOnline, 21 July 2005, http://news.bbc.co.uk/1/hi/uk/4703541.stm.

19 'Prevention and Suppression of Terrorism', *Hansard*, Column 490, 20 July 2006.

20 'Banned Islamists spawn front organisations', *Guardian*, 22 July 2006.

21 'Banned Islamists spawn front organisations', *Guardian*, 22 July 2006.

22 'Young Muslims and Extremism', Home Office-FCO Paper, 10 May 2004, p 9, http://www.timesonline.co.uk/article/0,,22989-1688872,00.html.

23 'The jihadist who needed no brainwashing to blow up Aldgate train', Ian Herbert and Kim Sengupta, *Independent*, 10 September 2005, http://news.independent.co.uk/uk/crime/article311539.ece.

24 'When I heard where the bombers were from I felt sick', *Guardian*, 24 June 2006, http://www.guardian.co.uk/uk_news/story/0,,1804867,00.html; Report of the Official Account of the Bombings in London on 7 July 2005, HC1087 (London: The Stationery Office), 11 May 2006.

25 'Prevention and Suppression of Terrorism', *Hansard*, Column 490, 20 July 2006.

26 'MI5 followed UK suicide bomber', BBC NewsOnline, 30 April 2007, http://news.bbc.co.uk/1/hi/uk/6417353.stm.

27 'Young Muslims and Extremism', Home Office-FCO Paper, 10 May 2004, p 9, http://www.timesonline.co.uk/article/0,,22989-1688872,00.html.

28 'Terrorists or tourists', *Guardian*, 26 June 1999, http://www.al-bab.com/yemen/artic/gdn42.htm.

29 Bartone PT & Kirkland FR, 'Optimal leadership in small army units', in Gal R & Mangelsdorff MD (eds), *Handbook of Military Psychology* (John Wiley & Sons, 1991).

30 Buunk BP, 'Affiliation, attraction and close relationships', in Hewstone M, Stroebe W & Stephenson GM (eds), *Introduction to Social Psychology* (Oxford: Blackwell Publishers, 1996).

31 van Avermaet E, 'Social influence in small groups', in Hewstone M, Stroebe W & Stephenson GM (eds), *Introduction to Social Psychology* (Oxford: Blackwell Publishers, 1996); Zimbardo P, *The Lucifer Effect: How Good People Turn Evil* (New York: Random House, 2007).

32 Janis I, *Victims of Groupthink* (2nd edition) (Boston: Houghton-Mifflin, 1982).

33 'Profile: Omar Khyam', BBC NewsOnline, 30 April 2007, http://news.bbc.co.uk/1/hi/uk/6149794.stm.

34 'When I heard where the bombers were from I felt sick', *Guardian*, 24 June 2006, http://www.guardian.co.uk/uk_news/story/0,,1804867,00.html.

35 'Badat "met Reid at London mosque"', *Evening Standard*, 28 November 2003.

36 Wilson M & Daly M, 'Competitiveness, risk taking, and violence: the young male syndrome', *Ethology and Sociobiology*, No. 6, 1985, pp 59–73.

37 Report of the Official Account of the Bombings in London on 7 July 2005, HC1087 (London: The Stationery Office), 11 May 2006.

38 'Terror fears on student radicals', BBC NewsOnline, 14 February 2006, http://news.bbc.co.uk/1/hi/uk_politics/4712722.stm.

39 Phillips M, *Londonistan* (London: Gibson Square Books, 2006), p 49.

40 'I spied on Abu Qatada for MI5', *Evening Standard*, 28 January 2005.

41 'I spied on Abu Qatada for MI5', *Evening Standard*, 28 January 2005.

42 'Profile: Abu Qatada, "An al-Qa'eda lynchpin"', *Daily Telegraph*, 8 May 2008, http://www.telegraph.co.uk/news/1939057/Profile-Abu-Qatada%2C-%27An-al-Qa%27eda-lynchpin%27.html; 'Cleric from London unmasked as inspiration

for Muslim terrorists', *Daily Telegraph*, 21 May 2003,
http://www.telegraph.co.uk/news/uknews/1430651/Cleric-from-London-unmasked-as-inspiration-for-Muslim-terrorists.html.

43 'Profile: Abu Qatada, "An al-Qa'eda lynchpin"', *Daily Telegraph*, 8 May 2008,
http://www.telegraph.co.uk/news/1939057/Profile-Abu-Qatada%2C-%27An-al-Qa%27eda-lynchpin%27.html.

44 'The Home Office case against Abu Qatada', *Daily Telegraph*, 27 February
2007, http://www.telegraph.co.uk/news/uknews/1543944/The-Home-Office-case-against-Abu-Qatada.html.

45 'Focus: My life as a spy at the heart of *al-Qaeda*', *Sunday Times*, 19 November
2006, http://www.timesonline.co.uk/article/0,,2087-2460306_7,00.html.

46 'Profile: Abu Qatada, "An al-Qa'eda lynchpin"', *Daily Telegraph*, 8 May 2008,
http://www.telegraph.co.uk/news/1939057/Profile-Abu-Qatada%2C-%27An-al-Qa%27eda-lynchpin%27.html.

47 'Cleric from London unmasked as inspiration for Muslim terrorists', *Daily
Telegraph*, 21 May 2003,
http://www.telegraph.co.uk/news/uknews/1430651/Cleric-from-London-unmasked-as-inspiration-for-Muslim-terrorists.html.

48 'Holocaust a punishment from God, said radical preacher', *The Times*, 14
January 2006.

49 'Focus: My life as a spy at the heart of *al-Qaeda*', *Sunday Times*, 19 November
2006, http://www.timesonline.co.uk/article/0,,2087-2460306_7,00.html.

50 'Defiant shouts end a strange saga of international intrigue', *Independent*, 10
August 1999.

51 'Focus: My life as a spy at the heart of *al-Qaeda*', *Sunday Times*, 19 November
2006, http://www.timesonline.co.uk/article/0,,2087-2460306_7,00.html.

52 '7/7 bomber linked to Israel pair', BBC NewsOnline, 9 July 2006,
http://news.bbc.co.uk/1/hi/uk/5161390.stm.

53 *Daily Telegraph*, 8 February 2006.

54 'Al Qaeda boss visited Blackburn', *Lancashire Evening Telegraph*, 15 June 2007,
http://www.lancashireeveningtelegraph.co.uk/display.var.1474143.0.al_qaeda_boss_visited_blackburn.php.

55 'Accused "influenced by Abu Hamza"', BBC NewsOnline, 25 July 2006,
http://news.bbc.co.uk/1/hi/uk/5214174.stm.

[56] Malik S, 'Society NS Profile – Omar Sharif', *New Statesman*, 24 April 2006, http://www.newstatesman.com/200604240017.

[57] 'Terror links of the Tottenham Ayatollah', *Sunday Times*, 24 July 2005, http://www.timesonline.co.uk/tol/news/uk/article547466.ece.

[58] Phillips M, *Londonistan* (London: Gibson Square Books, 2006), p 51.

[59] 'Profile: Omar Bakri Mohammad', BBC NewsOnline, 21 July 2005, http://news.bbc.co.uk/1/hi/uk/4703541.stm.

[60] 'Terror links of the Tottenham Ayatollah', *Sunday Times*, 24 July 2005, http://www.timesonline.co.uk/tol/news/uk/article547466.ece.

[61] Ronson J, *Them: Adventures with Extremists* (London: Simon and Schuster, 2002), p 22.

[62] 'I want to be a martyr says activist', *Manchester Evening News*, 6 April 2004, http://www.manchestereveningnews.co.uk/news/s/86/86545_i_want_to_be_a_martyr_says_activist.html.

[63] 'Profile: Omar Bakri Mohammad', BBC NewsOnline, 21 July 2005, http://news.bbc.co.uk/1/hi/uk/4703541.stm.

[64] Malik S, 'Society NS Profile – Omar Sharif', *New Statesman*, 24 April 2006, http://www.newstatesman.com/200604240017.

[65] 'Radical cleric "taught" bomb suspects', BBC NewsOnline, 2 May 2003, http://news.bbc.co.uk/1/hi/world/middle_east/2994497.stm.

[66] 'Kidnappers' call to London Imam', *Guardian*, 14 January 1999, http://www.politics.guardian.co.uk/yemen/Story/0,,209196,00.html.

[67] 'Cleric preached racist views', BBC NewsOnline, 24 February 2003, http://news.bbc.co.uk/1/hi/uk/2784591.stm.

[68] Malik S, 'My brother the bomber', *Prospect*, June 2007, http://www.prospect-magazine.co.uk/article_details.php?&id=9635.

[69] 'Profile: Omar Khyam', BBC NewsOnline, 30 April 2007, http://news.bbc.co.uk/1/hi/uk/6149794.stm.

[70] Report of the Official Account of the Bombings in London on 7 July 2005, HC1087 (London: The Stationery Office), 11 May 2006, p 23.

[71] 'Bombing claims a surprise to Derby', BBC NewsOnline, 1 May 2003, http://news.bbc.co.uk/1/hi/england/2991675.stm.

72 'Missile plot Briton sent to jail', BBC NewsOnline, 30 April 2007, http://news.bbc.co.uk/1/hi/uk/6206886.stm.

73 'Terror links of the Tottenham Ayatollah', *Sunday Times*, 24 July 2005, http://www.timesonline.co.uk/tol/news/uk/article547466.ece.

74 Malik S, 'My brother the bomber', *Prospect*, June 2007, http://www.prospect-magazine.co.uk/article_details.php?&id=9635.

75 'The jihadist who needed no brainwashing to blow up Aldgate train', Ian Herbert and Kim Sengupta, *Independent*, 10 September 2005, http://news.independent.co.uk/uk/crime/article311539.ece.

76 'When I heard where the bombers were from I felt sick', *Guardian*, 24 June 2006, http://www.guardian.co.uk/uk_news/story/0,,1804867,00.html; Report of the Official Account of the Bombings in London on 7 July 2005, HC1087 (London: The Stationery Office), 11 May 2006.

77 'When I heard where the bombers were from I felt sick', *Guardian*, 24 June 2006, http://www.guardian.co.uk/uk_news/story/0,,1804867,00.html.

78 'Bombing claims a surprise to Derby', BBC NewsOnline, 1 May 2003, http://news.bbc.co.uk/1/hi/england/2991675.stm.

79 'Path to extremism: How it started', BBC NewsOnline, 3 May 2007, http://news.bbc.co.uk/1/hi/uk/6619147.stm; Jon Ronson, *Them: Adventures with Extremists* (London: Simon and Schuster, 2002), pp 7–8.

80 CBS News, 25 March 2007, http://www.cbsnews.com/stories/2007/03/23/60minutes/main2602308_page3.shtml.

81 *Jane's International Security News*, 20 September 2001.

82 'Background: Birmingham's holy warriors', *Daily Telegraph*, 17 January 1999, http://www.telegraph.co.uk/htmlContent.jhtml?html=/archive/1999/01/17/nholy117.html.

83 'Airliner bomb trial: How MI5 uncovered the terror plot', *Daily Telegraph*, 9 September 2008, http://www.telegraph.co.uk/news/uknews/2709379/Airliner-bomb-trial-How-MI5-uncovered-the-terror-plot.html.

84 '"Astonishment" at terror verdicts', BBC NewsOnline, 9 September 2008, http://news.bbc.co.uk/1/hi/uk/7605583.stm.

85 'Prevention and Suppression of Terrorism', *Hansard*, Column 490, 20 July 2006.

86 'Inquiry over UK suicide bomb link', BBC NewsOnline, 1 May 2003, http://news.bbc.co.uk/1/hi/england/derbyshire/2990935.stm.

87 'Banned Islamists spawn front organisations', *Guardian*, 22 July 2006.

88 'We will drive Taliban supporters from our town: Muslim leaders speak out at fears of reprisals grow', *Luton Today*, 31 October 2001, http://www.lutontoday.co.uk/ViewArticle2.aspx?SectionID=541&ArticleID=2799 33; 'No tears for Luton's Muslim "martyrs"', *Luton Today*, 31 October 2001,http://www.lutontoday.co.uk/ViewArticle2.aspx?SectionID=541&ArticleID =279105; 'Three Luton men killed in US attack', *Luton Today*, 29 October 2001, http://www.lutontoday.co.uk/ViewArticle2.aspx?SectionID=541&ArticleID=2775 33.

89 'Fundamentalist: Muslim militants may have used the town as a training base', *Crawley Today*, 7 November 2001, http://www.crawleytoday.co.uk/ViewArticle2.aspx?SectionID=496&ArticleID=26 4044.

90 'Young Britons heed the call to arms for holy war', *Daily Telegraph*, 19 June 2001, http://www.telegraph.co.uk/news/main.jhtml?xml=/news/2000/12/29/nmus129. xml.

91 'Why I joined the British jihad – and why I rejected it', *Sunday Times*, 16 September 2007, http://www.timesonline.co.uk/tol/news/uk/article2459969.ece.

92 'Why I joined the British jihad – and why I rejected it', *Sunday Times*, 16 September 2007, http://www.timesonline.co.uk/tol/news/uk/article2459969.ece.

93 Malik S, 'Society NS Profile – Omar Sharif', *New Statesman*, 24 April 2006, http://www.newstatesman.com/200604240017.

94 'Blair bid to ban group "opposed"', BBC NewsOnline, 19 November 2006, http://news.bbc.co.uk/1/hi/uk/6162690.stm.

95 Horgan J, *The Psychology of Terrorism* (Oxford: Routledge, 2005), p 94.

96 Malik S, 'Society NS Profile – Omar Sharif', *New Statesman*, 24 April 2006, http://www.newstatesman.com/200604240017.

97 Malik S, 'My brother the bomber', *Prospect*, June 2007, http://www.prospect-magazine.co.uk/article_details.php?&id=9635.

98 Malik S, 'My brother the bomber', *Prospect*, June 2007, http://www.prospect-magazine.co.uk/article_details.php?&id=9635.

99 Taseer A, 'A British jihadist', *Prospect*, August 2005, http://www.prospect-magazine.co.uk/article_details.php?id=6992.

100 Report of the Official Account of the Bombings in London on 7 July 2005, HC1087 (London: The Stationery Office), 11 May 2006, p 23.

101 '7/7 bomber linked to Israel pair', BBC NewsOnline, 9 July 2006, http://news.bbc.co.uk/1/hi/uk/5161390.stm; Malik S, 'My brother the bomber', *Prospect*, June 2007, http://www.prospect-magazine.co.uk/article_details.php?&id=9635.

102 'How I escaped Islamism', *Sunday Times*, 12 August 2007, http://www.timesonline.co.uk/tol/comment/columnists/guest_contributors/article2241736.ece.

103 Malik S, 'My brother the bomber', *Prospect*, June 2007, http://www.prospect-magazine.co.uk/article_details.php?&id=9635.

104 CBS News, 25 March 2007, http://www.cbsnews.com/stories/2007/03/23/60minutes/main2602308_page3.shtml.

105 CBS News, 25 March 2007, http://www.cbsnews.com/stories/2007/03/23/60minutes/main2602308_page3.shtml.

106 'Young Britons heed the call to arms for holy war', *Daily Telegraph*, 19 June 2001, http://www.telegraph.co.uk/news/main.jhtml?xml=/news/2000/12/29/nmus129.xml.

107 Prepared text of Tuesday's portion of the Crown's opening statement in the trial of seven men alleged to have plotted to bomb London: Regina v Omar Khyam, Anthony Garcia, Nabeel Hussain, Jawad Akbar, Waheed Mahmood, Shujah-ud-din-Mahmood, Salahuddin Amin, 21 March 2006, *Ottawa Citizen*, http://www.canada.com/ottawacitizen/news/story.html?id=408dc2ed-d950-4ee5-a4b7-392eb5faaf34&k=75162.

108 'Profile: Anthony Garcia', BBC NewsOnline, 30 April 2007, http://news.bbc.co.uk/1/hi/uk/6149798.stm.

109 'School for veterans of Islam's holy wars', *Daily Telegraph*, 20 June 2001, http://www.telegraph.co.uk/news/main.jhtml?xml=/news/2001/02/09/wmid209.xml.

110 'Britons continue to ask: "Was Hosea Walker truly killed in an accident?"', *Yemen Times*, http://www.yementimes.com/00/iss29/front.htm; 'Moqbil Al-

Wadi'i to Yemen Times', *Yemen Times*,
http://www.yementimes.com/00/iss29/intrview.htm.

111 'Profile of a suicide bomber, An interview with a British-born Pakistani suicide bomber before he blew himself up in Tel Aviv provides insight into a new type of recruit for Islamist terrorist activities', Claudio Franco for ISN Security Watch, 21 July 2005, http://www.isn.ethz.ch/news/sw/details.cfm?ID=12263.

112 'We do not teach any terrorism in this place', *Daily Telegraph*, 16 July 2005.

113 'Pakistan to expel Madrassa foreigners', *Daily Telegraph*, 30 July 2005, http://www.telegraph.co.uk/news/main.jhtml?xml=/news/2005/07/30/ncleric130.xml.

114 'Britons fall victim to an Islamic dream', *Daily Telegraph*, 5 October 2001, http://www.telegraph.co.uk/news/main.jhtml?xml=/news/2001/10/05/ntal05.xml.

115 'Profile: Islamabad's Red Mosque', BBC NewsOnline, 6 July 2008, http://news.bbc.co.uk/1/hi/world/south_asia/7492283.stm.

116 Crumley B, 'High-alert holidays', *Time Magazine*, 14 December 2003, http://www.time.com/time/magazine/article/0,9171,561279,00.html.

117 'Suicide bombers flew to Pakistan together', *Daily Telegraph*, 19 July 2005, http://www.telegraph.co.uk/news/main.jhtml?xml=/news/2005/07/19/nbomb19.xml.

118 'We do not teach any terrorism in this place', *Daily Telegraph*, 16 July 2005, http://www.telegraph.co.uk/news/main.jhtml?xml=/news/2005/07/16/ncleric316.xml.

119 'West is to blame for bombers, say mullahs', *Daily Telegraph*, 15 July 2005, http://www.telegraph.co.uk/news/main.jhtml?xml=/news/2005/07/15/ncleric315.xml.

Chapter 6

Recruitment into Terrorist Networks and Cells

The security services have built a picture of terrorist activity in the UK that consists of tight cells or networks, often overlapping, that are operating within broader networks of politically radicalised individuals. Once an individual has been politically radicalised and has made a decision that he wants to become involved in terrorist activity, he faces the obstacle of actually joining a terrorist network or cell, which is not an easy task. Established terrorist networks and cells are careful about who they recruit; they ideally want individuals who are committed, skilled and discreet. Anthony Garcia, for instance, was initially considered to be a security risk by *mujahideen* in Pakistan because he was too tall, pale skinned and loud, and it seems to have been a personal decision by Omar Khyam to recruit him into the Ammonium Nitrate cell.[1] Opportunity is therefore a significant enabling or constraining factor on individuals seeking to engage in terrorism. An individual can be radicalised and ready to engage in terrorist violence, but it is not until they are actually recruited into a cell that they become an operational terrorist. Therefore, the length of time it takes some individuals to be recruited into terrorist cells may vary.

SELECTION AND RECRUITMENT

The problem for would-be terrorists is that they need to make contact with a recruiter who needs to be confident that they are worthy of recruitment. Terrorist recruiters move within radicalised networks and recruit selected individuals into terrorist cells. The cells in the dataset seem to have been recruited directly by their *emirs*. Barot individually recruited the members of the Gas Limos cell from a variety of personal social contacts. He first met Bhatti at Friday prayers at Brunel University; he met Feroze at a meeting about Kashmir in Blackburn, and Shaffi while working in Wembley. He also seems to have built trust by ingratiating himself with the families of both Bhatti and Feroze. Abu Hamza put together the Yemen 8 cell, while Omar Khyam recruited the members of the Ammonium Nitrate cell from the Crawley, Luton and East London wings of *al Muhajiroun*.

In many cases, bonds within the cells were strengthened by personal connections which pre-dated the creation of the cell. The Yemen 8 cell comprised three groups of friends: Kamel and Ghalain were very close friends; Shazad Nabi and Iyad Hussein were cousins, and it was their former schoolfriend, Malik Nasser Harhara, who was instrumental in persuading them to go to Yemen;[2] while Shahid Butt and Samad Ahmed were close friends from Birmingham. The Airline cell were also closely connected through friendship: Abdulla Ahmed Ali had known most of the other members of the cell at school or college. And the bonds of friendship and activism between the whole cell were strengthened by their work for a charity called the Islamic Medical Association, based in East London.[3] Several of the 21/7 cell had also been friends before their radicalisation, as had Mohammed Siddique Khan and Tanweer of the 7/7 cell.

The actions of family, friends and acquaintances may also have served as an inspiration for some of the dataset. Reference has already been made in Chapter 1 to Zaccarias Moussaoui's potential influence on Richard Reid. In addition, Anthony Garcia's older brother Lamine was his role model, and Anthony became involved in Islamism at the same time as Lamine did, from 1998.[4] Asif Hanif was a former schoolfriend of Zeeshan Siddique, a would-be *jihadi*, who was arrested in Pakistan in 2005. Omar Khyam was a friend of Yasir Khan, another Crawley man who was killed in Afghanistan in 2001;[5] and Suragah al Andalusi, who was killed during the US bombing of Tora Bora in Afghanistan in 2001, was a role model to Mohammed Siddique Khan.[6]

This illustrates how recruitment into terrorist activity in the UK is largely a 'bottom-up' process. There might be some direct recruitment activity by established *jihadi* and terrorist groups based overseas, but it seems the process in the UK is comprised largely of radicalised individuals and self-forming cells seeking to join the global *jihad*. In some cases, the cells are recruited and led by experienced terrorists such as Barot, who was networked with *al Qaeda* figures in Pakistan, but, in the majority of cases, the cells were recruited and led by novice terrorists who had little or no experience and only limited training, such as Mohammed Siddique Khan and Muktar Said Ibrahim. The contrast between the success of the 7 July bombings and the failure of the 21 July attacks highlights the hit and miss nature of these novice cells. The fact that most of the cells in the dataset were novices may account for their high failure rate.

GROOMING FOR JOINING TERRORIST CELLS

There appear to be two distinct but interconnected indoctrination and grooming processes at work among the dataset. At one level, they are indoctrinated with an extremist Islamist ideology, which justifies the use of violence for politico-religious objectives, but simple adherence to the ideology does not mean that an individual will necessarily prove willing to commit an act of violence. At another level, therefore, it seems clear that individuals need additional grooming or indoctrination in order to make the step change to being prepared to commit an act of violence. This will be explained in Chapters 8 and 9.

This ideological grooming is an incremental process. The role of personal mentors coupled with bonding with a group of fellow extremists appears to have been critical in the radicalisation of many members of the dataset. After initial contact, recruiters 'groom' their recruits through subsequent contacts, often privately in small groups until the individuals in the group begin feeding off each other's radicalisation.[7] The mentors doing the grooming vary from authority figures to other rank and file militants, and in Chapter 5 we have already identified the role of high-profile mentors such as Abu Hamza. In contrast, Salahuddin Amin was groomed by a young *jihadi* named Aftab, who some reports claim was his brother, who was later killed in Afghanistan. When Amin collected money for the *jihadis* overseas, he handed over the donations to Aftab, and in return Aftab provided Amin with *jihadi* videos and cassettes. Through Aftab's example and the content of those videos, it appears Amin was influenced to undergo military training and then to fight in Kashmir or Afghanistan.[8] In the case of the Gas Limos cell, it was Barot who, as *emir* of the cell, seems to have been the mentor who persuaded several members of the cell to engage in violence.

Salahuddin Amin's experience highlights the key role that *jihadi* and terrorist propaganda plays in this process. As we discussed in Chapter 5, the principal medium by which this propaganda is now disseminated is the internet, which has spawned a cottage industry of Islamist propagandists in the UK: Some download this propaganda on to DVDs and then disseminate it through community networks, with others involved in creating and uploading the material.

There have been a number of prosecutions in which internet propaganda material has featured prominently. In 2007, Younis Tsouli, Waseem Mughal and Tariq Al-Daour admitted inciting terrorist attacks against non-Muslims on websites and in emails. They ran a series of Islamist extremist websites and produced videos in support of violent *jihad*. For a time, Tsouli was the world's most wanted cyber-*jihadi*, operating under the online name *Irhabi* 007, which translates as terrorist 007. From 2004, he began posting extremist propaganda on websites, which brought him to the attention of *al Qaeda* in Iraq who were making videos but struggling to get them to a wider audience because of the size of the files and the difficulty of finding websites that could host them. Tsouli solved this problem for them, and the material was soon being disseminated across the internet and also in a format suitable for mobile phones. Tsouli also claimed that he had been asked by *al Qaeda* to translate the organisation's official e-book, *Thurwat al Sanam* (Tip of the Camel's Hump), into English. In 2004, *al Qaeda*'s media arm in Iraq, *al Sahab*, acknowledged its gratitude to *Irhabi* 007 for his role in helping it disseminate videos of insurgent attacks.[9]

The significance of the internet lies in the fact that it enables terrorist cells and networks to distribute their propaganda as and when they wish and in a completely unadulterated fashion, whereas, in the mainstream media, news editors determine how militant and terrorist messages are reported. Another advantage of the internet is that it cannot be controlled. No sooner is one website removed than another appears to take its place. Since 9/11, there has been an alarming proliferation of English-language websites aimed at targeting young Muslims in the West who do not speak Arabic or Urdu. One Islamist website uploaded a video in English entitled 'Advice to Muslims in Britain', in which an *al Qaeda* affiliate praises the 7 July attacks and calls on British Muslims to carry out more suicide attacks.[10]

There is no evidence that any British citizens have been radicalised solely through exposure to propaganda that they found on the internet, but there is evidence that militant networks and cells make extensive use of material that they find online. A number of the dataset possessed militant videos or DVDs that had been downloaded from the internet. A downloaded message from Osama bin Laden was discovered by police at Omar Sharif's home. The message, dated February 2003, declared that 'targeting the Americans and the Jews by killing them in any corner of the earth is the greatest of obligations and the most excellent of ways to gain nearness to Allah'.[11]

The extent to which some cells used the internet is staggering. Police investigating the Gas Limos cell seized 274 computers along with 2,000 computer disks, CDs and DVDs, and police investigating the Airline cell seized 400 computers along with 8,000 disks, CDs and DVDs. And the contents of the computers, hard drives and other media seized during the arrest of Tsouli, Mughal and al-Dour amounted to three terabytes of data, the equivalent of almost a third of the entire content of the US Library of Congress.[12]

The seizure of so many CDs and DVDs indicates that it may be the interface between the internet and alternative media which is the significant factor in spreading militant and terrorist propaganda to maximum effect. The easy availability of DVD rewriters means that militant videos can be downloaded from the internet and burned on to DVD for further distribution through personal contacts and networks. The internet might offer a mechanism for reaching a mass audience, but videotapes and DVDs are much more important in the indoctrination process because they enable small groups to view propaganda material in privacy, thus enabling recruiters and ideologues to exert face-to-face influence on individuals and exploit the small-group dynamics described in Chapter 5.

The internet also offers a communication forum to enable disaffected individuals to communicate with militant recruiters who can deepen this radicalisation even further. There is no evidence that activity in chat rooms contributed towards the radicalisation of any of the individuals in this study, but there is evidence that it does happen. It is believed that Atif Siddique, a student from Scotland who was convicted of collecting and distributing terrorist propaganda and setting up websites showing how to use weapons and make explosives in 2007, was radicalised over the internet by a man from the North of England.[13] However, virtually all of the dataset were already linked into established Islamist networks, and their indoctrination apparently took place face to face.

After ideological indoctrination, mentors gradually move on to what they claim is the religious justification for violent *jihad* in the *Qur'an* and the *Hadith*, and, if suicide attacks are the intention, the importance of martyrdom in demonstrating commitment to Islam and the rewards in Paradise for martyrs. The former *al Muhajiroun* recruiter Hassan Butt revealed that 'we were very well versed in the *Qur'an*, in the verses of the *Qur'an*, in the sayings of the Prophet that show that how it was permissible for people to go around killing innocent men, women and children'.[14]

The Official Narrative of the 7 July bombings suggests that, after mentors have indoctrinated their recruits with what they claim is a religious justification for violent *jihad* in the *Qur'an* and the *Hadith*, they will directly invite an individual to engage in terrorism. There is no evidence of overt compulsion in this final step; rather, they rely on the development of individual commitment and group bonding and solidarity.[15] However, the narrative underestimates both the role and value of training, and the incremental nature of many terrorists' involvement in terrorist violence.

SOCIALISATION INTO TERRORIST ACTIVITY

Gradual involvement in non-violent activities in support of terrorist violence is one way of incrementally socialising an individual into terrorist violence. This was true of many Provisional IRA recruits in Northern Ireland. Initially, new recruits would be involved in non-violent activity only, but would gradually be involved more and more around the periphery of violent activity before being directly involved in an act of violence. The same was also true for many members of the dataset, who are known to have been involved in non-violent terrorist activity, such as fundraising, couriering cash and equipment overseas, proselytising the Islamist ideology and providing logistic support, before being recruited into cells planning acts of violence.

The most common non-violent terrorist activity is fundraising, including through criminal activities, which is also a way of drawing them into illegal activity, testing their commitment to the cause and cementing their place in the network or cell. During one of several meetings between Omar Khyam and Mohammed Siddique Khan, Khyam told Khan that all of the members of his network were involved in scams to raise money, and he advised Khan to do the same.[16] Khan and Tanweer both followed Khyam's advice and became involved in fraud.[17] Individuals with links to *al Qaeda* or other *jihadi* groups are alleged to have raised hundreds of thousands of pounds by defrauding the social security benefits system, money from which has been traced to bank accounts that have funded Islamist fighters in conflicts including Afghanistan and Kashmir. In 2001, the police confirmed that a fraud ring had been operating undetected for more than five years through bank accounts set up by members of Supporters of *Sha'ria*. Many cases that were previously seen as run-of-the-mill benefit fraud are now believed to be much more significant. Anti-terrorist squad officers also examined the accounts of a government scheme to provide funding for adult education following suspicions that militants were exploiting it. The Department for Education suspended its Individual Learning Accounts programme following complaints that bogus 'providers' offering tertiary schooling had received large amounts of money illegally and were diverting it to *jihadi* and terrorist groups. In the early 1990s, Shahid Butt was accused of siphoning money to accounts linked with terrorist groups.[18] An accomplice stole National Insurance numbers belonging to immigrants and people who had died, and Butt then made claims for benefits under their names. Some of this stolen cash went to Supporters of *Sha'ria*. In June 1995, Butt was sentenced to 18 months in prison after pleading guilty to dishonestly obtaining property by deception.[19]

The other main mechanism for fundraising for terrorist and *jihadi* groups is through charity collections. There are numerous legitimate Muslim charities operating in Britain which help Muslim communities overseas, but there are other collections which raise funds to support fighters in overseas conflicts, much as collections for 'the cause' used to be made in Irish communities in the UK during the conflict in Northern Ireland. Khyam, for instance, worked to raise money and encourage support for the cause of the *jihadis* in Kashmir after returning to the UK from his first trip to Pakistan in 2000.[20]

Indeed, the provision of financial assistance is identified by militant groups and ideologues as one of the ways that an individual can engage in *jihad*. There is evidence of some Imams in Britain channelling money to *jihadi* groups in Kashmir, claiming that it is their duty to support their 'fighting brothers'. The Indian government claims that *Lashkar-e-Taiba* and *Jaish-e-Mohammed* raise up to £5 million a year in this way.[21]

There are also allegations of terrorist groups, including *al Qaeda*, using established charities to raise funds. National regulators in many countries have long been concerned that non-governmental organisations offer a convenient conduit for funding terrorism. The UK has frozen the assets of a number of charities and individuals on the grounds that they are funding terrorist activity. One volunteer who worked for the Kashmir International Relief Fund, a charity in East London that sends aid to refugees, argued that they had a duty to help their 'brothers' fighting in other countries.[22] Nevertheless, the Charity Commission, the UK's overseer body, has only found a handful of cases of charities being misused, and even those found to be channelling funds for terror are usually unaware of it.[23]

Several members of the dataset began the incremental process of being drawn into terrorist activity through charity work and fundraising for Muslim causes. At his trial, Anthony Garcia recounted how his involvement initially started by fundraising for militants in Kashmir. After having collected tens of thousands of pounds, he felt that he wanted to get more directly involved and sought to attend a military training camp in Pakistan. His defence at his trial was that he had procured the ammonium nitrate to make bombs in Kashmir: 'At the time I thought it was really the same as fundraising because I thought it was going to help people in Kashmir – to be used as an explosive, as a bomb ... It would be basically to protect the villages under attack from the Indian soldiers.'[24]

Abdulla Ahmed Ali went through a similar process of becoming disillusioned with aid work. He was shocked by the appalling conditions of the Afghan refugee camps in Pakistan, where he witnessed many people dying. He came to believe that aid work could not solve the problems of the people that he was trying to help, and that, in order to really help them, he had to tackle what he believed was the root cause of their problems – Western foreign policy.[25]

Involvement in fundraising can also lead to further non-violent terrorist activities, such as acting as a courier between facilitators in the UK and *jihadis* overseas. Both Mohammed Siddique Khan and Khyam personally delivered funds that had been raised in the UK for *jihadi* groups to contacts in Pakistan,[26] while Barot was responsible for communications between senior *al Qaeda* figures hiding in Pakistan and Afghanistan and sleeper cells in Britain and the US.[27] Other members of the dataset acted as facilitators and suppliers of equipment. Parviz Khan initially ran a logistics network in Birmingham, sending equipment to *jihadis* in Pakistan. He was so valuable in this role that his handlers refused to sanction his involvement in violent activity. Yet Khan became increasingly dissatisfied with this role, and conceived the plot to kidnap and behead a British soldier as an independent operation. Khan typifies the individuals who are driven to commit violence by their own beliefs rather than because they were selected, groomed or ordered to do it. Some others were also involved in disseminating terrorist propaganda, including the 7/7 cell.

Others, such as Abu Mansha, however, do not appear to have gone through such an incremental process of non-violent terrorist-related activity. The nature of the process required to indoctrinate and groom a particular individual impacts on the length of time it takes. Incremental processes imply that lengthy periods of time might be required, but government reports have indicated that an individual's involvement in violent terrorist activity can happen very quickly, and that in general terms the time it takes is getting shorter. MI5 reported that the speed of radicalisation of some of the 7/7 cell was unexpected. According to the Director General of MI5, the 7 July attacks showed that extremists could be created at any time through a very quick process.[28] However, it is unclear precisely what this means, because it is evident that all of the dataset were being indoctrinated with an Islamist ideology over a lengthy period, of years in most cases. Instead, it is clear that, for many members of the dataset, it was their final decision to engage in terrorist violence that happened very quickly. This is borne out by the case of Omar Sheikh who seems to have made the decision to join *Harkat ul-Mujahideen* over the very short space of time that he spent with the Convoy of Mercy in Bosnia. The Ammonium Nitrate cell came together over a number of years, but they appear to have reached the decision to engage in terrorist violence in the UK after a short period of debate in Pakistan during 2003.[29] Similarly, there is evidence that Germaine Lindsay became radicalised on his conversion to Islam while he was still at school, but his widow claimed that he did not become involved in terrorism until he fell under the influence of individuals he met towards the end of 2004,[30] less than a year before the 7 July bombings.

TERRORIST FACILITATORS

Because terrorist recruitment in the UK is a 'bottom-up' process of radicalised individuals seeking to join the *jihad*, facilitators who can make the connections between would-be *jihadis* and established *jihadi* and terrorist groups play a key role. Reports indicate that, since the 1990s, there have been a number of terrorist facilitators operating in the UK, who are networked with a range of *jihadi* and terrorist networks overseas. These individuals do not appear to comprise a connected and coherent recruitment operation, but rather act as individuals, each with their own contacts in the UK and overseas. Prior to 2001, *al Qaeda* operated a loose facilitating network in the UK, but there are also several others who are linked to other Islamist and *jihadi* groups overseas. The *al Qaeda* facilitators reported to Abu Zubeidah, a Palestinian who acted as the co-ordinator and gatekeeper for a number of the Afghan training camps. These facilitators included Abu Hamza and Abu Doha who both operated out of Finsbury Park mosque in the late 1990s.

Abu Hamza was the most high profile of these recruiters and facilitators. During his trial, the prosecution alleged that he was a recruiting sergeant for global terrorism, although he was not convicted of recruiting for terrorism. He claimed to have links with the Armed Islamic Group in Algeria and Egyptian Islamist groups, as well as groups in Bosnia,[31] and he also acted as a press officer for a number of terrorist groups, including the Islamic Army of Aden in Yemen.[32] In the late 1990s, the Islamic Army of Aden, which was led by Sheikh Abul Hassan Mehdar, was fighting to make Yemen an Islamic state. Hamza had personal links with Mehdar dating back to the war against the Soviet Union in Afghanistan, when they both fought with the Afghan *mujahideen*. Hamza's direct involvement with the Islamic Army of Aden was illustrated when the group seized a number of foreign hostages after the Yemen 8 cell had been arrested. During the ensuing stand-off between the kidnappers and the Yemeni security forces, Hamza and Mehdar had a number of satellite phone conversations in which Hamza reportedly told Mehdar not to harm the hostages.[33] There is no evidence that Hamza actually recruited the Yemen 8 cell into terrorism, but he does seem to have acted as a facilitator, linking the cell with the Islamic Army of Aden. The cell were actually recruited by a representative of the Islamic Army of Aden in the London offices of Supporters of *Sha'ria*. According to Ghalain, they were introduced to a man called Amin from Yemen, who showed them pictures of Mehdar, and then explained that the group had a camp in Abyan with about 400 members. Amin then showed them a printed announcement which sought recruits for the Islamic Army of Aden, after which Hamza asked them to go to Yemen.[34]

According to the FBI, however, Abu Hamza also had a direct personal link with Zubeidah. He had the power to refer recruits to Zubeidah for leadership training in the Afghan training camps. Ahmed Ressam, a member of a terrorist cell which planned to bomb Los Angeles airport on Millennium eve, recalled that, while he was training at Khalden camp in 1998, two new Algerian recruits arrived who had been selected for leadership training based on the recommendation of Hamza and another person. Ressam noted that recommendations from someone who is known and trusted were required for access to the training camps and for specialised training such as leadership training; one such person was Zubeidah. This is supported by evidence gathered by FBI agents working in Afghanistan who found dossiers at training camps in which Hamza was named as the referee for recruits.[35]

Hamza was also linked to the Training cell, which operated for 12 years before the members were arrested in 2006. The cell were led by Mohammed Hamid and Atilla Ahmet, who was Hamza's right-hand man before his arrest and conviction. They primarily recruited individuals off the street and indoctrinated them with an Islamist ideology in study meetings at Hamid's home and a bookshop that he owned. They also provided fitness and selection training in outdoor camps in the UK, before facilitating the travel of their best recruits to overseas training camps. In one conversation revealed during the trial, Hamid bragged to his latest batch of recruits of being well connected with *mujahideen* groups in Afghanistan, and that he had sent three men from Britain to fight, some of whom had become *shaheed*.[36] He was also recorded telling his recruits that 'as they wage war in our lands, you know it's *halal* [permissible] for you to do it here. You cannot say "yeah but brother, I didn't come from that land" … That's your family that's being put to the sword, that's your family's honour that's being put to the sword. That's Allah's honour being disgraced.'[37] Like Hamza, the cell were primarily focused on preparing recruits for fighting *jihad* overseas rather than terrorism in the UK. Nevertheless, they counted the 21/7 cell among their alumni, which again illustrates how indoctrination and facilitating contacts for overseas *jihad* can lead to terrorism in the UK.

Abu Doha was an experienced Algerian terrorist who operated as an *al Qaeda* recruiter and facilitator in the late 1990s. He was a senior figure in the Salafist Group for Call and Combat (GSPC), who built an extensive organisation among expatriate Algerians in the UK and overseas. Doha arranged for chosen recruits to attend training camps in Afghanistan and also personally supervised training there. He established a training camp exclusively for Algerian trainees and, in December 1998, met bin Laden in Kandahar to discuss co-operation between the GSPC and *al Qaeda*. Doha's mobile telephone number has been found in the notebooks and on computer disks seized from numerous *al Qaeda* suspects. Doha was accused of directing terrorist operations from London but not of targeting the city itself,[38] and was subsequently detained without trial under the Terrorism Act in 2001.

Evidence from the trial of the Ammonium Nitrate cell illustrates the critical role that lesser-known UK- and Pakistan-based facilitators play in recruiting groups and facilitating contacts and training. The key facilitator at the UK end was identified in the media as a Luton man, codenamed 'Q' by the police, who allegedly reported to al Qaeda figures in Pakistan, including Abd al Hadi al Iraqi, who was subsequently detained in Guantanamo Bay.[39] During the trial, it was alleged that, as Luton emerged as a powerbase for *jihadi* activism in the wake of 9/11, 'Q' became a significant rallying figure for a growing band of extremists. He is alleged to have linked the cell with military trainers in Pakistani and Afghan *mujahideen* groups, and to have organised fundraising for the Taliban and other *jihadi* groups. After the invasion of Iraq in 2003, 'Q' arranged for Khyam to return to Pakistan and meet Hadi, which is when Khyam offered his services as more than just a courier.[40] It was also alleged that 'Q' sent Mohammed Siddique Khan to deliver funds to Pakistan in July 2003, and it was on this trip that Khan first met Khyam, who arranged his first stint of terrorist training.[41] Despite these allegations, 'Q' has never been charged with a terrorist offence in the UK.

'Q' is also alleged to have had strong ties with Salahuddin Amin, who he initially met in Luton, but was living in Pakistan at the time of his arrest. Amin acted as a reciprocal facilitator in Pakistan, receiving money, equipment and men who he then sent on to *mujahideen* groups, *al Qaeda* or the Taliban.[42] He also had the necessary contacts to get advice on the technical aspects of constructing explosive devices.[43] Waheed Mahmood also played a role in arranging military training and helping British *jihadis* to enter Afghanistan.[44] Khyam, Amin and Mahmood were also reported to have developed links to a number of senior *mujahideen* figures in Pakistan, one of whom was a former Luton man known as Abu Munthir.[45]

A Syrian, who has been given British citizenship, is said by security sources to have arranged for Muktar Said Ibrahim to travel to Pakistan for terrorist training.[46] The US Treasury claims that the Syrian arranged for individuals to travel to Pakistan to meet senior *al Qaeda* individuals and undertake *jihadi* training, several of whom returned to the UK to engage in covert activity on behalf of *al Qaeda*. It also alleges that the Syrian facilitated the travel of UK-based individuals to fight in Iraq, and that he was involved in the radicalisation of individuals in the UK through the distribution of extremist media. In response, the Syrian has denied any involvement or even that his views were extreme, and he has not been prosecuted for involvement in terrorist activity.[47]

Some overseas *jihadi* or *mujahideen* groups also have established strong contacts in British Muslim communities. This is particularly true of militant groups fighting in Kashmir which have contacts in Pakistani communities, and Somali groups which are networked into the Somali community. In these instances, some respected community figures can act as facilitators. The Pakistani militant groups *Jaish-e-Mohammed* and *Lashkar-e-Taiba* have been exploiting contacts and networks in the expatriate community to actively recruit Britons since the early 1990s.[48] One Manchester-based cleric recruited members from his mosque for *Lashkar-e-Taiba* before it was banned in Britain.[49] In Oldham, Shafiq Ur Rehman, an Imam at the City's Ross Street mosque, was accused of recruiting and fundraising for the *Markaz-ud-Dawa-wal-Irshad* (MDI), a Fundamentalist organisation, of which *Lashkar-e-Taiba* is the military wing, although he claimed that he only raised money for MDI welfare schemes.[50]

Some *jihadi* groups have also used the internet as a virtual facilitator. Younis Tsouli, who was the first person in Britain to be convicted of incitement to commit an act of terrorism through the internet, was the administrator of *al Ansar*, a password-protected web forum where extremists communicated with each other. The forum's 4,500 users networked and shared practical information; some of the links were to instructions on making explosives. Among the discussions were details of how to get to Iraq to be a suicide bomber. Tsouli's message boards facilitated contacts that might otherwise not have happened.[51] However, there is no evidence that the members of the dataset relied solely on the internet to facilitate their introduction into terrorism.

A small number of the dataset first came into contact with facilitators and recruiters while they were overseas. Dhiren Barot had been politically radicalised in the UK by *Hizb ut-Tahrir* before his parents took him to India in an effort to remove him from the group's influence, but, after arriving in India, Barot sought out other Islamists and they facilitated his joining a *jihadi* group fighting in Kashmir.[52] How he became connected with *al Qaeda* remains unknown, but it was probably facilitated by a member of the group he fought with in Kashmir. In contrast, Abdulla Ahmed Ali travelled to Pakistan in the aftermath of 9/11 to work for the Islamic Medical Association in Afghan refugee camps, during which time he came into contact with *al Qaeda* recruiters, allegedly including Briton Rashid Rauf, who also helped train Muktar Said Ibrahim.[53] However, it is not known whether this contact had been arranged by facilitators prior to Ali leaving the UK.

These facilitators operate at the end of the radicalisation process, putting would-be terrorists in touch with those who can train them and form them into cells, or link them to *jihadi* groups. Some of them, such as Abu Hamza and the Training cell, were also engaged in the earlier phases of radicalising young men, but many of them were simply facilitators for young men who were already radicalised and committed to engaging in violent *jihad* or terrorism. What remains unknown is the extent to which these facilitators are linking British *jihadis* with *al Qaeda*. Reid, Badat and Barot are known to have been linked to *al Qaeda* before 9/11. However, since 9/11, the situation has become much less clear, although the British intelligence services believe that the 7/7, 21/7 and Airline cells were all linked to *al Qaeda*. In 2005, the leaders of all three cells are thought to have attended a gathering in Pakistan at which *al Qaeda* leaders brought together a group of young British *jihadis*. It is believed that they were then directed by Abd al Hadi al Iraqi, who is reported to have been *al Qaeda*'s number three, to attack the UK. The fact that the three plots share common features, such as the use of hydrogen peroxide bombs, also suggests that the cells were trained and directed by the same individual or group.[54]

INDEPENDENT OPERATORS

For radicalised individuals who are not recruited into terrorist cells or networks through the processes described above, there is the option of becoming lone operators. The threat from lone operators first assumed prominence in the US during the 1990s, following the 30-year bombing campaign by the 'Unabomber', Ted Kaczynski. Using Kaczynski as an inspiration, Christian far-right extremist groups developed the concept of 'leaderless resistance', by which individuals or cells would undertake terrorist action autonomously without reference to a command hierarchy. But, despite this concern, the threat from lone terrorists never materialised in the US. Since the war in Afghanistan in 2001, this perceived threat has assumed heightened prominence again, as *al Qaeda* sought to encourage independent terrorist action by locally based militant cells across the world, and the concept was rebranded as 'leaderless *jihad*'.[55]

After *al Qaeda* lost its Afghan bases and many of its senior leadership figures, it became more of a brand than a functioning organisation commanding and controlling terrorist operations worldwide. Its primary significance is as an idea, which inspires independent individuals and cells to action. With that end in mind, much of its activity moved to cyberspace where individuals with uncertain links to *al Qaeda* have tried to stimulate independent action from individuals and cells with no formal links. Messages purportedly from *al Qaeda* have been posted on a number of websites inciting violence, listing targets and encouraging independent cells to act on their own initiative. The internet is also a potentially useful tool in offering ideological encouragement as well as establishing a space where communities of like-minded individuals can meet and discuss the global *jihad*. As a result, the potential lone operator is never truly alone. Everything is therefore in place for lone operators to perpetrate acts of terrorist violence in Britain. These are individuals who share *al Qaeda*'s ideology but do not have direct contact with it.

However, it has also been alleged that the internet has given rise to a new phenomenon of 'self-radicalising kids' who are not members of established groups but are inspired by images and other propaganda on the internet to carry out their own attacks. These are young people driven by 'emotional rather than ideological' inspiration. They talk among themselves and some of them may start plotting; they are typically young people who spend their time on the internet and decide among themselves to plot an attack. They do not understand Islam; they are just emotionally inspired to do something. They are not particularly sophisticated, they do not form proper cell structures, and they do not have clear roles, such as one being designated as a bomber, or another as a fundraiser. They also lack professional skills; therefore, any attacks they might plan are most likely to be small scale, requiring few technical skills. However, as soon as they come into contact with experienced terrorists, they become more capable and more ideologically committed.[56]

A number of such lone operators have been convicted of non-violent offences under the Terrorism Act (2000), but the only members of the dataset who might potentially fit this model are Abu Mansha and Moinul Abedin. Mansha was being groomed by other individuals for a lone attack to murder a British soldier, but he was not part of an organised cell. Nor is there any evidence of Moinul

Abedin being linked into wider terrorist networks. However, there is evidence of all of the other cells and individuals being linked into wider networks of extremists.

Instead, radicalised individuals who are not recruited into terrorist cells might engage in unstructured violence which falls below the terrorism radar. As mentioned in previous chapters, this could also be manifest in forms of gang violence directed at non-Muslim targets. In particular, the number of violent anti-Semitic attacks in the UK has risen significantly in the 21st century, some of which have been blamed on Muslims.[57]

CONCLUSION

This analysis highlights the critical role of facilitators in linking would-be terrorists into established terrorist networks and cells. It also highlights how terrorist activity largely appears to be a 'bottom-up' process with radicalised individuals forming their own cells, and seeking out facilitators to acquire the necessary training and perhaps the resources to undertake terrorist attacks in the UK. For some members of the dataset, there was a gradual and incremental process of being drawn into terrorist activity, before making a sudden decision to perpetrate a terrorist attack in the UK. For others, however, the whole process of radicalisation and deciding to engage in terrorist violence appears to be very short.

Notes and references

[1] 'Profile: Anthony Garcia', BBC NewsOnline, 30 April 2007, http://news.bbc.co.uk/1/hi/uk/6149798.stm.

[2] '"Confession" statements attributed to the defendants', 14 June 2002, http://www.al-bab.com/yemen/hamza/statemts.htm.

[3] 'Air accused "planned bomb stunt"', BBC NewsOnline, 2 June 2008, http://news.bbc.co.uk/1/hi/uk/7431483.stm; '"Astonishment" at terror verdicts', BBC NewsOnline, 9 September 2008, http://news.bbc.co.uk/1/hi/uk/7605583.stm.

MARTYRDOM

[4] 'Profile: Anthony Garcia', BBC NewsOnline, 30 April 2007, http://news.bbc.co.uk/1/hi/uk/6149798.stm.

[5] 'Path to extremism: How it started', BBC NewsOnline, 3 May 2007, http://news.bbc.co.uk/1/hi/uk/6619147.stm.

[6] Report of the Official Account of the Bombings in London on 7 July 2005, HC1087 (London: The Stationery Office), 11 May 2006.

[7] Report of the Official Account of the Bombings in London on 7 July 2005, HC1087 (London: The Stationery Office), 11 May 2006.

[8] Prepared text of Tuesday's portion of the Crown's opening statement in the trial of seven men alleged to have plotted to bomb London. The rest of the statement was to be delivered on Wednesday: Regina v Omar Khyam, Anthony Garcia, Nabeel Hussain, Jawad Akbar, Waheed Mahmood, Shujah-ud-din Mahmood, Salahuddin Amin, 21 March 2006, *Ottawa Citizen*, http://www.canada.com/ottawacitizen/news/story.html?id=408dc2ed-d950-4ee5-a4b7-392eb5faaf34&k=75162; 'Town at the end of the terrorist trails', *Daily Telegraph*, 2 May 2007, http://www.telegraph.co.uk/news/main.jhtml?xml=/news/2007/05/02/nterror30 2.xml.

[9] 'Internet spreads terror in Britain', *Daily Telegraph*, 7 November 2007.

[10] 'Internet spreads terror in Britain', *Daily Telegraph*, 7 November 2007.

[11] 'Omar's message from bin Laden', *Derby Telegraph*, 10 October 2005, http://www.thisisderbyshire.co.uk/displayNode.jsp?nodeId=124615&command= displayContent&sourceNode-124519&contentPK=13288727&moduleName= InternalSearch&forname=sidebarsearch.

[12] 'Gordon Brown plans to double 28-day detention limit for suspected terrorists', *The Times*, 26 October 2007, http://www.timesonline.co.uk/tol/news/politics/article2741689.ece.

[13] 'Student "was part of Canadian terror plot"', *The Times*, 18 September 2007, http://www.timesonline.co.uk/tol/news/uk/crime/article2477567.ece.

[14] CBS News, 25 March 2007, http://www.cbsnews.com/stories/2007/03/23/60minutes/main2602308_page3.shtml.

[15] Report of the Official Account of the Bombings in London on 7 July 2005, HC1087 (London: The Stationery Office), 11 May 2006.

[16] 'Revealed: Bomber transcript', BBC NewsOnline, 1 May 2007, http://news.bbc.co.uk/1/hi/uk/6611803.stm.

17 'MI5 knew of bombers' plan for Holy War', *Sunday Times*, 22 January 2006.

18 'Benefit fraud ring funds Islamic terrorists', *Daily Telegraph*, 17 November 2001,
http://www.telegraph.co.uk/news/main.jhtml?xml=/news/2001/11/18/nbenef18.xml.

19 'Benefit fraud ring funds Islamic terrorists', *Daily Telegraph*, 17 November 2001,
http://www.telegraph.co.uk/news/main.jhtml?xml=/news/2001/11/18/nbenef18.xml.

20 'Profile: Omar Khyam', BBC NewsOnline, 30 April 2007,
http://news.bbc.co.uk/1/hi/uk/6149794.stm.

21 'Britons send £5m to Kashmir terrorists', *Daily Telegraph*, 9 June 2002.

22 'Britons send £5m to Kashmir terrorists', *Daily Telegraph*, 9 June 2002.

23 'Charities in terror fund spotlight', BBC NewsOnline, 15 October 2003,
http://news.bbc.co.uk/1/hi/business/3186840.stm.

24 'Terror suspect says he did buy fertiliser', *The Times*, 26 September 2006,
http://www.timesonline.co.uk/article/0,,2-2374710.html.

25 '"Astonishment" at terror verdicts', BBC NewsOnline, 9 September 2008,
http://news.bbc.co.uk/1/hi/uk/7605583.stm.

26 'MI5 followed UK suicide bomber', BBC NewsOnline, 30 April 2007,
http://news.bbc.co.uk/1/hi/uk/6417353.stm.

27 'The web of terror in London', *Evening Standard*, 6 August 2004.

28 'The web of terror in London', *Evening Standard*, 6 August 2004.

29 'Men convicted over UK bomb plot', BBC NewsOnline, 30 April 2007,
http://news.bbc.co.uk/1/hi/uk/6195914.stm.

30 'Nightmare', *Huddersfield Daily Examiner*, 6 July 2006,
http://ichuddersfield.icnetwork.co.uk/0100news/0100localnews/tm_method=full%26objectid=17340559%26siteid=50060-name_page.html.

31 'On Yemen's death row', *Guardian*, 17 January 1999,
http://www.guardian.co.uk/yemen/Story/0,2763,209259,00.html.

32 'Terrorists or tourists', *Guardian*, 26 June 1999, http://www.al-bab.com/yemen/artic/gdn42.htm.

[33] 'On Yemen's death row', *Guardian*, 17 January 1999, http://www.guardian.co.uk/yemen/Story/0,2763,209259,00.

[34] '"Confession" statements attributed to the defendants', 14 June 2002, http://www.al-bab.com/yemen/hamza/statemts.htm.

[35] 'Militant cleric had links with al-Qa'eda chiefs, says FBI report', *Daily Telegraph*, 24 June 2003, http://www.telegraph.co.uk/news/uknews/1433959/Militant-cleric-had-links-with-al-Qa%27eda-chiefs%2C-says-FBI-report.html.

[36] 'UK "terrorism camps" revealed', BBC NewsOnline, 26 February 2008, http://news.bbc.co.uk/1/hi/uk/7190323.stm; 'The radicaliser and the bombers', BBC NewsOnline, 26 February 2008, http://news.bbc.co.uk/1/hi/uk/7231492.stm; 'Top extremist recruiter found guilty', 26 February 2008, http://news.bbc.co.uk/1/hi/uk/7193128.stm.

[37] 'Top extremist recruiter found guilty', 26 February 2008, http://news.bbc.co.uk/1/hi/uk/7193128.stm.

[38] '"Architect of terror" held in British jail cell', *Daily Telegraph*, 9 January 2003, http://www.telegraph.co.uk/news/uknews/1418311/%27Architect-of-terror%27-held-in-British-jail-cell.html.

[39] 'British terror cell plotted to kill thousands of shoppers in Bluewater with a devastating fertiliser bomb', *The Times*, May 1, 2007, http://www.timesonline.co.uk/tol/news/uk/crime/article1729043.ece.

[40] 'Questions over "plot mastermind"', BBC NewsOnline, 1 May 2007, http://news.bbc.co.uk/1/hi/uk/6248803.stm; 'Profile: Omar Khyam', BBC NewsOnline, 30 April 2007, http://news.bbc.co.uk/1/hi/uk/6149794.stm.

[41] 'Questions over "plot mastermind"', BBC NewsOnline, 1 May 2007, http://news.bbc.co.uk/1/hi/uk/6248803.stm.

[42] 'Questions over "plot mastermind"', BBC NewsOnline, 1 May 2007, http://news.bbc.co.uk/1/hi/uk/6248803.stm.

[43] 'Profile: Salahuddin Amin', BBC News Online, 30 April 2007, http://news.bbc.co.uk/1/hi/uk/6149790.stm.

[44] 'Al-Qaeda's target', *Ilford Recorder*, 30 March 2006, http://www.ilfordrecorder.co.uk/search/story.aspx?brand=GVSROnline&category=vgreenhithe&itemid=WeED30%20Mar%202006%2015:10:08:323&tBrand=GVSROnline&tCategory=search.

[45] 'Path to extremism: How it started', BBC NewsOnline, 3 May 2007, http://news.bbc.co.uk/1/hi/uk/6619147.stm.

[46] 'Fixer for 21/7 plot free in London', *The Times*, 15 July 2007, http://www.timesonline.co.uk/tol/news/uk/crime/article2076241.ece.

[47] 'Londoner named as Al-Qaeda "banker"', *Sunday Times*, January 2007, http://www.timesonline.co.uk/article/0,,2087-2535240,00.html.

[48] '"Holy warrior" casts light on dark links to Pakistan', *The Times*, 18 July 2005, http://www.timesonline.co.uk/tol/news/uk/article545253.ece.

[49] 'Britons send £5m to Kashmir terrorists', *Daily Telegraph*, 9 June 2002.

[50] 'Terror link mullah fights on', *Manchester Evening News*, 12 October 2001.

[51] 'Al-Qaeda's 007', *The Times*, 16 January 2008, http://women.timesonline.co.uk/tol/life_and_style/women/the_way_we_live/article3191517.ece.

[52] Husain E, *The Islamist* (London: Penguin, 2007), p 131.

[53] 'Airliner bomb trial: How MI5 uncovered the terror plot', *Daily Telegraph*, 9 September 2008, http://www.telegraph.co.uk/news/uknews/2709379/Airliner-bomb-trial-How-MI5-uncovered-the-terror-plot.html.

[54] The identify of Abdul Hadi al-Iraqi is uncertain. At least two *jihadis* are known to have used the name. One was arrested in Afghanistan in 2002, and another was reported to have been detained in Guantanamo Bay in 2007. 'Analysis: How the plan was put together', *The Times*, September 9, 2008, http://www.timesonline.co.uk/tol/news/uk/crime/article4708700.ece?token=null&offset=12&page=2; 'Airline bomb trial: Five potential suicide bombers "still at large"', *Daily Telegraph*, 9 September 2008, http://www.telegraph.co.uk/news/uknews/2707241/Airline-bomb-trial-Five-potential-suicide-bombers-still-at-large.html.

[55] Sageman M, *Leaderless Jihad: Terror Networks in the Twenty-First Century* (Philadelphia: University of Pennsylvania Press, 2008).

[56] '"Terror kids" inspired by net are West's big threat', *The Times*, 7 November 2007, http://www.timesonline.co.uk/tol/news/uk/crime/article2821101.ece.

[57] 'Rising UK anti-semitism blamed on media', *Guardian*, 25 January 2005, http://www.guardian.co.uk/media/2005/jan/25/raceandreligion.television.

Chapter 7

Training

As with all terrorist groups, the Islamist cells and networks operating in the UK normally select their recruits very carefully, and one of the primary methods through which all terrorist groups do this is training. There are well-structured systems of training for would-be British *jihadis*, starting with basic selection training in the UK itself, followed by basic military training overseas for engaging in *jihad*, and for the few who agree to engage in terrorist activity in the UK there are camps which specialise in training terrorist skills, including bomb making. The amounts of training that the members of the dataset received varied. Richard Reid and Saajid Badat had access to the permanent *jihadi* camps in Afghanistan prior to 9/11 and appear to have received training in some of the specialist terrorist training camps that used to exist there. Since the loss of the Afghan camps, training is carried out in the new, smaller camps in the tribal areas of Pakistan which border Afghanistan, and recruits seem to attend for short periods of time, sometimes weeks, but sometimes only days. The majority of the dataset attended these newer, smaller camps.

INITIAL SELECTION

UK-based training focuses on physical training as a way of testing the commitment of new recruits. The limitations of training in Britain mean that firearms training and practising bomb making is difficult, so training focuses primarily on physically preparing would-be *jihadis* to test whether they are physically ready for the rigours of fighting in *jihad* overseas. Many individuals and cells in the dataset used gyms and joined martial arts clubs as part of the process of physically preparing themselves for *jihad* and terrorism.[1] These are everyday leisure pursuits for many young British men, so would-be recruits do not stand out in any way by pursuing these activities.

Beyond this personal physical preparation, however, there have also been many examples of structured group training at Islamist training camps around the UK. Evidence of the existence of *jihadi* training camps in Britain first began to emerge in the mid-1990s, and, in the late 1990s, one group from Birmingham was organising training weekends in Wales, where they were taught how to assemble an automatic weapon.[2]

Also in the late 1990s, Abu Hamza used to lead training weekends which taught participants martial arts, parachuting, paintballing, escape and evasion, fitness, security, surveillance, mountaineering, map-reading and scuba diving.[3] Some journalists dismissed these activities as little more than adventure holidays, but it is apparent that they were actually being used as selection weekends to identify candidates for proper military training abroad. One of the venues used by Hamza was the *Jameah Islameah* school in Sussex, and there were reports that five members of the Yemen 8 cell had used camping facilities at the school for training in survival techniques and martial arts prior to departing for the Yemen.[4] Security services informant Reda Hussaine stated, 'I watched young Muslims at Finsbury Park mosque in London in the late 1990s being prepared for journeys to military camps … money was raised for their air fares by selling books and films in stalls at the mosques. Those who were chosen to go were the most fanatical – and the most obedient.'[5]

Hamza himself was a graduate of the Afghan training camps and so was capable of leading this training and identifying the most suitable candidates to go abroad. Similarly, *al Muhajiroun* operated training camps at a gym and scout hut in a forestry centre just outside Crawley, as well as in Luton and the East End of London.[6] In 1999, it was reported that 2,000 Muslims a year were attending *al Muhajiroun* training camps in order to learn hand-to-hand combat and survival skills. At these camps, they were encouraged to seek real military training in countries such as Yemen and Afghanistan.[7]

In contrast, the Mullah Crew used to organise their own training to physically strengthen themselves and bond the group, often through outdoor activities such as paintballing, climbing and canoeing. The Official Narrative of the 7 July bombings stated that:

Camping, canoeing, white-water rafting, paintballing and other outward bound type activities are of particular interest because they appear common factors for the 7 July bombers and other cells disrupted previously and since. Khan and others from the youth centre and bookshop arranged many of these. Khan and Tanweer were known to have attended a camping trip in the UK with others in April 2003, and a white-water rafting trip just weeks before the bombings. Such trips are varied in location and informal: there is no particular centre or centres where they are based. There is no firm evidence about how such trips might have been used. But it is possible that some trips were used to identify candidates for indoctrination. It is worth noting that for some extremist activities – e.g. fighting overseas – physical fitness and resilience are essential. They may also be used to help with bonding between members of cells already established, or for more direct indoctrination or operational training and planning.[8]

The other main organisers of terrorist training in the UK were the Training cell led by Mohammed Hamid and Atilla Ahmet, who were convicted in 2008 of incitement to murder and receiving and organising terrorist training. The cell used to put raw recruits through intensive training and indoctrination, which included outward-bound-type activities, martial arts, paintballing and bonding exercises at locations across the UK.[9] The training was extreme and macho, and involved endurance in bad weather and group bonding.[10] These camps were a selection process to identify the most promising recruits who would be sent overseas for military training. Thousands of recruits are believed to have been through the cell's training camps, and Hamid boasted that a number of them had fought in *jihad* overseas. However, the only members of the dataset who are known to have attended them are the 21/7 cell.

It is not known how many of the dataset went through this type of selection training in Britain, but it is reasonable to assume that the majority of them did simply because it seems to be a standard activity for the radicalised networks of which they were part. However, very few of the dataset went straight from this basic training into terrorism, with the majority undergoing additional military and terrorist training overseas. This suggests that terror cells only recruit individuals who have received proper training, and that even cells which have formed at grass-roots level will seek training before actually trying to engage in terrorism. Even after receiving military training overseas, a number of cells continued to engage in these activities in order to maintain and strengthen the bonds between the members of the cell.

INTERNET TRAINING MATERIALS

UK-based training is facilitated to a certain extent by terrorist training manuals that *al Qaeda* and other Islamist terrorist groups have posted on the internet. Perhaps the best known of these manuals is *al Qaeda's Encyclopedia of Islamic Jihad*, while Abu Hamza possessed a copy of the *Encyclopaedia of Afghan Jihad*. These manuals have been widely disseminated among radicalised networks in the UK, and a number of people have been convicted of possessing them. Among the *jihadi* material which Younis Tsouli, Waseem Mughal and Tariq al-Daour disseminated over the internet were PowerPoint presentations such as 'The Illustrated Booby Trapping Course' and details of how to make car bombs and suicide vests.[11] The easy availability of this material enables cells which emerge at grass-roots level, but which lack the contacts with experienced terrorists, to acquire the necessary skills to engage in terrorism without needing to interface with wider networks of experienced terrorists or a command hierarchy. In other words, it has the potential to facilitate the growth of 'leaderless *jihad*'.

While many of the dataset possessed *jihadi* propaganda, very few of them were found to be in possession of these online training materials. Aadel Yahya of the 21/7 cell possessed a CD which contained chapters on explosives and chemicals including hydrogen peroxide, one of the key components of the bombs used by the 21/7 cell.[12] Qaisir Shaffi of the Gas Limos cell also possessed an extract from a terrorist handbook which included formulae for preparing explosives.[13] The only cell that possessed a significant amount of this material was the Ammonium Nitrate cell. Anthony Garcia possessed an extract from an *al Qaeda* manual entitled *Means of Communication and Transportation* and a document describing the use of landmines, missiles, grenades, machine guns, combat stress control and sniper weapons,[14] and Jawad Akbar had details of bomb-making formulae, which had been downloaded from the internet, on his laptop.[15]

The effectiveness of these virtual training manuals for teaching unskilled radicals the necessary skills to make them effective terrorist operators is debatable. The prosecutor of the Ammonium Nitrate cell claimed that it would take someone a matter of seconds to find the details of how to make an ammonium nitrate-based bomb on the internet, but he added the significant caveat – only if the person knew what they were doing.[16] This suggests that terrorists also need face-to-face training from skilled instructors in order to be able to use the information contained in these manuals to maximum effect. This is illustrated by the fact that it took a considerable amount of experimentation for scientists working at the Forensic Explosives Laboratory to create viable bombs equivalent to those that the Airline cell intended to use. However, face-to-face training in bomb making, which requires testing practice devices, can only really take place overseas for security reasons. The fact that the majority of the dataset went overseas for military training before attempting to perpetrate their attacks indicates that they were not prepared to rely on internet training materials alone.

OVERSEAS TRAINING CAMPS

A key milestone in the radicalisation of the majority of the dataset was their attendance at overseas training camps. The majority of the members of the dataset spent limited amounts of time in training camps and attended camps in Pakistan and Afghanistan, but some of them also attended camps in other, more low-profile countries. The Yemen 8 cell were trained by the Islamic Army of Aden in Yemen; Shahid Butt had previously received military training in Bosnia during the war there; and Ghalain and Kamel might also have received training in Albania in the summer of 1998.[17] This was the time of the war in Kosovo, and the Kosovo Liberation Army had training bases in northern Albania. Muktar Said Ibrahim attended a training camp in Sudan, and Dhiren Barot received training in the Philippines, where there are a number of terrorist and guerrilla groups operating among the Muslim population. Khaled Sheikh Mohammed, one of *al Qaeda's* most senior figures, also ordered Barot to Kuala Lumpar in Malaysia to learn about *jihad* from Hambali, who at that time was a major figure in Islamist terrorism in Southeast Asia.[18] Barot was even reported to be the author of a terrorist training manual describing the use of remote-controlled explosives, grenades and automatic weapons, and was an instructor at *mujahideen* training camps in Afghanistan before returning to Britain.[19]

Prior to 9/11, there was an extensive network of training camps in Afghanistan, run by a wide range of different *jihadi* and terrorist groups, including *al Qaeda*. The first member of the dataset to head overseas for military training was Omar Sheikh, who attended a *Harkat ul-Mujahideen* camp in Afghanistan in 1993, where he was trained in weapons, hand-to-hand combat, surveillance methods, the art of disguise and how to plan an attack.[20] The main training camp for foreign fighters in Afghanistan was Khalden, operated by Abd al

Rab al Rasul Sayyaf, an Afghan warlord and Islamic scholar, but it was not an *al Qaeda* camp or a terrorist training camp. The camp was for recruits who could not speak fluent Arabic, so lectures were mainly conducted in English and Urdu. It is not known how many Britons passed through Khalden, but both Richard Reid and Saajid Badat are known to have been trained there. Equally, not all British *jihadis* would have attended Khalden, and the precise camp to which a recruit was sent was probably determined by the *jihadi* group to which his British-based facilitator was connected.

The curriculum at Khalden involved both military training and ideological indoctrination and was geared to preparing its recruits for *jihad*, not terrorism in the West. The camp itself consisted of a compound of four tents and four stone buildings. Recruits were provided with basic military training based on methods that American advisers and the Pakistani Inter-Services Intelligence had introduced to the Afghan *mujahideen* during the war against the Soviet Union in the 1980s. However, spiritual preparation took up as much, if not more, of the time.[21] Early each morning, the recruits were called to formation, then sent to pray. After a meal, they went through strength and endurance training. Veterans of the war against the Soviet Union taught self-defence and hand-to-hand combat, using knives, garrottes and other weapons. Trainees practised with small arms, assault rifles and grenade launchers, and were schooled in the use of explosives and landmines.[22] Bin Laden was a frequent visitor to the camp, where he would deliver long sermons about how these men were to be in the vanguard of his war against America and its allies.[23]

The Khalden curriculum of ideological instruction and basic military training did not particularly equip its graduates for terrorist operations in the West. For that, there were networks of other camps in Afghanistan which provided specialist terrorist training. *Al Qaeda* operated a number of such camps, of which one of the most infamous was Darunta, near Jalalabad. At Darunta, recruits received detailed and intensive instruction in bomb making, including how to make a wide range of explosives from scratch, including black powder, RDX, tetryl, TNT, dynamite, C2, C3, C4, Semtex, nitroglycerine and others, all of which the recruits learned how to construct from everyday products that could be purchased in shops. They were also taught terrorist fieldcraft, such as how to blow up trains, cars, buildings and aircraft.[24] Apart from Reid and Badat, it is not known how many other Britons might have been trained in these specialist *al Qaeda* terrorist training camps. It is believed that talent spotters at Martyrs House, the *al Qaeda* headquarters in Peshawar, would identify suitable candidates, who would then be taken over the border to the camps in Afghanistan. Others might have been recommended to *al Qaeda* by facilitators in the UK, or talent spotted by *al Qaeda* operatives who visited training camps run by other groups. The whole network of camps in Afghanistan was shut down following the war in 2001–02, which led to the growth of a network of smaller camps in Pakistan. Since 2001, most would-be British *jihadis* now appear to head to the tribal areas of Pakistan's North West Frontier Province for training.

Different individuals in the dataset therefore received different levels and types of training depending upon who their contacts were. It also indicates that *jihadis* who attended training overseas did not necessarily learn all of the skills that they required to become effective terrorist operators. The Yemen 8 cell, for instance, received only two weeks of basic military training that consisted of learning to fire various weapons, including machine guns and rocket-propelled grenades, and the use of explosives, before being sent on their mission.[25] This training gave them sufficient skills to perform their mission, but they could hardly be described as being highly trained or experienced terrorists.

In the new camps in the tribal areas of Pakistan, the training is much more truncated and focuses primarily on teaching basic military skills and basic bomb making. Unlike the former camps in Afghanistan, therefore, the role of such training camps in ideologically indoctrinating recruits is probably quite limited. In fact, the evidence suggests that it was precisely because they were politically radicalised that the members of the dataset chose, and were selected, to go abroad for training. This was confirmed by Hassan Butt in an interview for the American TV station CBS. Asked at what point he would say to a recruit that it was time to head to Pakistan for military training, he replied, 'Never. I would never say that, ever. It's not me forcing them. I mean, the network never, never pushes people in that way. We believe that if the person is convinced, has the conviction themself to come up to you and say they wanna go training, then they are the type of person who will most likely take that one step further and will be the reliable foot soldiers for you.'[26]

Similarly, Tanweer's relatives in Pakistan claim that he was already radicalised when he arrived in the country. Osama bin Laden 'was his hero, and everything he did was right', recalled his cousin, Asfaq Ahmed.[27] Nevertheless, it is possible to argue that their radicalisation was deepened through this training, and they became hardened through contact with serious players in the *jihadi* world.[28]

Details of the training that the dataset received in Pakistan are sketchy but fairly consistent. All of the Ammonium Nitrate cell attended training camps in Pakistan. Omar Khyam first received training in the mountains of Kashmir in 2000,[29] where he learned everything he needed for guerrilla warfare in Kashmir including training in the use of AK47s, light machine guns, pistols, rocket-propelled grenades, sniper rifles, climbing and crawling techniques and reconnaissance.[30] In the summer of 2003, Khyam took Garcia and Jawad Akbar to a training camp in Pakistan.[31] At his trial, Garcia tried to downplay the significance of this training, claiming that the camp was just a field where they were only allowed to fire guns on the last day for fear of disturbing local villagers.[32] Evidence at his trial, however, suggested that Garcia's experience was very different, and that, because he had previous training, he taught those with less experience how to dismantle and reassemble weapons.[33] Only Amin and Khyam appear to have received some limited training in bomb making, on a two-day training course in 2003.[34] This suggests that they were only trained to make the type of bomb that they would use for their mission, which is in marked contrast to the extensive and high quality of the training that the recruits at Darunta received. This limited training indicates that the members of the Ammonium Nitrate cell were taught the bare minimum required to carry out their mission, and their firearms training was of no use for the mission they planned in Britain. There is no evidence that they were trained in terrorist fieldcraft, which, coupled with their lack of experience, may have contributed to the failure of their mission.

The exact details of the training received by members of the 7/7 cell on various trips to Pakistan and possibly Afghanistan is unclear, but it seems likely that both Mohammed Siddique Khan and Tanweer attended several short training courses from the late 1990s onwards. It is also believed that Khan had visited Pakistan, and possibly Afghanistan, on a number of occasions since the late 1990s, but there is no confirmation and no details of all these trips. However, Khan received training in the use of assault rifles, light machine guns and rocket-propelled grenades, in a remote part of Pakistan close to the Afghan border during a two-week visit in July 2003, although it is unclear whether he met *al Qaeda* figures during that trip. When Khan and Tanweer visited Pakistan again between November 2004 and February 2005, it is possible that they went up to the border areas with Afghanistan or over the border for training, but there is no firm evidence of this, although some reports suggested that Khan attended a training camp run by *Harkat ul-Mujahideen* between November and December 2004, where he received lessons in handling weapons and explosives.[35] Again, it is unclear who they might have met in Pakistan, but it is assumed that they had some contact with *al Qaeda* figures.[36] Pakistan's Inter-Services Intelligence believes that Khan spent much of his time liaising with an *al Qaeda* operative, identified as Mohammed Yasin, alias Ustad ('the teacher') Osama, an explosives specialist with *Harkat-e-Jihad*. Yasin is believed to have prepared British Muslims to fight in Afghanistan and Bosnia, and it is suspected that he might have trained Khan to produce the sort of homemade bombs used in the London attacks.[37] While full details of the training they

226

received are unclear, it does seem that it would have included terrorist fieldcraft. The Official Narrative of the 7 July bombings reported that they planned their attack meticulously and maintained good security awareness, including careful use of mobile phones and the use of hire cars for a number of sensitive activities associated with the planning of the attacks.[38] Given that they were not experienced terrorists, this indicates that they received good training. The British intelligence services also believe that the same people trained Mohammed Siddique Khan, Muktar Said Ibrahim and Abdulla Ahmed Ali, the *emirs* of the 7/7, 21/7 and Airline cells, respectively. All three of them are known to have been in Pakistan in 2005, and are believed to have attended a meeting with senior *al Qaeda* figures.[39] The fact that all three plots used hydrogen peroxide bombs also indicates that they may have been trained by the same people.

While many members of the dataset attended various training camps in Pakistan, it is extremely difficult to ascertain who was actually running those camps. In some cases, it even seems as though some cells organised their own training. According to Junaid Babar, the main prosecution witness at the trial of the Ammonium Nitrate cell, he and a British man called Sajil Shahid set up a terrorist training camp in the Malakand district of Pakistan in 2003.[40] Babar claims that the Ammonium Nitrate cell and Mohammed Siddique Khan attended this camp. This 'do it yourself' approach suggests that British terrorist cells might not have automatic access to the training facilities of the more established *jihadi* groups in Pakistan. It is also likely that the quality of training in these DIY facilities might have been quite poor. However, it is clear that members of the dataset also attended other training camps at different times, which were run by established *jihadi* groups, including *al Qaeda*. This was seemingly confirmed in a conversation between Khyam and Mohammed Siddique Khan in 2004, shortly before Khan was due to fly to Pakistan for training. Khyam advised him, 'The only thing, one thing I will advise you, yeah, is total obedience to whoever your emir is whether he is *Sunni*, Arab, Chechen, Saudi, British, total obedience.' He also warned that the consequences of disobedience could be decapitation.[41]

The military training that the members of the dataset received in overseas terror camps was therefore a significant milestone in their journey to violent extremism. The acquisition of skills is a key step in the incremental process towards engaging in violence through providing an increased sense of control and power.[42] It also seems that terrorist recruiters look for individuals who have gone through this training process. But, despite this, there does seem to be a small number of important exceptions among the dataset; only Barot and Jalil of the Gas Limos cell are known to have attended training camps in Pakistan and there have been no reports of Lindsay or Hasib Hussain attending training camps. Similarly, of the 21/7 cell, only Muktar Said Ibrahim, the *emir* of the cell, is known to have received military training overseas.[43] It also seems that individuals who attend overseas training camps are not automatically recruited into terror networks or cells. Hassan Butt claimed that, following training in Pakistan, recruits had to be patient, and one day they might be recruited into a network.[44]

However, not all of these camps are run by *al Qaeda* and not all are terrorist training camps. In some cases, individuals appear to be attending training camps centred on training fighters for conflicts in places like Kashmir or Central Asia. Terrorist recruiters may talent spot Westerners from these camps and offer them the chance to move on to more specialised terrorist training.[45]

Notes and references

[1] Feroze, Tanweer and Shahid Butt all learned hand-to-hand fighting skills in martial arts clubs. Muktar Said Ibrahim used to attend the gym in prison. The Mullah Crew used a gym known locally as the '*al Qaeda* gym', and in the weeks before the 7 July bombings Lindsay also become a frequent visitor to a local gym. The Walthamstow-based members of the Airline Cell also used to attend a gym in Walthamstow.

[2] 'Background: Birmingham's holy warriors', *Daily Telegraph*, 17 January 1999, http://www.telegraph.co.uk/htmlContent.jhtml?html=/archive/1999/01/17/nholy117.html.

3 'Terrorists or tourists', *Guardian*, 26 June 1999, http://www.al-bab.com/yemen/artic/gdn42.htm.

4 'Islamic school trained U.K. police before raid', *New York Times*, 5 September 2006, http://www.iht.com/articles/2006/09/05/news/britain.php; *Kent and Sussex Courier*, January 1999; Hansard, 11 January 1999: Columns 25–26, http://www.publications.parliament.uk/pa/cm199899/cmhansrd/vo990111/debtext/90111-06.htm#90111-06_spnew1.

5 *Daily Mail*, 3 September 2005.

6 Ronson J, *Them: Adventures with Extremists* (London: Simon and Schuster, 2002), p 44; 'Path to extremism: How it started', BBC NewsOnline, 3 May 2007, http://news.bbc.co.uk/1/hi/uk/6619147.stm.

7 *Sunday Times*, 17 January 1999.

8 Report of the Official Account of the Bombings in London on 7 July 2005, HC1087 (London: The Stationery Office), 11 May 2006.

9 'Police swoop on Britain's first "jihad training camp"', *Evening Standard*, 3 September 2006, http://www.thisislondon.co.uk/news/article-23365480-details/Police+swoop+on+Britain's+first+'jihad+training+camp'/article.do.

10 'Britain's first "school for martyrs" raided by police', *Independent*, 3 September 2006, http://news.independent.co.uk/uk/crime/article1325480.ece.

11 'Internet spreads terror in Britain', *Daily Telegraph*, 7 November 2007, http://www.telegraph.co.uk/news/main.jhtml?xml=news/2007/11/07/nterror107.xml; 'Al-Qaeda's 007', *The Times*, 16 January 2008, http://women.timesonline.co.uk/tol/life_and_style/women/the_way_we_live/article3191517.ece.

12 'Terrorist jailed over failed July 21 bomb plot', *Daily Telegraph*, 6 November 2007, http://www.telegraph.co.uk/news/main.jhtml?xml=/news/2007/11/06/nterror106.xml.

13 'Man in court on terror charge', *Evening Standard*, 25 August 2004.

14 Prepared text of Tuesday's portion of the Crown's opening statement in the trial of seven men alleged to have plotted to bomb London. The rest of the statement was to be delivered on Wednesday: Regina v Omar Khyam, Anthony Garcia, Nabeel Hussain, Jawad Akbar, Waheed Mahmood, Shujah-ud-din Mahmood, Salahuddin Amin, *Ottawa Citizen*, 21 March 2006, http://www.canada.com/ottawacitizen/news/story.html?id=408dc2ed-d950-4ee5-a4b7-392eb5faaf34&k=75162.

15 'Profile: Jawad Akbar', BBC NewsOnline, 30 April 2007,
http://news.bbc.co.uk/1/hi/uk/6149788.stm.

16 'Men "stored 600kg bomb material"', BBC NewsOnline, 16 May 2006,
http://news.bbc.co.uk/1/hi/uk/4774981.stm.

17 'Terrorists or tourists', *Guardian*, 26 June 1999, http://www.al-bab.com/
yemen/artic/gdn42.htm.

18 'Profile of Dhiren Barot', *Channel 4 News*, 7 November 2006,
http://www.channel4.com/news/special-reports/special-reports-
storypage.jsp?id=3838.

19 'The web of terror in London', *Evening Standard*, 6 August 2004.

20 'Manhunt for public school kidnapper', *Guardian*, 9 February 2002,
http://www.guardian.co.uk/pakistan/Story/0,2763,647495,00.html; 'Islamic
militancy appealed to Pearl's killer', The Associated Press, 15 July 2002,
http://www.usatoday.com/news/world/2002/07/15/2002-07-15-saeed-
profile_x.htm.

21 'Spy lifts lid on al-Qaeda', BBC NewsOnline, 16 November 2006,
http://news.bbc.co.uk/1/hi/uk/6156180.stm; Bruce Crumley, 'High-Alert
Holidays', *Time Magazine*, 14 December 2003,
http://www.time.com/time/magazine/article/0,9171,561279,00.html.

22 'British-born Muslim admits plot to blow up airliner', *Independent*, 1 March
2005.

23 'Mountain camp trained British terror recruits', *The Times*, 29 November
2003,
http://www.timesonline.co.uk/tol/news/uk/article1029381.ece.

24 'Focus: My life as a spy at the heart of *al-Qaeda*', *Sunday Times*, 19 November
2006, http://www.timesonline.co.uk/article/0,,2087-2460306_7,00.html.

25 'Terrorists or tourists', *Guardian*, 26 June 1999, http://www.al-bab.com/
yemen/artic/gdn42.htm.

26 CBS News, 25 March 2007,
http://www.cbsnews.com/stories/2007/03/23/60minutes/main2602308_page3.sh
tml.

27 'Police investigation: How many more are out there?', *Independent*, 27
February 2007, http://news.independent.co.uk/uk/crime/article301236.ece;
'Britain Under Attack', *Dispatches*, Channel 4 TV,
http://www.channel4.com/news/articles/dispatches/britain+under+attack/656252.

28 'The jihadi house parties of hate', *Sunday Times*, 6 May 2007,
http://www.timesonline.co.uk/tol/news/uk/article1752338.ece.

29 'Terror accused "ran away" to join jihad', *The Times*, 14 September 2006,
http://www.timesonline.co.uk/article/0,,2-2357829.html.

30 'Profile: Omar Khyam', BBC NewsOnline, 30 April 2007,
http://news.bbc.co.uk/1/hi/uk/6149794.stm.

31 'Court told how terror suspect "missed his mum"', ICSurreyonline.com, 15
November 2006,
http://icsurreyonline.icnetwork.co.uk/0100news/0400crawley/tm_headline=court
-told-how-terror-suspect—missed-his-mum-&method=full&objectid=18100955
&siteid=50101-name_page.html.

32 'Accused admits buying fertiliser for bomb, but "not to use here"', *Guardian*,
27 September 2006,
http://www.guardian.co.uk/alqaida/story/0,,1881756,00.html.

33 Prepared text of Tuesday's portion of the Crown's opening statement in the
trial of seven men alleged to have plotted to bomb London. The rest of the
statement was to be delivered on Wednesday: Regina v Omar Khyam, Anthony
Garcia, Nabeel Hussain, Jawad Akbar, Waheed Mahmood, Shujah-ud-din
Mahmood, Salahuddin Amin, *Ottawa Citizen*, 21 March 2006,
http://www.canada.com/ottawacitizen/news/story.html?id=408dc2ed-d950-
4ee5-a4b7-392eb5faaf34&k=75162.

34 'Accused "helped make test bomb"', BBC NewsOnline, 24 July 2006,
http://news.bbc.co.uk/1/hi/uk/5210870.stm.

35 'The jihadist who needed no brainwashing to blow up Aldgate train', Ian
Herbert and Kim Sengupta, *Independent*, 10 September 2005,
http://news.independent.co.uk/uk/crime/article311539.ece.

36 Report of the Official Account of the Bombings in London on 7 July 2005,
HC1087 (London: The Stationery Office), 11 May 2006; 'MI5 followed UK
suicide bomber', BBC NewsOnline, 30 April 2007,
http://news.bbc.co.uk/1/hi/uk/6417353.stm.

37 'Pakistan: the incubator for al-Qaeda's attacks on London', *Daily Telegraph*,
23 July 2005,
http://www.telegraph.co.uk/news/main.jhtml?xml=/news/2005/07/24/nterr224.
xml&page=3.

38 Report of the Official Account of the Bombings in London on 7 July 2005,
HC1087 (London: The Stationery Office), 11 May 2006, p 25.

[39] 'Airline bomb trial: Five potential suicide bombers "still at large"', *Daily Telegraph*, 9 September 2008,
http://www.telegraph.co.uk/news/uknews/2707241/Airline-bomb-trial-Five-potential-suicide-bombers-still-at-large.html.

[40] 'How many more are out there?' BBC NewsOnline, 30 April 2007,
http://news.bbc.co.uk/1/hi/programmes/newsnight/6607647.stm.

[41] 'Revealed: Bomber transcript', BBC NewsOnline, 1 May 2007,
http://news.bbc.co.uk/1/hi/uk/6611803.stm.

[42] Horgan J, *The Psychology of Terrorism* (Oxford: Routledge, 2005), p 99.

[43] 'The four guilty July 21 bombers', *Daily Telegraph*, 10 July 2007,
http://www.telegraph.co.uk/news/main.jhtml?xml=/news/2007/07/10/nplot310.xml; 'How MI5 left ringleader free to acquire recruits and explosives', *The Times*, 11 July 2007,
http://www.timesonline.co.uk/tol/news/uk/crime/article2056474.ece.

[44] 'Suicide bomber recruitment in the UK', BBC NewsOnline, 10 February 2004,
http://news.bbc.co.uk/1/hi/uk/3475929.stm.

[45] 'Al-Qaeda resurgent six years on?', BBC NewsOnline, 11 September 2007,
http://news.bbc.co.uk/1/hi/world/middle_east/6988356.stm.

Chapter 8

Killing Enabling Factors

Killing is not easy and very few people are willing or able to kill another person. There is evidence that a number of British Islamists have been unwilling to engage in acts of violence, and acts of terrorist violence in particular. Some have refused to even countenance the idea of using violence, and one of the catalysts for Ed Husain to leave *Hizb ut-Tahrir* was his witnessing the murder of Ayotunde Obanubi by fellow members of the group. Parviz Khan approached a number of associates to join his plot to murder a British soldier, but none of them agreed. Others who initially agreed to take part in violent attacks subsequently pulled back from the brink, sometimes right up to the very moment of the planned attack. Saajid Badat pulled out a matter of weeks before his planned attack, while Manfo Asiedu of the 21/7 cell was on his way to the Underground station with his bomb when he decided to pull out. Others have drawn distinctions between different forms of violence and refused to commit certain types of attack. Abu Omar, for instance, was prepared to fight for the Taliban, but was opposed to terrorist attacks such as 9/11, the murder of US journalist Daniel Pearl and the 7 July bombings, which he describes as 'disgusting'.[1] While he was in Afghanistan in 2001, Omar argued furiously with Kazi Rahman over whether innocent civilians should be murdered for the sake of *jihad*.[2]

233

MARTYRDOM

While most research has focused on why murderers choose to commit murder, very little has been carried out on why ordinary people kill. Most people would not commit acts of extreme violence even if they could do so without being caught or punished. This self-regulation is due to the transmission of cultural and moral values that place great value on human life and discourage killing. Most people subscribe to a set of moral values that they are loath to contravene as these values define their own self-image and sense of self-worth. While individuals will vary in their morality around many issues, such as the illegal use of controlled drugs or tax evasion, most people believe that killing someone else is immoral. In order for someone to kill another human being, a change in the psychological state of the individual is necessary.

In wartime, the state sanctions the killing of enemy combatants, therefore it is a natural presumption that a combat soldier will have no problem in killing the enemy. The reality is somewhat different as history is littered with examples of soldiers who chose not to kill the enemy in battle. One of the most often cited examples is the battle of Gettysburg during the American Civil War.[3] After the battle, over 27,000 single-shot muskets were recovered from the battlefield, about 24,000 of which were still loaded. This is not all that surprising, as the owners may have been killed, captured or routed before they had the chance to fire the round they had loaded. The interesting statistic is that half of these muskets had been loaded more than once without having been fired, and a quarter had between three and ten shots in them. The largest number of rounds loaded in a single musket was 23. These statistics clearly indicate that thousands of combatants went through the well-rehearsed drills of loading their weapons but then subsequently failed to fire them in order to kill the enemy. Instead, they must have pretended to fire and then reload an already loaded weapon. Lieutenant Colonel Grossman interprets these statistics as an indication that the soldiers were not trying to kill the enemy and were reluctant to even fire in their general direction in case they accidentally hit someone. Given that this was a civil war with Americans fighting Americans, it is understandable that there was a widespread reluctance to kill. Despite this, it is not an unusual finding.[4]

The seminal study on the reluctance to kill in combat was *Men Under Fire* by General 'Slam' Marshall, who spent the Second World War documenting the experiences of US combat troops as an official US army historian. Marshall and his team had unprecedented access to soldiers immediately after they had been in combat. The most surprising finding was that less than 25 per cent of those soldiers had actually fired their weapons. This is not to say that the other 75 per cent were cowards and ran away. These men were doing other things that were equally dangerous, such as recovering injured comrades or delivering messages. Individual soldiers who could see the enemy and had to decide whether they wanted to kill them were faced with an immediate moral and personal dilemma. When faced with this dilemma, many of them simply could not overcome their ingrained cultural belief that killing another human was wrong. Numerous officers and NCOs reported that they had to physically move between their troops ordering them to fire their weapons, otherwise none of them would do so. However, soldiers firing a weapon that required more than one person to use, such as a machine gun, were more likely to do so. Therefore, where there was more than one person involved in using a weapon to kill the enemy, that weapon was much more likely to be used. Similarly, soldiers using weapons that killed at a greater distance so that they did not have to see the enemy, or more importantly the enemy being killed, had no such problem in firing their weapons or dropping their bombs. It would appear that the immediacy of the killing was the problem for these soldiers. As we will describe below, there are ways to overcome the reluctance to kill and these killing enabling factors are the key to understanding how acts of terror are committed.

Subsequent researchers have questioned whether Marshall's statistics were accurate, as the implications for the military were so profound.[5] Regardless of the actual number of soldiers who fired their weapons, no one has been able to refute the central argument of the findings that some soldiers were reluctant to kill the enemy. The US military were not slow to react to these findings and this is obvious in Marshall's subsequent work during the Korean War, where the number of soldiers using their weapons increased to 55 per cent. By the time of the Vietnam War, only five per cent of combat soldiers did not fire their weapon at the enemy.[6] In fact, killing the enemy was uppermost in their minds. Dr Nadelson treated Vietnam veterans suffering from post-traumatic stress disorder (PTSD) and describes how many of them actually enjoyed killing in combat. For these veterans, nothing in the rest of their lives ever compared to the experience of combat. It is a common assumption that the horrors of combat and killing the enemy are the traumas that cause PTSD. Nadelson found that the problem for some of his veterans was actually readjusting to civilian life, and rather than detesting the war it seems they fondly remembered it as the best time of their lives and were more than willing to return to combat.[7]

The reluctance to kill observed during the Second World War was reduced during the second half of the 20th century so that modern soldiers are now more willing to kill the enemy. Grossman and others ascribe this change in the behaviour of soldiers to the application of psychology to their basic training. The main change appears to be the conscious use of psychological principles to desensitise the recruits. Glenn describes how at the beginning of the 20th century soldiers were arriving in France to fight the First World War with little or no training in how to fire their weapons, so it is not surprising that they had not been desensitised to the effects of those weapons. Many commanders had to create training packages for these soldiers so that they could fight effectively. In the Second World War, the situation does not appear to have improved significantly, and even during the Vietnam War there was still a perceived need for soldiers to receive additional training with their weapons. However, the key difference at the time of the Vietnam War was that the additional training was required to *reduce* the firing of weapons rather than increase it. One of Marshall's recommendations had been to make weapons training more realistic and this is what happened. Using the principles of conditioning developed by psychologists, training attempted to replicate the battlefield experience so that the soldiers learned how to behave in battle. Glenn refers to this conditioning process as 'battlefield inoculation' where the training immunises the soldier against the shock of unexpected events in combat.[8] This training initially focused on preventing confusion and fear in the soldiers, so this may explain why firing rates were so low. Training developed to include shooting reflexively at more realistic targets that resembled enemy combatants.[9] Grossman argues that, even if the principles of psychological theory were not applied deliberately, this is what the military were doing.[10]

While this research refers to soldiers in combat situations, it is of direct relevance to terrorism. Islamist terrorists perceive themselves to be fighting a global war against the enemies of Islam, for the very future of Islam. Their immediate objectives are to drive what they perceive to be foreign invaders from Muslim lands, and free Muslims from the 'oppression' of manmade laws by fighting to implement *Sha'ria* law. In the minds of Islamist terrorists, these objectives are equivalent to the actions of the armies that freed Europe from the control of Nazi Germany. Mohammed Siddique Khan and Reid both claimed to be soldiers, and it is reasonable to assume that the others saw themselves as warriors in the international *jihad*, since that is part of the rhetoric of Islamist terrorist groups. As we saw in Chapter 7, many of the terrorists had been through training camps both in the UK and abroad. The training that they received in these camps would have worked to condition and desensitise them to killing.

NATURAL BORN KILLERS

Several authors have argued that there are some individuals who are best described as 'natural born killers' because they do not experience the usual resistance to killing.[11] These individuals are often called either 'psychopaths' or 'sociopaths' as their behaviour is considered abnormal. The psychiatric disorder from which this terminology stems is currently called antisocial personality disorder.[12] The essential diagnostic feature is a 'pervasive pattern of disregard for, and violation of, the rights of others that begins in childhood or early adolescence and continues into adulthood'. The sufferer would not conform to social norms that govern lawful behaviour and therefore many fall foul of the law and experience incarceration. In order to further their own aims, many sufferers are skilled liars and extremely manipulative, so consequently many people do not notice their antisocial behaviour. Their decision making is extremely impulsive with little regard for the future consequences of their actions, particularly for other people. When things do go wrong and other people suffer, they tend to show little remorse for the consequences of their actions. They tend to be indifferent to the pain and suffering of others and provide superficial rationalisations to explain why they hurt others. Often the blame for their behaviour is transferred on to their victims because they 'deserve it, are stupid, or helpless'. Coupled with this transferring of blame is the minimising of the harmful consequences of their actions. These diagnostic criteria clearly suggest that an individual suffering with antisocial personality disorder would not have any difficulty killing someone else.

It is a common error to view psychiatric disorders as either present or absent, as this is how most of us view medical problems. In reality, most psychiatric disorders comprise a set of symptoms that are present in the normal population and it is only the severity of those symptoms that determines whether someone has a psychiatric disorder. Psychiatric symptoms are basically dimensional and every one of us can be located on those dimensions. For example, anxiety and depression are common human emotions that all of us experience from time to time, yet it is unusual for those symptoms to interfere with our day-to-day lives for extended periods of time. This is why the diagnosis of psychiatric disorders involves an appraisal of the extent or severity of the symptoms rather than their mere presence. Therefore, a normal individual could display some of the symptoms of antisocial personality disorder without necessarily qualifying for the diagnosis. It is important to note that the diagnostic criteria for antisocial personality disorder are based on people who display such abnormal behaviour that they have come to the attention of psychiatrists. There are likely to be many normal people who find themselves in situations where having the symptoms of antisocial personality disorder is actually a good thing. Psychopathy researchers have suggested that many function very well, particularly in the corporate world, and attain senior management positions.[13]

For many years, researchers into terrorism have argued that terrorists are not psychiatrically disturbed, as there is little evidence of any psychiatric disorders in the vast majority of the terrorists that they have studied.[14] Their analyses are, to a certain extent, correct, as individuals with psychiatric disorders pose risks for terrorist organisations, because they generally have difficulties working in teams and their lack of impulse control makes them a security risk. However, they fail to take account of the difference between the functional and dysfunctional nature of some psychiatric symptoms. That is, some psychiatric symptoms may be functional in some situations and dysfunctional in others, thus it is important to take account of the context in which the individual operates. Some of the symptoms of antisocial personality disorder would be useful for a terrorist; for example, to be able to kill without remorse and to lie and manipulate others would appear to be useful traits for individuals who have to act covertly and commit acts of terror. Providing that the terrorist is able to function within the cell or organisation, it is likely that these psychopathic traits would be sought out rather than eradicated. It is more likely that disruptive individuals would be weeded out and this is why clinical cases of antisocial personality disorder or any other psychiatric disorder are not found among the terrorists studied. What is more likely to be found are individuals with the symptoms of antisocial personality, but these symptoms are not so severe and disruptive that they warrant a diagnosis of the disorder.

Natural born killers are individuals who behave in a similar way to patients with antisocial personality disorder, but their behaviour is less pronounced and more functional because of the circumstances in which they find themselves. Because of this, they are not suffering from a psychiatric disorder and are essentially normal people. They find themselves in the situation where they are faced with the moral dilemma of killing other human beings and respond by killing without remorse. This is similar to Dyer's concept of the 'natural soldier', an individual who excels at being a soldier but does not enjoy killing. These individuals kill to get the job done and tend to congregate in special forces units. In these situations, killing is normal. As we discussed in Chapter 1, the fundamental attribution error overemphasises the dispositional and underemphasises the situational explanations for other people's behaviour. It would therefore be wrong to label these individuals as 'psychopathic killers', as this focuses on the individual's disposition and ignores the situation. Other terrorism researchers have correctly argued that using the psychopathic killer explanation is an oversimplistic and circular method of explaining terrorist behaviour. The evidence used to support these explanations is clearly subject to both the fundamental attribution error and confirmation bias. Despite this, it is obvious that otherwise normal people are behaving in an abnormal way, so therefore psychopathology will always be an attractive explanation for terrorist behaviour.

DIFFUSION OF RESPONSIBILITY

The acceptability of killing in combat lies in the fact that the state or another authority figure has sanctioned that killing. They are also able to reduce the reluctance to kill by providing leadership and a justification for killing. The role of the leader is to assume the responsibility for the actions of their followers and in return the followers are expected to obey their leader. Obedience to authority is considered the single most powerful psychological tool in enabling killing. Several different types of authority figure can be identified in respect of the dataset: the leaders of their individual cells; players in the international *jihad* in Pakistan with whom they had contact; and the religious figures or ideologues who provide the theological justification for terrorist violence.

Numerous psychological studies have been published on the role of authority figures in making people do what they would not otherwise do. The seminal experiments by Stanley Milgram are the most infamous studies on the use of authority to make ordinary people kill another person. In the classic Milgram experiment, an ordinary person answers an advert to participate in a study of memory at Yale University in return for $4. Upon arrival at the research laboratory, the participant is met by the experimenter (actually an actor) and another participant (another actor). The experimenter explains to the two participants that the purpose of the experiment is to examine whether punishment can be used to improve learning and memory. The experiment requires a teacher and a learner so the two participants are asked to draw lots. The outcome is rigged so that the participant plays the teacher and the actor plays the learner. The experimenter and the teacher escort the learner into an adjacent room where they are strapped into a chair and electrodes are attached to their body. The experimenter explains to the teacher that the punishment is electric shocks delivered through these electrodes and gives the teacher a sample shock to demonstrate. The learner does not actually receive any shocks as this part of the experiment is a deception. The teacher is then taken into another room and introduced to the shock generator which has 30 switches on it. Each switch corresponds to a different intensity of shock from the lowest at 15V through to the highest at 450V. Each switch also has a descriptor, for example 255V is described as 'intense shock' and 450V is described with only 'XXX'. The two experimental rooms are connected by an intercom so the teacher can only hear the learner. The experimental task consists of the teacher asking the learner to memorise a set of word pairings and then testing the learner by providing one half of the pair as a stimulus. The learner must respond with the other word in the pair. The teacher is asked to punish an incorrect response with an electric shock and to increase the level of shock with each successive mistake. As the actor deliberately makes mistakes, it is not long before the teacher is increasing the shock levels. As the shock intensity increases, the learner starts to complain about the pain of the shocks. These complaints become increasingly desperate until they cease all together. Eventually, the learner refuses to answer the questions and the experimenter instructs the teacher to continue administering the shocks as no answer is an error of omission and so therefore is also incorrect. If the teacher refuses to continue with the experiment, the experimenter (who is standing behind them) tells them to continue by using four phrases: 'please continue', 'the experiment requires that you continue', 'it is absolutely essential that you continue', and finally, 'you have no other choice, you must go on.' The experiment is terminated when the teacher refuses to continue or they administer three shocks of the highest intensity.[15]

The key question in the Milgram experiment is how many teachers would continue to administer shocks in the knowledge that they were harming the learner. Zimbardo describes how Milgram asked a group of psychiatrists to predict how many of the teachers would see the experiment through to the end. In line with the accepted wisdom of natural born killers, they predicted that, on average, around 1 per cent would engage in such blatantly 'sadistic' behaviour. Most of us would like to think that we would not see this experiment through to the end either. In reality, over 60 per cent of the teachers continued with the experiment and administered three shocks of the highest intensity despite the feedback coming from the learner. This basic finding has been replicated by other researchers from around the world, with minor variations in the number of teachers willing to see the experiment through to the end.[16] This clearly indicates that obedience to authority is universal and not the product of any one culture. The original purpose of this experiment was to investigate how seemingly ordinary people could have perpetuated the Holocaust. It is clear that obedience to authority may have been a contributing factor to the genocide.

The influence of the authority figure in the Milgram experiment can be modified by subtly altering the experimental situation.[17] The most obvious way is to change the authority of the experimenter. Milgram did this by conducting an experiment in a rundown office rather than the rather more prestigious Yale University building he had used before. He found that obedience was not significantly affected, although there was a slight drop. The key variable appeared to be the physical presence of the experimenter, as the level of obedience did drop significantly when the participant spoke to the experimenter over the phone. In fact, many of the participants told the experimenter that they were administering shocks when they were not. This is mirrored in the real world by individuals who appear to obey authority but actually seek to undermine that authority if they do not agree with the instructions. This disobedience is also facilitated by the tasks required of the participants. If the participants were required to physically hold the learner's hand on the shock plate, then obedience was dramatically reduced. Physical proximity and undeniable responsibility appear to overcome the obedience to authority.

The presence of other participants appears to impact on the participants' interpretation of their own role. As we discussed in Chapter 5, conformity is a powerful psychological process in small groups such as terrorist cells. The presence of peers who obeyed the authority figure increased obedience and, likewise, the presence of peers who disobeyed reduced obedience. In one interesting twist on the presence of peers, the experimenter leaves the room before instructing the participant to increase the shock with each error. Instead, the experimenter instructs a second participant (another actor) to take charge and this new authority figure subsequently decides to increase the shock levels once the experimenter has left. Around 20 per cent of the participants obeyed the new authority figure despite their being of equal status. In this particular experiment, the new authority figure was instructed to take over administering the shocks if the participant refused. Some of the participants actively resisted this, which suggests that the participants were aware of what was going on in the Milgram experiment.[18] The interesting question is why they did not resist the authority figure in the other versions of the experiment. The most likely explanation is that we are socialised to obey authority throughout our lives, and it is only in exceptional circumstances that we will question it.

Leaders are able to remove direct responsibility from the individual for their actions and the obedience to authority is a common defence in war crimes trials. The Milgram experiment clearly indicates that normal people subtly progress through to committing extreme acts without overtly questioning the authority that instructs them to do so. It is reasonable to assume that, if the participants were asked to deliver the highest level of shock immediately, obedience would have been low. The reluctance to kill in combat would support this assumption. That is, the Milgram experiment worked because of the subtle use of incremental pain that could be rationalised by the participants with each successive increment. Part of this rationalisation would have been the commitment that they had already made to the experiment.

In this context, it is tempting to argue that the dataset were heavily influenced by leaders, the most obvious being the *al Qaeda* leadership. There is much discussion of a connection to *al Qaeda*, but the direct links between any of our dataset and recognised members of *al Qaeda* are limited. The influence of the leader would have to be at the level of the *emirs* that ran the individual cells. As discussed in Chapter 5, the individuals' commitment was to their *emirs* and the cells. When Mohammed Siddique Khan and Omar Khyam discussed Khan's attendance at a training camp in Pakistan, Khyam advised him to be totally obedient to his *emir*. This same sense of obedience can be seen in the Gas Limos cell. Barot, the *emir*, was a charismatic individual who personally recruited the cell, and as a professional terrorist with links to *al Qaeda* figures in Pakistan he was a much more serious player in British Islamist terror networks than the other members of his cell.

At another level, religious figures also played a significant role in motivating the dataset and providing the 'religious' justification for their actions. At the international level, there are ideologues, such as bin Laden and al Zawahiri, who issue *fatwas* which provide a rationale and justification for terrorist attacks. While there is no evidence that any of the dataset ever met bin Laden, he was clearly an inspiration, and his words and example have been used as a justificatory mechanism by a number of the dataset. At national level, several members of the dataset are linked with British-based religious ideologues such as Abu Hamza, Abu Qatada, Omar Bakri Mohammed and Abdullah el Faisal.

The role of these individuals was to provide a theological justification for terrorist violence. Hassan Butt stated in an interview that:

one day I may even be called a terrorist, if Allah permits me. That is something it would be an honour to be called ... There is a speech by the Prophet in which he says: 'Allah gave me five things. One of them was the power to strike fear, to strike terror into the heart of the enemy from a mile's distance', and this was a reference to a battle he had commenced. The way the warriors had prepared themselves was so terrifying that the enemy didn't even turn up to the battle. Besides that, in the *Qur'an* the word *irhab* is the root word for terror in Islam, and *irhabiyun* is the word for terrorist. Allah mentions the word in the *Qur'an* many times – the one who strikes terror into their hearts is an *irhabiyun*. If I could have that title Islamically then I would be more than happy to take it and be proud of it. But unfortunately, I haven't reached that level yet.[19]

Evidence from the dataset indicates quite clearly that increased belief in the religious justification for violence, through adherence to an Islamist ideology, was a feature along the path to the violent radicalisation of virtually all of these individuals.

While leaders remove direct responsibility, peers are able to share and therefore reduce the burden of responsibility. This explains why crew-served weapons, such as artillery and heavy machine guns, were much more likely to be used in the Second World War than personal weapons. This analogy is directly applicable to a terrorist cell planning a non-suicide bombing. In the case of the Ammonium Nitrate and Gas Limos cells, different members of the cells performed different functions, such as procuring materials, reconnaissance, planning or simply acting as gofer for the *emir* of the cell. Individually, each of these functions would not cause death or destruction, but when combined they might do so.

Many veterans recall the intense bonds that existed between them and their comrades. Nadelson reports that it was common for his patients to refer to other soldiers and veterans as 'my people', as a distinct group that shared a bond of loyalty and understanding that no one else could. Even if the individual did not want to take part in killing, pressure to conform ensured that they did so. Many soldiers awarded medals for bravery state that their actions were in support of their friends, and the desire not to let their mates down appears to be the strongest motivation for soldiers to fight. These intense bonds are replicated to a great extent in terrorist cells, particularly those that isolate themselves from the community. This was illustrated by the three members of the 7/7 cell who came from Beeston. In the years leading up to the 7 July bombings, their lives became increasingly narrow; they associated with a small network of radicalised individuals and socialised in a limited number of venues in a small area of the town. However, not all of the cells in the dataset isolated themselves from society in this way, particularly those who had family lives and jobs, or those whose members lived in different towns. In these cases, training seems to have been used to intensify the bonds between the members of individual cells, particularly outward-bound-type activities which can be easily and discreetly arranged in the UK. The Yemen 8 and Ammonium Nitrate cells, in particular, trained together as cells, both in the UK and overseas.

VIOLENT MEDIA

There is plenty of controversy surrounding the issue of violent media in the generation of violent behaviour in society, and there is substantial evidence that exposure to such violent media can have a negative effect.[20] Killing has always been a popular topic for authors and it has fascinated people ever since Homer wrote *The Iliad*. Tales of heroes and villains fighting in mortal combat are prevalent throughout the world, and there is a seemingly endless supply of films and TV shows that graphically portray such tales. Computer games take this graphic violence to a new level as the player is able to assume the mantle of the hero and slay their enemies in order to achieve victory. People all over the world are avid consumers of these violent media and the impact of this consumption is difficult to gauge. What is certain is that people are learning that violence and killing can secure victory against almost impossible odds.

There is a considerable amount of extremely violent *jihadi* material circulating within the UK, much of which has been downloaded from the internet and further disseminated by email, DVD and mobile telephones. A number of members of the dataset were reported to have possessed violent media. For instance, a computer belonging to members of the Ammonium Nitrate cell contained video files showing the execution of a Russian soldier, a Taliban execution and an execution by firing squad in Iran.[21] Mohammed Siddique Khan and Tanweer's network in Beeston produced numerous DVDs from material downloaded from the internet, including horrific material from Iraq, Afghanistan and the Middle East, focused particularly on the killing and maiming of children in operations by the American and Israeli military.[22] Among other propaganda material, Abu Mansha owned a DVD of the beheading of British hostage Ken Bigley in Iraq.[23] The impact of this violent media was explained by Salahuddin Amin who admitted that he had watched videos about the conflicts in Chechnya and Bosnia. Those videos showed 'a lot of killing' of innocent children, women and old people and they had made him feel 'angry'.[24]

Exposure to violent media will reinforce any cognitive distortions that the individual has regarding the instrumental use of violence and desensitises them to its effects. One of the key mechanisms involved in this process is social learning, where the individual learns how to behave from significant others, such as family, peers and role models. The most famous psychological experiments on social learning and aggression involved young children observing the aggressive behaviour of an adult towards an inflatable clown doll (called 'Bobo'). Bandura and colleagues provided the children with a room full of different toys, but the adult only interacted with Bobo by making hostile comments and striking it. Sometimes the adult was rewarded for their 'good' behaviour by the psychologist with chocolate. When the children were subsequently placed in the room with the different toys, their behaviour was observed. Invariably, the children would imitate the adult if they observed that adult being rewarded for their aggressive behaviour. In a slight variation of this study, the adult was either praised or chastised and the variation in the psychologist's response to the adult influenced the children's behaviour. However, in order for these effects to be seen, the psychologist had to be present; therefore, when there was no mechanism for either reward or sanction for their behaviour, the children tended to ignore the Bobo doll. Despite this, the effect was long lasting and could be observed for several months afterwards. Some controversy surrounds these experiments as it is not clear whether the children were actually displaying aggression or rough-and-tumble play. However, there is little doubt that, if an individual learns that violent behaviour is normative and appropriate, they are more likely to use violent behaviour when provoked.

Building on social learning theory, Huesmann proposed that, when young children are exposed to violent media, they learn scripts – a set of concepts that have been learned and linked to form a plan of how to behave – from it. For example, if young children learn that heroes prevail over their adversaries through violence, they will resort to violence in order to triumph over their own adversaries. Therefore, in conflict situations, the violence script is used to define the situation and guide behaviour.[25] Many combat veterans recall how the actions of fictional characters in combat influenced their own behaviour in combat.[26]

Violent imagery not only provides a script to guide behaviour, but it also desensitises the individual so that the thought or sight of death is no longer shocking. As detailed above, being physically exposed to battlefield inoculation was sufficient to reduce the shock of combat. Being psychologically exposed to the act of killing and its aftermath may also be sufficient to reduce the aversion towards killing. This exposure can make killing seem normal and, once it is considered normal, the moral restraints are removed. The Theory of Planned Behaviour[27] explains how such moral restraints are removed by the shaping of intentions and behaviour through three psychological factors: attitudes, beliefs and self-efficacy. The intention to kill is affected by the individual's attitudes towards the act, which are a function of the personal consequences of killing and the emotional value of those consequences. The decision to kill is determined by the individual's beliefs about what is normal behaviour. Self-efficacy is the perception of control over the successful completion of a particular behaviour. It plays a crucial and independent role in shaping behavioural intentions. Therefore, if an individual feels that killing someone else will lead to a positive outcome for them and that this is a normal way to get that positive outcome, they become likely to kill that person if they have the means to do so. The repeated exposure of the dataset to *jihadi* videos of executions, combat and bombings would have provided all of these reinforcements. The perceived success of Islamist attacks in Lebanon, Iraq and Chechnya will show that the 'infidel invader' can be fought and defeated using the weapons of the resistance fighters. While this behaviour may not be normal for the wider Muslim population, it may be considered justifiable resistance within the militant Islamist community.

DEHUMANISATION

One of the most pervasive killing enabling factors is dehumanisation, where the target of instrumental violence is believed to be less than human. Dehumanisation serves several functions for the individual as it explains the conflict, provides a sense of superiority and justifies their violent behaviour. Dehumanisation undermines the normal moral restraints on violent behaviour and makes violence towards the target group morally acceptable. This protects the individual from the psychological costs and consequences of their violent behaviour towards the target group. Dehumanisation is most often discussed in relation to ethnicity and race, often in the context of immigration and genocide.[28] The outsiders are usually portrayed as primitives who lack intelligence, self-restraint, morality and culture. Their behaviour is associated with impulsivity, criminality and unrestrained sexuality. As moral values are normally used to determine humanity, the symbolic threat posed by the outsiders is sufficient to devalue their humanity. Ultimately, dehumanisation is an extreme example of the group conflict we discussed in Chapter 2.

Dehumanisation is most obvious in the language used by the individuals concerned; for example, the Hutu extremists in Rwanda referred to the Tutsi minority as 'cockroaches'. This terminology seeks to attribute extremely negative characteristics to the target group with the purpose of excluding them from the rest of humanity. The use of this language is normally emotionally laden (usually contempt or fear) and culturally determined, and emphasises discriminatory rejection of the target group. The phraseology usually incorporates two inhuman categories: animals or other subhuman beings; or superhuman beings, such as monsters, demons and devils. The use of language by an individual or group that dehumanises any other individual or group within society indicates an increased threat of violent behaviour by that individual or group, and such language will create the impression that these beliefs are normal and morally acceptable.

As we discussed in Chapter 5, the term *kuffar* is used as a culturally derogatory term, particularly by the Islamists. In the view of these groups, *kuffar* are considered to be less than Muslims, and the West is portrayed as being Islamophobic and engaged in a war against Islam. One journalist who visited an *al Muhajiroun* safe house in Lahore before the authorities closed it down said that recruits from Britain referred to Indians as 'subhumans' and were violently opposed to homosexuals and Jews.[29] Among the dataset, Jawad Akbar, in particular, is known to have had a deep hatred of non-Muslims, and told his wife that, 'when we kill the kuf, this is because we know Allah hates the kufs.'[30] The 'martyrdom' videos of the Airline cell are also peppered with references to the *kuffar*. Umar Islam even declared that it was an obligation on Muslims to wage *jihad* against the *kuffar*.[31] There is also evidence that some criminal gangs are being radicalised by viewing crime directed against the *kuffar* as being morally acceptable.[32]

Dehumanisation of non-Muslims appears to have been an integral part of the indoctrination and training of the members of the dataset. Mohammed Hamid and Atilla Ahmet would bombard their recruits with insults about the *kuffar* and the alleged religious obligation to fight the *kuffar*. At one meeting, Ahmet claimed, 'Allah says they [the *kuffar*] are cowards. It's an obligation for Allah to fulfil *jihad*. Allah says it is quite easy for him to punish the *kuffar* … but Allah says "No, I've left you to fulfil that duty if you really believe it."'[33]

Parviz Khan even went so far as to teach his five-year-old son to dehumanise and hate the US and followers of other religions. In one recorded conversation in May 2006, Khan made his son stand in front of him with his hands by his side and demanded:

'Who do you kill?'
'America kill,' said the boy.
'Who else you kill?' asked Khan.
'Bush I kill,' said the boy.
'And who else?' demanded Khan.
'Blair kill, both people kill.'

'Who else you kill?' asked Khan.

'Saddam, Saddam,' said the boy.

Then the pair began chanting at each other.

Khan said, '*Kuffar*,' and the boy replied, 'Kill.'

Khan said, '*Mushrik* [polytheists],' and the boy replied, 'Kill.'

Then it continued with: 'Hindu? ... Kill ... *Sheedi* [blacks]? ... Kill ...
Pathan [thieves]? ... Kill ... *Sharab* [alcohol]? ... Kill ... And who
do you love? ... Sheikh Osama bin Laden, I love.'[34]

This dehumanisation is often given theological legitimacy by quoting
selected passages from the *Qur'an* and the *Hadith*. Suragah al
Andalusi, who is considered to have been a powerful influence on
Mohammed Siddique Khan, quoted the following verse in his last will
and testament:

> And verily, you will find them [the Jews] the greediest of
> mankind for life and [even greedier] than those who – ascribe
> partners to Allah [and do not believe in Resurrection –
> Magicians, pagans, and idolaters, etc]. Everyone of them wishes
> that he could be given a life of a thousand years. But the grant
> of such life will not save him even a little from [due]
> punishment. And Allah is All-Seer of what they do.[35]

The dehumanisation of non-Muslims is a central theme in the
discourse of Islamist ideologues based in the UK. Omar Bakri
Mohammed helped organise a seminar after the 9/11 attacks in
favour of the 'Magnificent 19' and went on to call the 7 July bombers
the 'Fantastic Four'. Documents produced by *al Muhajiroun* claimed,
'Terrorism is a part of Islam' and 'Allah made it obligatory to prepare
and to terrify the enemy of Allah ... The *kuffar* of USA and UK are
without doubt our enemy. There is no such thing as an innocent *kafir*,
innocence is only applicable for the Muslims. Not only is it obligatory
to fight them, it is *haram* [religiously forbidden] to feel sorry for
them.'[36] Similarly, Abu Hamza once declared, 'Killing a *kafir* who is

252

fighting you is OK. Killing a *kafir* for any reason, you can say it, it is OK – even if there is no reason for it.'[37]

This gives the dehumanisation a theological legitimacy, which, coupled with the fact that it is being delivered by an authority figure, makes it extremely powerful.

Notes and references

1 'Do you want to become a martyr, the al Qaeda chief asked ...', *Evening Standard*, 31 March 2008, http://www.thisislondon.co.uk/standard/article-23469193-details/Do+you+want+to+become+a+martyr%2C+the+al+Qaeda+chief+asked.../article.do.

2 'British al-Qaeda recruit talks exclusively to the Daily Mirror', *Daily Mirror*, 1 April 2008, http://www.mirror.co.uk/news/topstories/2008/04/01/british-al-qaeda-recruit-talks-exclusively-to-the-daily-mirror-89520-20369334/.

3 Grossman D, *On Killing: The Psychological Cost of Learning to Kill in War and Society* (Boston: Back Bay Books, 1996); Nadelson T, *Trained to Kill: Soldiers at War* (Baltimore: Johns Hopkins University Press, 2005).

4 Grossman D, *On Killing: The Psychological Cost of Learning to Kill in War and Society* (Boston: Back Bay Books, 1996).

5 Glenn RW, *Reading Athena's Dance Card: Men against Fire in Vietnam* (Annapolis: Naval Institute Press, 2000).

6 Glenn RW, *Reading Athena's Dance Card: Men against Fire in Vietnam* (Annapolis: Naval Institute Press, 2000).

7 Nadelson T, *Trained to Kill: Soldiers at War* (Baltimore: Johns Hopkins University Press, 2005).

8 Glenn RW, *Reading Athena's Dance Card: Men against Fire in Vietnam* (Annapolis: Naval Institute Press, 2000).

9 Glenn RW, *Reading Athena's Dance Card: Men against Fire in Vietnam* (Annapolis: Naval Institute Press, 2000).

10 Grossman D, *On Killing: The Psychological Cost of Learning to Kill in War and Society* (Boston: Back Bay Books, 1996).

11 Grossman D, *On Killing: The Psychological Cost of Learning to Kill in War and Society* (Boston: Back Bay Books, 1996); Nadelson T, *Trained to Kill: Soldiers at War* (Baltimore: Johns Hopkins University Press, 2005).

MARTYRDOM

[12] American Psychiatric Association, *Diagnostic and Statistical Manual of Mental Disorders*, 4th Edition Text Revised. American Psychiatric Association, Washington, DC, 2000.

[13] Hall JR & Benning SD, 'The "successful" psychopath: Adaptive and subclinical manifestations of psychopathy in the general population', in Patrick CJ (ed),Handbook of Psychopathy (New York: Guilford Press, 2006); 'Is your boss a "corporate psycho"?', BBC NewsOnline, 13 January 2004, http://news.bbc.co.uk/1/hi/business/3392233.stm.

[14] Horgan J, *The Psychology of Terrorism* (Oxford: Routledge, 2005); Silke A, 'Cheshire-cat logic: The recurring theme of terrorist abnormality in psychological research', *Psychology, Crime & Law*, No. 4, 1998, pp 51–69.

[15] van Avermaet E, 'Social influence in small groups', in Hewstone M, Stroebe W & Stephenson GM (eds), *Introduction to Social Psychology* (Oxford: Blackwell Publishers, 1996); Zimbardo P, *The Lucifer Effect: How Good People Turn Evil* (New York: Random House, 2007).

[16] Zimbardo P, *The Lucifer Effect: How Good People Turn Evil* (New York: Random House, 2007).

[17] van Avermaet E, 'Social influence in small groups', in Hewstone M, Stroebe W & Stephenson GM (eds), *Introduction to Social Psychology* (Oxford: Blackwell Publishers, 1996).

[18] van Avermaet E, 'Social influence in small groups', in Hewstone M, Stroebe W & Stephenson GM (eds), *Introduction to Social Psychology* (Oxford: Blackwell Publishers, 1996).

[19] Taseer A, 'A British jihadist', *Prospect*, August 2005, http://www.prospect-magazine.co.uk/article_details.php?id=6992.

[20] Anderson CA & Bushman BJ, 'Human aggression', *Annual Review of Psychology*, No. 53, 2002, pp 27–51; Dill KE & Dill JC, 'Video game violence: A review of the empirical literature', *Aggression and Violent Behavior*, No. 3, 1998, pp 407–28.

[21] Prepared text of Tuesday's portion of the Crown's opening statement in the trial of seven men alleged to have plotted to bomb London: Regina v Omar Khyam, Anthony Garcia, Nabeel Hussain, Jawad Akbar, Waheed Mahmood, Shujah-ud-din-Mahmood, Salahuddin Amin, 21 March 2006, *Ottawa Citizen*, http://www.canada.com/ottawacitizen/news/story.html?id=408dc2ed-d950-4ee5-a4b7-392eb5faaf34&k=75162.

[22] 'When I heard where the bombers were from I felt sick', *Guardian*, 24 June 2006, http://www.guardian.co.uk/uk_news/story/0,,1804867,00.html.

23 'Man jailed for plot to kill Iraq war hero', *Guardian*, 26 January 2006, http://www.guardian.co.uk/terrorism/story/0,12780,1695690,00.html?gusrc=rss.

24 'Accused "influenced by Abu Hamza"', BBC NewsOnline, 25 July 2006, http://news.bbc.co.uk/1/hi/uk/5214174.stm.

25 Huesmann LR, 'Psychological processes promoting the relation between exposure to media violence and aggressive behaviour by the viewer', *Journal of Social Issues*, No. 42, 1986, pp 125–40.

26 Nadelson T, *Trained to Kill: Soldiers at War* (Baltimore: Johns Hopkins University Press, 2005).

27 Ajzen I, *Attitudes, personality, and behaviour* (Homewood, Illinois: Dorsey Press, 1988).

28 Haslam N, 'Dehumanisation: An integrative review', *Personality and Social Psychology Review*, No.10, 2006, pp 252–64.

29 'Terror links of the Tottenham Ayatollah', *Sunday Times*, 24 July 2005, http://www.timesonline.co.uk/tol/news/uk/article547466.ece.

30 Prepared text of Tuesday's portion of the Crown's opening statement in the trial of seven men alleged to have plotted to bomb London: Regina v Omar Khyam, Anthony Garcia, Nabeel Hussain, Jawad Akbar, Waheed Mahmood, Shujah-ud-din-Mahmood, Salahuddin Amin, 21 March 2006, *Ottawa Citizen*, http://www.canada.com/ottawacitizen/news/story.html?id=408dc2ed-d950-4ee5-a4b7-392eb5faaf34&k=75162; 'Profile: Jawad Akbar', BBC NewsOnline, 30 April 2007, http://news.bbc.co.uk/1/hi/uk/6149788.stm.

31 'Bin Laden "inspired bomb plotter"', BBC NewsOnline, 10 April 2008, http://news.bbc.co.uk/1/hi/uk/7340606.stm.

32 'From jail to jihad', *Dispatches*, Channel 4 TV, 16 June 2008.

33 'Top extremist recruiter found guilty', 26 February 2008, http://news.bbc.co.uk/1/hi/uk/7193128.stm.

34 'Plot leader "groomed children for terrorism"', *Daily Telegraph*, 18 February 2008, http://www.telegraph.co.uk/news/main.jhtml?xml=/news/2008/02/18/nkidnap2 18.xml.

35 *Qur'an* 2:96.

36 'Cleric preaches that violence is part of Islam', *Daily Telegraph*, 1 May 2007, http://www.telegraph.co.uk/news/main.jhtml?xml=/news/2007/05/01/nplot901.xml.

37 'Key to proving Hamza's hate', BBC NewsOnline, 7 February 2006, http://news.bbc.co.uk/1/hi/uk/4670906.stm.

Chapter 9

Martyrdom

Martyrdom is central to our understanding of why the dataset chose to engage in terrorist activity. Ramzi Mohammed of the 21/7 cell, for instance, wrote in a letter to his family: 'I beg Allah to accept this action from me ... for verily he grants martyrdom to whomever he wills ... My family, don't cry for [me]. But indeed rejoice in happiness and love what I have done for the sake of Allah for he loves those who fight in his sake.'[1] Similarly, Muktar Said Ibrahim possessed a notebook in which the principles of the 21 July operation were laid out, which stated that it was designed to achieve 'martyrdom in the path of God'.[2]

The martyr is an almost universal concept in both religious and national histories from around the world. Throughout recorded history, the altruistic self-sacrifice of the martyr for the greater good is revered. The actions of martyrs are ingrained into the history and folklore of the communities for which they died through repeated remembrances and retelling of stories. This imbues them and their deeds with a measure of historical immortality. However, self-sacrifice in battle is not the only way for an individual to become a martyr. Syed Qutb, the Islamist ideologue whose work has heavily influenced the global *jihad* and the members of the dataset, is considered to be a martyr after being hanged by the Egyptian authorities in 1966. The same is true of Abdullah Azzam who was murdered in 1989. Communities ascribe the status of martyr to the individual, therefore it is the discourse within the wider community that determines such status. Community support is an absolutely central requirement for achieving martyrdom. Terrorist and insurgent organisations have sought to use religious or national identities to garner support for their causes and therefore martyrs become central to their discourse as well. The ultimate aim of these organisations is to subvert religious or national identities so that they provide justification for their actions. As we discussed in Chapter 8, it is necessary for terrorists to use killing enabling factors so they can overcome the resistance to killing. These killing enabling factors must resonate with their target audience (i.e. potential supporters and recruits) in order for them to be effective.

The Arabic word *shahid* does not mean sacrificing one's life; rather, it means 'being present' or an 'observer', in the sense of a person who bears witness to the truth. For Muslims, martyrs occupy a special status akin to that of prophets, righteous men and just Imams. In the eyes of many ordinary Muslims, a martyr endows his entire community with grace and purity, and his immediate family becomes the object of admiration.[3]

The notion of martyrdom (but not suicide attacks) is a feature of the mainstream discourse of Muslim communities in the UK. In his speech entitled 'The globalised suffering of the Muslims', Riyadh al Huq argued that:

Masjid al Aqsa is under siege and the Prophet has identified the cause of our weakness: Allah will cast into your hearts ... the love of the *dunya* and the dislike of death. And the love of life and the dislike of death. When the love of the world sets in the heart of Muslims, when we love our luxury, when we love our comfort, when we have become so accustomed to, and so fond of this easy life, especially here in the West and in other parts of the world, how can any Muslim hope to meet Allah in a good way? How can any Muslim hope to look forward to sacrificing his wealth, his family, his children, his time and most importantly his life in the way of Allah? It cannot happen. First, [dislike of] death has to die in the heart of the Muslim. But if there's a love of life, that can never happen. That will inevitably lead to the dislike of death.[4]

In a sermon about Israel, he called upon his congregation to 'be willing to sacrifice anything that may be required of us.' The *al Aqsa* mosque in Jerusalem must be liberated and 'we are willing to die in the process.' When called upon, 'we will consider it an honour and a privilege to shed our blood.'[5]

He argued that Muslims have become weak because they have developed 'the love of life and the dislike of death'. Their faith is being tested and for Islam to prevail the believer must be willing, even eager, to sacrifice his life 'in the way of Allah'. Muslims are living in that era 'before the day of reckoning' when, as prophesised, 'the truthful will be rejected and the liar will be believed'. In this time of darkness, 'adhering to the fundamentals of Islam … is considered extremism and the struggle against oppression is called terrorism'.[6]

For our dataset, the discourse on martyrdom was framed by the *Qur'an* and how it is interpreted. There are 12 verses in the *Qur'an* which deal directly with martyrdom. They imply that a person who becomes a *shahid* does not really die, but actually receives their reward in the afterlife. Central to their interpretation was the individual obligation of every Muslim to wage *jihad* in defence of the people, lands and religious institutions of Islam. In this narrative, *jihad* means a defensive war fought against powerful foes besieging Muslim lands.

Jihad can be conceived as a process of affirming faith, which has a sacrificial quality. The act of martyrdom is therefore a testament of faith, and God and the public bear witness to it. It affirms the strength of the *shahid*'s faith, courage and bravery and their right to belong to their own close community. It also demonstrates to the enemies of the faith that, although there may be a disparity in their material strength, they are actually fighting an equal fight because it is the *shahid* rather than the enemy who possesses the greater faith and courage. To those Muslims whom the terrorists hope to motivate, it becomes impossible to ignore what the martyr believes in. It is also intended to have a shaming effect on those Muslims who realise that this act has been committed on their behalf. The act of martyrdom therefore also presents a challenge to those Muslims who have not joined the fight.[7]

The case of Parviz Khan illustrates how some individuals are driven by a sense of needing to do more to affirm their faith because God will ultimately bear witness to their actions on the day of judgement. Even though he operated a logistics network that provided valuable supplies for *jihadis* in Pakistan, Khan feared that he would be damned at the time of judgement because his only notable achievements were a handful of good performances for his Sunday league football team. He confided to a friend, 'There is no answer, Brother was a good footballer ... centre midfield ... it's not going to be good enough ... not good enough. I know if I die now, if I die tonight, if I am not working for Islam full time ... pure hypocrite.'[8] These fears were the major driver for Khan's planning to perpetrate an act of violence rather than just provide logistic support to *jihadis* in Pakistan.

The dataset believed that Muslims who are killed waging *jihad* to counter persecution and injustice are rewarded by God as *shaheed*. The *Qur'an* and the *Hadith* clearly outline the benefits of martyrdom, which include remission of one's sins at the moment the *shahid*'s blood is shed; immediate admission into heaven, so *shaheed* do not suffer the punishment of the tomb; the privilege of accompanying prophets, saints and righteous believers; marriage to heavenly maidens (*houri al-ayn*); the right to intercede with God on behalf of seventy relatives; protection against the pain of death; and entry into the highest gardens of heaven (*jannat al-firdaous*).[9] It is also suggested that the immediate families are given similar privileges including being spared the pain of death, remission of sins, exemption from the punishment of the tomb and the final judgement, intercession on behalf of their co-religionists, marriage to *houri al-ayn* and a place in *jannat al-firdaous*.[10]

This process of demonstrating faith to fellow radicals is evident from the case of Suragah al Andalusi, who was killed by a US airstrike in Afghanistan in 2001. His last will and testament takes the form of a message to the *ummah*. Quoting selectively from the *Qur'an*, al Andalusi argues that *jihad* and martyrdom are evidence of supreme religious commitment, and that martyrs will be rewarded in the after life.[11] For instance, 'Think not of those who are killed in the Way of Allah as dead. Nay, they are alive, with their Lord, and they have provision. They rejoice in what Allah has bestowed upon them of His Bounty, rejoicing for the sake of those who have not yet joined them, but are left behind [not yet martyred] that on them no fear shall come, nor shall they grieve.'[12]

The concept of martyrdom is central to contemporary *jihadi* ideology and discourse. For militant Islamists, *jihad* as armed struggle provides the basis for the ideology of martyrdom, in which violent death on the battlefield and not the inward sacrifice of the believer occupies a central place.[13] Sheikh Abdullah Azzam worked hard to inculcate his volunteers with a desire for martyrdom, repeatedly stressing its rewards and quoting the single *Hadith* in which the Prophet assures the *shahid* absolution from all sins, 72 beautiful virgins and permission to bring 70 members of their families into Paradise with them.[14]

In his last will and testament, al Andalusi quoted several passages by Azzam including: 'It is with the likes of all these martyrs that nations are established, convictions are brought to life and ideologies are made victorious'; and 'Indeed, the manuscripts of history are not scribed except with the blood of these martyrs, except with the stories of these martyrs, except with the examples of these martyrs.'

The words of al Andalusi have been posted on *jihadi* websites for anyone to read, and seem to have had a profound effect on Mohammed Siddique Khan, whose own last will and testament draws heavily on that of al Andalusi.

SUICIDE AND SUICIDE TERRORISM

Suicide is typically defined as the conscious effort to end one's life. Psychologist Edwin Shneidman identified four kinds of people who intentionally end their own lives. The 'death seeker' clearly intends to die when they attempt to commit suicide; however, this intention may be temporary. The 'death initiator' is attempting to hasten the process of dying that they believe has already started, such as a chronic fatal illness. The 'death ignorer' does not believe that their death will be the end of their existence but instead believes that by dying they will exist in a better place. The 'death darer' is actually ambivalent about dying despite attempting to kill themselves and often the suicidal behaviour is used to gain attention or punish others. The common strand to all of these categories is that the suicidal behaviour is abnormal. This is how most societies view suicide and many countries around the world have made attempting suicide a criminal act. Indeed, even the phrase 'to commit suicide' implies that one is carrying out a criminal act rather than choosing to end one's life.[15]

Suicide is often portrayed as the act of depressed, lonely people who are seeking a way of ending the torment of their lives. To a certain extent, this may explain why a large number of people become suicidal. Emile Durkheim wrote a seminal study of suicidal behaviour that focused on the relationship between the individual and society. Durkheim argued that the attachment of the individual to family and/or society determines the probability of that individual's committing suicide, as people with more attachments are less likely to kill themselves. This best describes egoistic suicide which occurs when society has little or no control over the individual because they are not concerned by its norms or rules due to their poor social integration. According to Durkheim, those who are isolated, alienated and/or non-religious are more likely to commit an egoistic suicide as a rejection of the society around them. When society fails to provide the individual with social support then anomic suicide occurs. Society provides stable structures, such as religion and family, to offer social support and give meaning to one's life. When these are absent the individual lacks a sense of belonging and purpose, and this social state is known as anomie (meaning 'without law'). Bizarrely, this can occur through the sudden acquisition of wealth and/or status as well as the sudden loss of both. The key is the suddenness of the change in social circumstances rather than simply a negative change. The anomic suicide is therefore the act of an individual who has been let down by society. In contrast to both egoistic and anomic suicides, individuals who are well integrated into society sacrifice their lives for the good of others as the supreme act of altruism. Altruistic suicide is very common if the definition of suicide is broad; for example, there are countless examples of soldiers who willingly sacrifice their lives for their comrades.[16]

Suicide is normally considered a psychiatric problem, which then becomes the frame of reference most commentators use to understand suicide. Investigations of why someone killed themselves usually start from this premise and look for signs of abnormality in the background of the individual. Suicide is common in most psychiatric disorders, with around one in 10 sufferers of the most common disorders committing suicide.[17] As most psychiatric disorders are precipitated by stressful life events, such as bereavement, divorce or unemployment, most analyses focus on identifying these stressors. A common misconception in these analyses is that stress *per se* is the problem; however, it is, in fact, the way in which the individual copes with such stress that is the key to the subsequent pathology. Common sources of stress are serious illnesses, abusive relationships/environments and occupational stress. Against this background of coping with the stresses and strains of everyday life, there sometimes appears to be a shift in thinking. Shneidman argues that individuals lose their sense of perspective as they become preoccupied with their problems and as a result see suicide as the only effective solution. This shift in thinking is best described as hopelessness, the pessimistic belief that things will never improve, and many clinicians believe that hopelessness is the best indicator of suicidal intent. Coupled with the sense of hopelessness is dichotomous thinking, where the individual views problems and their solutions as either/or questions, for example the only way to end the pain of living is to commit suicide. This dysfunctional thinking is also susceptible to the contagion effect, where the behaviour of others acts as reinforcement. As we discussed earlier, significant others can exert a powerful influence over the individual through the mechanisms of social learning. Interpreting the actions of others favourably will encourage some individuals to act in the same way, particularly if they are vulnerable, even if it means committing suicide.

Applying this understanding of suicide to the behaviour of our dataset illustrates the limitations of viewing suicide terrorism as abnormal. As we discussed in previous chapters, none of them exhibited the acute psychiatric problems normally associated with suicidal behaviour. Most of them were well integrated into their families, religion and social groups or communities. While some were unemployed or had low-paid jobs, none of them appeared to be experiencing extreme poverty. There is little or no evidence that any of them saw suicide as a means of escaping their problems. Robert Pape argues that suicide terrorists are actually committing altruistic suicide as they believe their behaviour is for the greater good. In order to understand this argument, we need to examine the background of suicide terrorism in the Middle East. Despite a long history of suicide attacks throughout the world, the reference point for our dataset is Lebanon in the 1980s.[18]

At around 6.20 a.m. on 23 October 1983, a truck bomb drove through the gates of the US Marine Corps Headquarters at Beirut International Airport. The driver detonated the explosives it carried, collapsing the four-storey building and killing 241 Marines. About two minutes later, another suicide truck bomb was exploded underneath the French army barracks about 6km away, levelling the eight-storey building and killing 58 paratroopers. These two near simultaneous attacks are widely considered to have led to the withdrawal of the International Peacekeeping Force that had occupied Beirut in the aftermath of the 1982 Israeli invasion of Lebanon. Eventually, the campaign of suicide attacks also led to the withdrawal of the Israeli Defence Force. It is widely believed that these two suicide attacks were conducted by *Hezbollah*, although the Islamic *Jihad* actually claimed responsibility. Ultimately, for our analysis, it is not important who actually did it; the key point is that previously weak paramilitaries were able to force not one, but three modern military forces to withdraw from Lebanon. The implications of this attack for resistance fighters throughout the world were obvious.

Hezbollah is universally seen as an Islamist terrorist or resistance group, but Pape's analysis of their 41 suicide attackers between 1982 and 1986 found that very few could be described as Islamists. In fact, the majority (27) were socialists or communists and three were Christians. Only eight of the attackers could be described as Islamists as they were affiliated with the Islamic *Jihad*. The important question is: why did these individuals volunteer to die for *Hezbollah*? As with our dataset, these suicide attackers did not fit the usual profile of someone who commits suicide. The more likely explanation put forward by Pape is that these individuals saw the ultimate goal of their suicide attack as the expulsion of foreign occupiers from the Lebanon. In this context, these suicides are best described as altruistic suicides, as the attack serves the interests of the nation over the interests of the individual. Caution needs to be exercised in this simplistic interpretation, as there are many rewards associated with these suicide attacks and therefore selfless sacrifice may not be the sole motivation. As it is the wider community that assigns the status of martyr to the individual rather than the individual themselves, the mainstream discourse within a community creates the conditions for martyrdom. *Hezbollah* ensures that their members who are killed during combat or in 'martyrdom' operations are remembered and revered by the community. Posters are put up and streets are renamed after those who have been martyred. 'Martyrdom' videos are made and aired on news channels and the internet. As we saw in previous chapters, acquiring this status could be a powerful motivation and therefore achieving such status will attract some individuals.

The 'martyrdom' videos of Mohammed Siddique Khan, Tanweer and the Airline cell support this notion. In their videos, they make it clear that their acts are a response to Western actions in Muslim countries and are designed to bring an end to Western oppression of Muslim peoples. But there is more than this to the actions of the dataset, whose ultimate goal is the establishment of Islamic states in the Muslim world. This could also be described as being altruistic, because in the Islamist ideology they believe that by establishing Islamist regimes they will be freeing mankind from the oppression of manmade laws and ushering in a period of human rights and dignity for all mankind.

Hezbollah's example is widely believed to have inspired the two longest campaigns of suicide terror in recent years, in the Palestinian territories and Sri Lanka. The Liberation Tigers of Tamil Eelam ('Tamil Tigers') are often credited with having conducted the largest number of suicide attacks prior to the ongoing insurgency in Iraq.[19] The Tamil Tigers are seeking a Tamil homeland (Eelam) in the North and East of Sri Lanka, and so are therefore a nationalist movement, who portray themselves as a secular organisation and so disavow religious motivations for their resistance. This indicates that suicide attacks are not the sole preserve of religious resistance movements; however, the Tamil Tigers do exploit religious differences between the various communities in Sri Lanka. There is strong community support for suicide attacks among the Tamil population, although war weariness may have reduced this support in recent years.[20] Again, the Tamil Tigers go to great lengths to ensure that their martyrs are celebrated by the community with a national day of celebration on 5 July, Heroes Day, and there are posters, parades and monuments to the martyrs.

In the Palestinian territories of the West Bank and Gaza Strip, there are numerous organisations that have used suicide attackers. The most high-profile of these organisations is *Harakat al Muqawamah al Islamiyya* (Islamic Resistance Movement or *Hamas*) which currently governs the Gaza Strip. Bloom argues that the use of suicide attacks by Palestinian organisations involves a process of outbidding where suicide attacks are used to gain support from the community. The use of suicide attacks drew popular support from the Palestinian government towards the Islamist resistance groups and this tactic became so successful that secular groups, such as the Marxist Democratic Front for the Liberation of Palestine, started using the terminology of *jihad* and conducting suicide attacks.[21] Pape argues that the apparent success of *Hamas* and Islamic *Jihad* in forcing the Israeli Defence Force to withdraw from the Gaza Strip in 1994 and West Bank towns in 1995 demonstrated to the Palestinians the effectiveness of suicide attacks.[22] This obviously created the impetus for the outbidding process described by Bloom, because these other groups did not start using suicide attacks until the second *intifada* began in 2000. One factor in this process was the lack of support for suicide attacks within the community prior to the start of the second *intifada*. Once it had begun, however, community support was high, despite the obvious negative impact on the community from Israeli counter-strikes. Again, the celebration of the martyrs was commonplace, with the added dimension of financial, as well as spiritual, rewards for the *shaheed* and their families. In the Gaza Strip, where there is widespread unemployment and extreme poverty, the financial rewards offered for the surviving family of the *shaheed* may contribute to the decision to undertake a martyrdom operation.

The examples of *Hezbollah*, the Tamil Tigers and the various Palestinian groups clearly show that, if the conditions are right, communities will support the use of suicide attacks even if it is to their own detriment. However, within the wider Muslim population of the UK, this is not the case. The so-called 'martyrs' are not celebrated within the Muslim population of the UK as they are in the Palestinian territories, Sri Lanka and Lebanon. Indeed, there is widespread renunciation from the majority of the Muslim population for acts of terrorism in the UK. Instead, the memory of those who die is kept alive within the collective memory of the radicalised networks of which they were part and the *ummah*. One of the main ways of doing this is through *jihadi* websites such as Islamic Awakening and Caravan of Martyrs, which have entries for a number of British 'martyrs'. This means that the analysis of suicide attacks outside of the UK may not be directly applicable to the situation in the UK. One key difference is the lack of an overt group or groups (based in the UK) taking responsibility for the suicide attacks and seeking support from the community.

For global *jihadis*, their community is the *ummah*; they celebrate their martyrs though their propaganda, which is disseminated through the internet and in books. Much of the *jihadi* propaganda that is circulating in the UK is a celebration of the *shaheed*. However, at least one of the British *shaheed* is actively celebrated in overseas communities. Every year a ceremony is held at the grave of Shehzad Tanweer in his home village in Pakistan. Members of his family and up to 400 guests celebrate his life and remember him as a martyr. People are invited to join in blessing Tanweer's soul by reading verses from the *Qur'an* and those present are called on to remember him as a *shahid*. His epitaph bears the inscription *'La ilaha il Mohammed dur rasool Allah'*, which means 'There is no God but Allah, and Mohammed is his messenger.'[23]

Our dataset clearly identified with Islamic resistance movements and Islamist terrorist groups in overseas conflicts and felt a strong connection to the *ummah*, but there is no clearly identifiable resistance or terrorist organisation within the UK. There is much discussion of a connection between British terrorist cells and *al Qaeda*, but only a few members of the dataset had proven links with recognised members. Instead, as discussed previously, joining the global *jihad* is primarily a 'bottom-up' process of radicalised individuals in the UK seeking training to undertake terrorist attacks in the UK. Several cells and individuals were networked with *jihadis* abroad, but the extent to which those *jihadis* directed the dataset is unclear. All that is known for certain is that they trained them with the skills required to undertake their missions. Sageman argues that a decentralised, leaderless grouping of self-radicalising cells now characterises the transnational Islamist terror threat.[24] In this context, terrorists are inspired to act by the example of others and are not directed by any group or individual. Kirby argues that, although the 7/7 cell were essentially one of these self-radicalising cells, their actions were 'the perfect realisation' of *al Qaeda*'s aim of inspiring Muslims to embrace the *jihad* and attack apostate regimes and foreign occupiers.[25] This suggests that it will be difficult to truly understand the relationship between self-radicalising cells and the wider transnational Islamist terror networks. The role of the internet in globalising Islamism is central to this relationship as it allows the widespread transnational community of Islamists to maintain contact with each other. As we discussed in previous chapters, the internet also provides access to violent media, propaganda and technical 'know how' to conduct acts of terrorism. Despite this, it is important not to overstate the significance of the internet in the radicalisation of our particular dataset. These groups were tied to physical entities, such as ideologues, mentors and other radicalised individuals, in settings such as mosques, bookshops, student Islamic societies and street gangs, rather than existing solely in cyberspace.

If we view the radicalised networks of individuals both in the UK and overseas as the *ummah*, then it is possible that the dataset perceived they had the necessary community support for their actions. As we discussed previously, the *ummah* is an idealised transnational community of the faithful bound together by their faith. The *ummah* bind these individuals to the wider struggle against 'apostate' rulers in Muslim countries and the *kuffar*, so their attacks are part of the ongoing transnational struggle supported by those international communities rather than their national community. In effect, the opinions of their non-radicalised peers who reject their actions are not important to them. It is within the radicalised communities of which they were part that these individuals would expect to find support for their actions. Sageman argues that these individuals are the 'rock stars of young Muslim militants', who seek to 'impress their friends with their heroism and sacrifice'.[26] Unfortunately, this terminology potentially trivialises what is a central motivation for human behaviour. As we discussed previously, social identity and status form the bedrock of our self-esteem. It is perfectly normal for young people to aspire to acquire social status from their peers and challenges to such social status will be robustly countered. The immediate constituency of our dataset were the radicalised networks that existed around them. They acquired status within these networks and ultimately these networks would celebrate their martyrdom.

This is evident from the rhetoric of a range of radical politico-religious groups that operate, and have previously operated, in the UK. *Hizb ut-Tahrir* insists that it does not support suicide bombings, but it has posted documents on its website which called suicide bombers martyrs,[27] as have dozens of its leaflets over the past decade. One, which was posted on the party's website in 2004 under the title 'And kill them wherever you find them', declared:

> Today the *mujahideen* in Palestine provide us with the best of examples. The youth are competing in the martyrdom operations. Young girls have started to compete with the young men for martyrdom. Mothers are pushing their sons to become *shaheed*, and they make *sujood* [religious prostration] in thanks to Allah when they hear the news of the martyrdom of their sons. A new dawn is beginning to rise on this *umma* in which *iman* [belief], *jihad*, martyrdom and victory prevail against the *kuffar*, their agents and tools. Is it not time that you yearned for *jannah* [Paradise]? ... If you neglect this duty then you will bear the sin of remaining silent, and you will be humiliated and disgraced.[28]

The *al-Ghuraba* website contained many links, including to one website which hosted articles justifying suicide bombings.[29] Another declared that the *kuffar* were trying to 'wipe out [Muslims] from the face of the earth ... cover the land with our blood through martyrdom, martyrdom, martyrdom'.[30] A spokesman for *al-Ghuraba* explicitly refused to condemn the 7 July bombings and declared, 'what I would say about those who do suicide operations or martyrdom operations is they're completely praiseworthy.'[31]

In this context, the role of religious authority figures is important because they can sanction an act of martyrdom; in particular, their religious injunctions enable 'martyrdom operations' by providing a theological justification for why it is not suicide. Suicide is forbidden in Islam, so without clerical sanction it would be much more difficult for these individuals to engage in 'martyrdom operations'. But martyrdom was a key element of the discourse of British-based Islamist ideologues and it is alleged that Omar Bakri Mohammed incited followers of *Hizb ut-Tahrir* and *al Muhajiroun* to commit acts of violence, including suicide bombings.[32] At one *al Muhajiroun* meeting, he gave a lesson entitled 'The virtue of the self-sacrifice operation', in which he said that 'people like to call it suicide bombing ... We call it self-sacrifice. You must fight for the way of Allah – to kill first and be killed.'[33] He also declared that the British *jihadis* who died in Afghanistan in 2001 were martyrs,[34] and described Omar Sharif as a martyr who had died in the cause of Muslim lands and Muslim people: 'I knew Sharif very well and he used to attend regularly at my sessions. He was my brother and I am very proud of him and any Muslim who will do the same as he did.'[35] Sheikh Abdullah el Faisal preached to his audiences that their reward for becoming martyrs would be a place in Paradise,[36] while Abu Hamza, when asked about suicide bombing by a member of his audience during another lecture, replied, 'It is not called suicide ... this is called martyring, because if the only way to hurt the enemies of Islam except by taking your life for that then it is allowed.'[37]

Notes and references

[1] 'Ramzi Mohammed: Father of two who left a suicide note', *The Times*, 10 July 2007, http://www.timesonline.co.uk/tol/news/uk/crime/article2051431.ece.

MARTYRDOM

2 'Muktar Said Ibrahim: From robbery and indecent assault to bomb plot leader', *The Times*, 10 July 2007, http://www.timesonline.co.uk/tol/news/uk/crime/article2051428.ece.

3 Ansari H, 'Attitudes to jihad, martyrdom and terrorism among British Muslims', in Abbas T (ed) *Muslim Britain: Communities under Pressure* (London: Zed Books, 2005), p 150.

4 Riyadh al Huq, 'Speech: The globalised suffering of the Muslims', *The Times*, 6 September 2007, http://www.timesonline.co.uk/tol/comment/faith/article2401855.ece?token=null&offset=48.

5 'The homegrown cleric who loathes the British', *The Times*, 7 September 2007, http://www.timesonline.co.uk/tol/news/uk/article2402998.ece.

6 Riyadh al Huq, 'Speech: The globalised suffering of the Muslims', *The Times*, 6 September 2007, http://www.timesonline.co.uk/tol/comment/faith/article2401855.ece?token=null&offset=48.

7 Burke J, *Al-Qaeda: The True Story of Radical Islam* (London: Penguin, 2004), pp 34–35.

8 'Profile: Parviz Khan', *Guardian*, 18 February 2008, http://www.guardian.co.uk/uk/2008/feb/18/uksecurity3.

9 Hafez MM, 'Dying to be martyrs: The symbolic dimension of suicide terrorism', in Pedahzur A (ed), *Root Causes of Suicide Terrorism: The Globalization of Martyrdom* (Oxford: Routledge, 2006).

10 Ansari H, 'Attitudes to jihad, martyrdom and terrorism among British Muslims', in Abbas T (ed), *Muslim Britain: Communities under Pressure* (London: Zed Books, 2005), p 150.

11 Suragah Al-Andalusi: The Last Will and Final Testament, http://www.islamicawakening.com/viewarticle.php?articleID=713&pageID=235&pageID=234&.

12 *Qu'ran* 3:169–70.

13 Ansari H, 'Attitudes to jihad, martyrdom and terrorism among British Muslims', in Abbas T (ed), *Muslim Britain: Communities under Pressure* (London: Zed Books, 2005), p 151.

14 Burke J, *Al-Qaeda: The True Story of Radical Islam* (London: Penguin, 2004), p 74.

[15] Shneidman ES (ed), *Comprehending Suicide: Landmarks in 20th-century Suicidology* (American Psychological Association, 2001).

[16] Durkheim E, 'Suicide: A study in sociology', summarised in Shneidman ES (ed), *Comprehending Suicide: Landmarks in 20th-century Suicidology* (American Psychological Association, 2001).

[17] American Psychiatric Association, *Diagnostic and Statistical Manual of Mental Disorders*, 4th Edition Text Revised. American Psychiatric Association, Washington, DC, 2000.

[18] Pape R, *Dying to Win: Why Suicide Bombers Do It* (New York: Random House, 2005).

[19] Bloom M, *Dying to Kill: The Allure of Suicide Terror* (New York: Columbia University Press, 2006); Pape R, *Dying to Win: Why Suicide Bombers Do It* (New York: Random House, 2005).

[20] Bloom M, *Dying to Kill: The Allure of Suicide Terror* (New York: Columbia University Press, 2006); Pape R, *Dying to Win: Why Suicide Bombers Do It* (New York: Random House, 2005).

[21] Bloom M, *Dying to Kill: The Allure of Suicide Terror* (New York: Columbia University Press, 2006).

[22] Pape R, *Dying to Win: Why Suicide Bombers Do It* (New York: Random House, 2005).

[23] 'Relatives of July 7 bomber hold PARTY at his grave to "celebrate his life"', *Evening Standard*, 7 July 2008, http://www.thisislondon.co.uk/news/article-23511590-details/Relatives+of+July+7+bomber+hold+PARTY+at+his+grave+to+%27celebrate+his+life%27/article.do.

[24] Sageman M, 'Radicalization of global Islamist terrorists', Evidence to the United States Senate Committee on Homeland Security and Governmental Affairs, 27 June 2007.

[25] Kirby A, 'The London bombers as "self starters": A case study in indigenous radicalization and the emergence of autonomous cliques', *Studies in Conflict and Terrorism*, No. 30, 2007, pp 415–28.

[26] Sageman M, 'Radicalization of global Islamist terrorists', Evidence to the United States Senate Committee on Homeland Security and Governmental Affairs, 27 June 2007.

[27] 'Blair bid to ban group "opposed"', BBC NewsOnline, 19 November 2006, http://news.bbc.co.uk/1/hi/uk/6162690.stm.

28 Malik S, 'Society NS Profile – Omar Sharif', *New Statesman*, 24 April 2006, http://www.newstatesman.com/200604240017.

29 'Profile: Omar Bakri Mohammad', BBC NewsOnline, 21 July 2005, http://news.bbc.co.uk/1/hi/uk/4703541.stm.

30 *Sunday Times*, 7 August 2005.

31 'Prevention and Suppression of Terrorism', *Hansard*, Column 490, 20 July 2006.

32 Phillips M, *Londonistan* (London: Gibson Square Books, 2006), p 51.

33 'Suicide bomber recruitment in the UK', BBC NewsOnline, 10 February 2004, http://news.bbc.co.uk/1/hi/uk/3475929.stm.

34 'Cleric preaches that violence is part of Islam', *Daily Telegraph*, 1 May 2007, http://www.telegraph.co.uk/news/main.jhtml?xml=/news/2007/05/01/nplot901.xml.

35 'British suicide bomber identified', *Daily Telegraph*, 20 May 2003, http://www.telegraph.co.uk/news/main.jhtml?xml=/news/2003/05/20/nbomb20.xml.

36 'Cleric preached racist views', BBC NewsOnline, 24 February 2003, http://news.bbc.co.uk/1/hi/uk/2784591.stm.

37 'Key to proving Hamza's hate', BBC NewsOnline, 7 February 2006, http://news.bbc.co.uk/1/hi/uk/4670906.stm.

Chapter 10

conclusion: The Rationality of Martyrdom

The purpose of our analysis is to explain why our dataset were prepared to commit acts of terrorism and why some of them were prepared to make the ultimate sacrifice for what they believed. The most natural reaction to terrorism is that the perpetrators are 'abnormal', as no 'normal' person would do such a thing. Thinking along these lines may reinforce our faith in the rest of humanity but, unfortunately, the evidence to support such faith is lacking. The much more consistent pattern of behaviour emerging from history is that many 'normal' people are willing and able to perpetrate acts of terrorism, mass murder and even genocide. As we discussed in Chapter 1, this may be due to the disposition of the people committing such crimes or to the situation in which they find themselves. As we discussed in Chapter 8, the Milgram experiment clearly shows that the majority of us can potentially be manipulated into perpetrating such crimes by authority figures. The troubling question for all of us is how we would react if we were in such a situation.

In order for us to answer that question, we need to think about our own psychological processes and in particular how we make decisions. The most simplistic description of the decision-making

275

process is economic. We are all faced with countless decisions every single day, some incredibly trivial, some life changing, but the psychological process is the same. Each decision maker is attempting to obtain the best outcome they possibly can from the choices in front of them, and to do so they must evaluate the costs and benefits of the outcome of each choice. The choice with the most advantageous ratio of costs to benefits will provide the best possible outcome. A good example is buying a new car, as the benefits of the car are easily articulated (e.g. good aesthetics, good reliability, low fuel consumption, right size for garage, high status value) and so are the costs (e.g. poor aesthetics, purchase price, high fuel consumption, poor reliability, wrong size for garage, low status value). While we would like to maximise our choice and purchase the perfect car that is beautiful to look at and cheap to purchase and run, the reality is that this perfect car does not exist, and we have to make compromises. Therefore, each car we look at will have a different cost/benefit ratio that we will have to analyse in order to make our decision. In traditional economics, this cost/benefit analysis would be logical and based on the economics of the different cost/benefit ratios presented by each choice, commonly called Rational Choice theory. The logical nature of this analysis and thus the final decision has defined rationality since the Ancient Greek philosophers. By extraction, failure to follow purely logical deductive reasoning when making decisions is irrational. Most of us would describe irrational behaviour as simply not logical.

A good example of irrational behaviour is addiction to drugs. On the face of it, most of us would view people dependent on drugs as irrational. It does not appear to make much sense to use drugs such as heroin and crack cocaine that effectively destroy your life. At the most basic level, every addict makes continuous decisions about whether to use drugs or lead a drug-free life. Even at the very first opportunity to use drugs, the potential addict is faced with this decision. Given the widespread cultural taboos against the illegal use of drugs that are communicated through every possible mechanism of social learning (such as the media, schools, religious institutions and the family), it is just not credible to argue that young people are unaware of the consequences of using drugs. Young people must decide to use drugs knowing the risks that they take. As we discussed in Chapter 1, there are numerous stable and systematic errors in judgements that we all make. In this context, the most salient cognitive error is the optimism bias, where the decision maker believes that the negative impact of their decision will not happen to them. Smokers are a good example. Smoking will most likely kill the smoker through one of a number of smoking-related diseases or severely reduce the quality of their lives through ill-health, yet many people start smoking and continue to smoke. Many smokers rationalise their addiction by arguing that the negative consequences of smoking are not certain and that, as one of their relatives who smoked lived to a ripe old age, they too may not experience any negative consequences.

The reason why the optimism bias is so effective in undermining our decision making is that the outcomes of our decisions are in the future, even if only microseconds, and, as such, these outcomes are actually uncertain. Therefore, we are, in fact, making judgements based on probability. The addict is making a decision based on the certainty of the drug's effects after consuming it versus the uncertainty of a successful and healthy drug-free life. This decision has a temporal component and therefore the decision maker is gambling on the future outcome of their decision.

The inability to delay gratification is a core feature of impulsive behaviour. According to the model of delay discounting, impulsivity is defined as the choosing of smaller immediate rewards over larger rewards to be received after some delay. That is, the value of a delayed reinforcer is reduced in value, or considered to be worth less, compared to the value of an immediate reinforcer because of the time taken to receive the reward. Accordingly, self-control, the opposite of impulsive behaviour, means engaging in behaviour which leads to larger delayed rewards.

One reason why the delayed rewards are considered to be worth less than the immediate rewards is the time perspective of the decision maker.[1] While it is generally considered that the passage of time is objective in that minutes, hours and days are fixed in duration, the actual perception of time is subjective. How the individual conceptualises time is also subjective and there is considerable evidence that different people's time perspective varies. Some people clearly live for the moment and do not consider the future. They tend to be hedonists who focus on acquiring the good things in life. Some people are mired in the past and constantly refer back to their former selves, sometimes reflecting on past glories and sometimes ruminating on past mistakes. What has happened to these people in the past casts a long shadow into their future. Still others look to the future, sometimes looking forward to the great things ahead of them and sometimes perceiving the future to be bleak and empty. The former will plan for the future at the expense of the present, while the latter will live for the moment as they do not perceive themselves to have a future. Many members of teenage street gangs also fit into this category because they believe that they will probably be murdered by rival gang members before they reach adulthood. These differences in time perspective explain why some people are unable to delay gratification. The hedonists do not think of the future, as it is something that they will think about when it happens, and they see no point in delaying gratification. Those who are fatalistic about the future do not think about it because they believe there is no future, and their view that there is no point in delaying gratification is based on their belief that they will not be here to reap the benefits. Egoistic and anomic suicides would be more common in people who are fatalistic about the future.

By looking at the decision making of drug addicts from the perspective of the drug addict themselves, it is possible to see the rationality of the decision to use drugs. If there is nothing in the future that is worth working for, then there is no real incentive to work for it. On the other hand, if drugs provide an immediate sense of wellbeing and happiness, then there is an incentive to use drugs. The short-term risks of using drugs are uncertain, as there is the possibility of an overdose, while the short-term benefits are certain, as the drug will have its effect. The long-term risks of using drugs are also uncertain, as your life may be cut short or it may not, but the long-term benefits of not using drugs are also uncertain, as you are not guaranteed a successful and healthy life. In this very oversimplified model of the decision to use drugs, it is clear that the only certainty in this decision is that drugs will provide an immediate benefit if you take them. For young people with a bright future, the probability of success in their lives is high; however, for some young people with more limited prospects, the probability is much lower.

To put these decisions into context, we need to look at the development of drug dependency. Drug addicts do not decide that they want to become drug addicts. Instead, they are faced with a series of decisions whether to use drugs or not. When they first come into contact with drugs, the decisions will be different to ones they make once they have become addicted, although the basic decision is the same, but the contingencies in the cost/benefit analysis have changed. In the beginning, young people are faced with making decisions over smoking cannabis. Most young people have a fairly benign view of cannabis and so large numbers of them smoke it. After a while they may come into contact with other, more dangerous, drugs, such as ecstasy or cocaine. As they are already using cannabis, they may be more well disposed to using these drugs. Their friends may also use them and they can probably afford them. For some young people they will begin to use drugs more often than not. Soon their friends may be replaced by new, drug-using ones. Eventually, they will come into contact with heroin or crack cocaine. Up to this point they have been using drugs that they feel they have some 'control' over in that they can continue a normal life. This sense of control is transferred on to heroin or crack cocaine so the potential addict optimistically believes that they will control their use rather than the desire for drugs controlling them. Unfortunately for the drug user they do not realise that the drugs undermine their self-control and so they eventually become addicted. So, while the young person may not have set out to become a drug addict, with each successive decision, the incremental process occurs. Obviously, it is not a foregone conclusion that every cannabis smoker will become a heroin addict, as there is much more to addiction than the simplistic model that we describe here. However, the rationality of addiction indicates that martyrdom can also be the result of rational decision making.

We need to view the decision to become a martyr from the perspective of the individual and use that as our frame of reference for understanding how and why they made their decisions. As we discussed in Chapter 2, we have both a cognitive (i.e. rational) and emotional connection to our social identities. Therefore, the emotional identification with the social identity of Islamist martyr will affect the cost/benefit analysis of martyrdom. For the potential martyr, the benefits of martyrdom must be greater than the costs of the martyrdom operation. From the outside looking in, it is hard to empathise with the belief that one will achieve more in death than one ever would in life. This is because we are focusing on the act of martyrdom as a single decision, when in fact it is a series of much smaller, less consequential decisions (as it is with using drugs). As we described in Chapter 8, the Milgram experiment only succeeded because the decision to 'kill' was an incremental process of smaller decisions that effectively bound the participant to continuing with the experiment. We must therefore understand these small, incremental decisions if we are to understand martyrdom.

THE THREE PHASES OF ISLAMIST TERRORISM IN THE UK

In order to understand the actions of our dataset we must first accept that each one of them made a decision to become an Islamist terrorist. However, it is highly unlikely that they woke up one morning and decided to run off to Afghanistan and train to become a *mujahideen* or a *shahid*. As described above, the most basic model of decision making is the cost/benefit analysis provided by Rational Choice theory. The cost/benefit analyses involved in these decisions will be influenced by a range of risk and protective factors. A risk factor indicates the individual is vulnerable to making the decision to engage in violent extremism, while a protective factor reduces the vulnerability of the individual. As the number of risk factors increases, so does the individual's vulnerability but it does not make it inevitable that they will become a violent extremist. It will probably be impossible to truly know why any individual becomes a violent extremist, as the only person who can answer that question may not be aware themselves. By identifying risk and protective factors, we can begin to understand the process of becoming a violent extremist.

Risk Factors for Passive Recruitment

British society is riven with endemic social problems, such as crime, unemployment, inequality and discrimination. We are all exposed to these problems, even if only through watching the news on television or reading a newspaper, and they become talking points in our everyday lives. As we discussed in Chapters 2, 3 and 4, there are some social problems facing British Muslims that may provide an impetus for them to do something more than merely talk about such problems. For the purposes of understanding the process of radicalisation, we will call these passive recruitment factors, which comprise any event or social problem that resonates with the social identity and experiences of British Muslims. The reason that we have termed these factors 'passive' is that they exist for the entire Muslim population of the UK and therefore it is not something over which the individual has any control. As we discussed in Chapter 6, Islamist recruiters may exploit these passive factors to attract potential recruits into their networks or organisations through their propaganda. Up to the point that the individual decides to act upon their response to these factors, the influence is still passive.

Religious Knowledge

There is evidence that individuals with limited religious knowledge may be more vulnerable than others to radicalisation with a violent Islamist ideology. Among the dataset, Omar Sharif and the six converts to Islam particularly demonstrated this risk factor. Yet the dataset also includes individuals who had been well schooled in Islam from a young age by mainstream Imams, such as Tanweer, Badat and Hanif.

Nevertheless, increased religious observance was a feature of the radicalisation of many of the dataset.[2] In many cases, this was a reflection of their rediscovering Islam after leading a Westernised lifestyle, often involving alcohol and drugs. As described in Chapter 2, it would be wholly wrong to suggest that increasing religious observance *per se* poses a risk factor for violent extremism. Instead, our analysis clearly shows that increased religious observance may be subverted by radical and militant Islamists through the exploitation of the individuals' lack of religious knowledge and language skills. It is therefore the subversion of increasing religious observance among those with limited knowledge of Islam that constitutes the risk factor.

Social Identity

The diversity within the Muslim population of the UK indicates that there is no uniform sense of Muslim social identity. Some sections of the Muslim population are still developing an understanding of how to reconcile their faith and Islamic social identity with living in a secular multicultural society that poses modern social challenges. Some young Muslims find that the traditionalism of their parents' generation and their view of Islam do not equip them for dealing with these challenges, leading to generational and cultural conflicts within Muslim communities. For some, their reaction can be to look for an alternative brand of Islam to the one their parents taught them. Part of the allure of Islamism is that it provides a more prominent form of Islamic social identity. For young South Asians in particular, Islamism offers an alternative to the *biradri* system, which seems to empower them and challenges the more traditional elements of their culture, through encouraging the active participation of women, rejecting arranged marriages and opposing honour killings. Neither fully Western nor Eastern, this discourse of alternative Islamist identity is 'supra-cultural' and identifies with an idealised *ummah*. It is also profoundly anti-Western.

Social Status

Social status is an important element of both individual and group social identity, and seemingly trivial challenges to this social status can lead to violent behaviour. Real and perceived status inequalities can generate significant inter-group animosity and conflict. Real and perceived inter-group conflict is a common feature in the social background of the dataset, some of whom became involved with gang violence, particularly in 'defending' Muslim communities against racist attacks, but also in responding to apparent indications of 'disrespect' with violence.

International Politics

Awareness of international affairs is one of the main risk factors for passive recruitment into radical political groups and terrorist networks. Among the main issues have been the wars in Bosnia, Kosovo, Chechnya, Kashmir and Somalia in which Muslims are seen to be suffering as a result of the unwillingness of the international community to intervene. But there are also broader concerns about the underlying motivations of Western and US foreign policy, in terms of being anti-Islamic and neo-colonialist in seeking to spread US cultural hegemony throughout the Muslim world, and control the natural resources of Muslim nations. These concerns were also heightened after 9/11, as a result of US (and British) policies in the 'war on terror'.

British Foreign Policy and the 'War on Terror'

British foreign policy in the 'war on terror' has led to the increased alienation of many Muslims from the political mainstream.

Opposition to the wars in Afghanistan and Iraq is one of the issues on which the views of radical political and religious groups dovetail with the mainstream discourse of the Muslim population. Militant Islamist and terrorist groups have exploited these sentiments with rhetoric about an Islamic duty to fight for justice and to protect the *ummah*, as well as claims that these wars are part of a wider war on Islam, a modern-day crusade. These conflicts have added impetus to the politicisation of young Muslims, and fostered increased levels of activism.

It is a reasonable assumption that all of the dataset were angry about the war on terror and were opposed to the British government's policy of supporting the US, but it was not the catalyst which triggered the start of their political radicalisation because virtually all of them were radicalised prior to 9/11. A few members of the dataset were involved in terrorism before 9/11, but British involvement in the 'war on terror' can be viewed as a trigger for many of the others to either engage in terrorist violence or redirect their violence towards terrorism in the UK. In particular, Mohammed Siddique Khan and Khyam initially sought to fight in *jihad* overseas, and it was not until after the invasion of Iraq that they were persuaded to become terrorists in the UK.

Counter-Terrorism Policy in the UK

The other significant aspect of the 'war on terror' that has impacted on the radicalisation of young British Muslims is domestic counter-terrorism policy. Relations between the Muslim population and the police have worsened since 9/11 and the 7 July bombings, as anti-terrorism legislation has been increasingly strengthened and used against individuals and cells operating within the Muslim population. Muslim communities are increasingly concerned about the use of anti-terrorism legislation and claim that they are being disproportionately targeted. As a result, many British Muslims feel that their communities are being unfairly tarnished with the suspicion of terrorism.

CONCLUSION: THE RATIONALITY OF MARTYRDOM

Community Defence

In order to counter threats directed towards their communities, some individuals are taking it upon themselves to defend them. This leads to the formation of street gangs for the purpose of fighting real and perceived threats from outside, which is one of the initial ways that individuals can be socialised into the use of violence. To a certain extent, the existence of these gangs is an indication of young Muslims' disillusionment with the way that their elders handle issues affecting the younger generation and their alienation from their traditional communities, as it is an indication of their alienation from wider society.

These gangs are not necessarily ideologically driven. Among the dataset, Shahid Butt was a member of this type of gang. This lack of an ideological foundation has meant that many of these gangs have subsequently descended into criminal activity as overt physical threats from racists have diminished, as happened with Butt's gang. In contrast, some other gangs are ideologically driven. For some second- and third-generation Muslims who are more prepared than their parents' generation to confront injustice and racism, the confrontational ideology of militant groups could be perceived to reflect the reality of the situation in which they live and offer solutions to it. These gangs have wider agendas than just community defence, and they tend to reject mainstream society and enforce separatism between Muslim communities and those living adjacent to them. Mohammed Siddique Khan and Tanweer both belonged to a gang of this nature. In addition, some radical Islamist groups have also acted like gangs. Ed Husain described how members of *Hizb ut-Tahrir* and the Young Muslim Organisation UK, which was part of *Jamaat-e-Islami*, could be as violent in defending their 'turf' as any of the street gangs in his East London neighbourhood.

It is important to stress that Muslim street gangs are not necessarily a breeding ground for terrorists and individuals who engage in street violence will not necessarily go on to become involved in terrorism. Nevertheless, membership of a gang often reflects alienation from

285

their own community leaders as well as wider society, and these are exactly the kind of individuals that radical Islamist groups and terrorist cells try to recruit.

The Mainstream Media

The mainstream media is one of the key actors informing and influencing public opinion. Media reporting of the 'war on terror' has evoked a considerable reaction from the Muslim population of the UK. This has focused around four main issues: exposing the government's rationale for the invasion of Iraq; reporting the suffering of Muslim civilians in Afghanistan and Iraq; reporting of the domestic terror threat; and reporting *al Qaeda* propaganda. Importantly, a reporting bias that emphasises atrocities committed by Western forces (e.g. in Abu Ghraib) while under-reporting atrocities committed by their opponents (e.g. crimes committed in Saddam's prisons) facilitates the construction of narratives whereby Muslims perceive themselves to be targeted, and Western actions to be illegitimate.

In reporting the domestic terrorism threat, the UK media is frequently accused by British Muslims of having an anti-Muslim bias. This criticism falls into four broad groups: sensationalism; insensitive use of terminology such as 'Muslim terrorism'; lack of publicity given to the release of terror suspects; and outright errors in reporting which are not corrected. The principal question is to what extent media reporting contributes to the radicalisation of UK Muslims. Many Muslims believe that the media is demonising both them and their religion, and as a result is whipping up 'Islamophobia' within the wider population of the UK. The record of the media in reporting the 'war on terror' is open to criticism on a number of points, and, while not all of the criticism that is directed its way might be considered to be valid, it is the perception within the Muslim population that is crucial, and it largely perceives the media to be hostile.

CONCLUSION: THE RATIONALITY OF MARTYRDOM

The Internet

The significance of the internet in the radicalisation process lies in the fact that it enables terrorists to disseminate propaganda when they want to, and in a completely unadulterated fashion. In the mainstream media, news editors determine how militant and terrorist messages are reported, thereby lessening their impact. What the internet offers the individual are opportunities for finding additional information and viewpoints beyond what appears in that mainstream media, particularly information from outside of the UK. There is no evidence that any members of the dataset were radicalised either solely or partly through exposure to propaganda that they found on the internet, but a number of them possessed terrorist propaganda videos or DVDs that had been downloaded from the internet.

This suggests that it is the interface between the internet and alternative media which is a significant factor in the effective spreading of militant and terrorist propaganda. The easy availability of DVD rewriters means that militant videos can be downloaded from the internet and burned on to DVD for distribution through personal contacts and networks. While the internet offers a mechanism for reaching a mass audience, videos and DVDs are perhaps more important in the radicalisation process because they allow recruiters and small groups to view and discuss this propaganda material in secrecy, enabling recruiters to exert face-to-face influence on individuals and exploit small-group dynamics.

The internet also offers a communication forum to enable disaffected individuals to communicate with militant facilitators and recruiters who can deepen this radicalisation even further. There is evidence that some individuals who have been prosecuted for non-violent terrorist offences may have been wholly or partly radicalised through contacts made on the internet. However, virtually all of the dataset were already part of Islamist networks, and their indoctrination took place face to face, with mentors and Islamist ideologues.

While much attention has focused on the internet, the mainstream media probably had a much more significant impact on starting the process of radicalisation of the dataset. This was due to the full and frank reporting of conflicts such as those in Chechnya, Iraq and Afghanistan, which fully exposed the suffering of Muslim civilians.

Risk Factors for Active Recruitment

The first 'decision point' occurs when the individual decides that the passive recruitment factors they experience require them to actually *do* something in order to rectify the situation. This decision could be considered the point at which the individual becomes radicalised. For the purposes of this model, radicalised individuals are political rather than violent. This is also a decision that we can clearly identify in the individual's behaviour, for example they may join one of the radical groups that we discussed in Chapter 5. Again, for the purposes of understanding the process of radicalisation, we will call these active recruitment factors. An active recruitment factor will be the active participation of the individual in any of the groups and networks that exist in the UK which may bring them into contact with transnational Islamists. Active recruitment occurs when an individual actively seeks out or is sought out by violent extremists. During an individual's interaction with these violent extremists, they may decide that violence is the only answer to the problems facing them. Some opinion polls suggest that approximately one per cent of the Muslim population of the UK might have supported the 7 July bombings, and up to 14 per cent might believe that it is right to use violence for political ends. But 14 per cent of British Muslims have not engaged in terrorist violence. This suggests that there are other factors underlying why only some individuals seek to join terrorist groups or agree to do so when approached by a terrorist recruiter. The decision to use violence to attain political goals defines the violent extremist for the purposes of this model.

CONCLUSION: THE RATIONALITY OF MARTYRDOM

Charity Work

One way of making the transition from passive support for a cause to active involvement in it is by engaging in charity work. For Muslims, donating money to charity is one of the pillars of Islam. However, for some members of the dataset, involvement in charity work can be argued to have been part of the incremental process of activism, and was an important first step in moving from passive to active support for Islamist causes. In many instances, this charity work merely involved relief work for suffering Muslim civilians, but transnational terrorist or *mujahideen* groups have also raised funds in the UK under the guise of charity work. Several members of the dataset have been identified as raising funds for radical groups or *jihadis* overseas.

Participation in Radical Political Groups

Islamist activity in the Muslim population of the UK has primarily been linked to a number of high-profile individuals and the radical political and religious groups associated with them, notably *Hizb ut-Tahrir*, *al Muhajiroun* and Supporters of *Sha'ria*. There are also other local groups or networks, which have no names or labels, such as the one which Mohammed Siddique Khan and Tanweer were part of in Beeston. These are not terrorist groups, but they share similar ideologies, beliefs and goals. Joining such groups and networks is a significant act for an individual in moving from passive to active support for a militant cause or ideology. It demonstrates both a heightened level of commitment and also a willingness to act on their convictions. For a number of individuals in the dataset, therefore, involvement with these groups can be seen as a significant milestone in their radicalisation.

These groups have an Islamist ideology which is political in nature but is firmly rooted in the religion of Islam. While they pursue political goals, such as opposition to Western foreign policy in the Middle East, they also reject manmade laws and believe that Muslims should live in states governed by *Sha'ria* law. Consequently, they also argue that Muslim regimes which do not govern according to *Sha'ria* law are 'apostate' and should be overthrown. Significantly, their beliefs and actions are justified by reference to the *Qur'an* and other Islamic concepts, such as the *ummah*. However, the way they use the *Qur'an* is often partial, with passages taken out of historical context, thereby enabling them to adapt the meaning to suit their political purposes. It is therefore impossible to separate the political from the religious aspects of their ideological belief systems, which is why it is commonly defined as 'political Islam'. This synthesis of politics and Islam is best reflected in *Hizb ut-Tahrir*'s objective of re-establishing the *caliphate*. These groups promote ideological hatred of the West, but they also use Islam to generate religious hatred between their supporters and non-Muslims.

The same people are often linked to a range of different groups, which often tend to be loose associations rather than organisations in the traditional sense. These groups and networks intersect with each other to comprise an amorphous nationwide network of radicalised networks. This nationwide network provides the groundswell of radicalised individuals that terrorist recruiters and facilitators tap into, and within which smaller terror cells and networks exist.

Involvement with such organisations does not automatically presuppose socialisation into terrorist activity; for example, Ed Husain left *Hizb ut-Tahrir* without ever engaging in terrorist activity. Instead, for many young Muslims looking to rebel against their taught values, the wider community or the government, involvement in these groups can simply provide a cathartic and vocal 'pressure valve' for anxieties, frustrations and a sense of helplessness. On the other hand, it might also be the case that would-be terrorists might view the activities of these groups as 'pointless pontification and debate' and simply by-pass them as they seek to join a terrorist group or network. Nevertheless, these groups and their members did interface with terror groups, recruiters and facilitators, and participation in such groups can be a significant stepping stone in the process of becoming a violent extremist.

CONCLUSION: THE RATIONALITY OF MARTYRDOM

Social Status

The status of the individual's social identity can be a key motivation for their behaviour. There is considerable evidence that members of the dataset sought and acquired status from their activities within radicalised networks.

Active Recruiters

Some individuals are active recruiters for networks of violent extremists and transnational terrorist organisations. These individuals typically have extensive experience of working within such networks and organisations, and some have direct experience of previous conflicts. They move within the networks of radicalised individuals and recruit selected individuals into terrorist cells. Many of the cells in the dataset seem to have been recruited directly by their *emirs*.

There appear to be two distinct but interconnected recruitment processes at work among the dataset. At one level, they are indoctrinated with an extremist politico-religious ideology. This ideology justifies the use of violence for religious and political ends, but adherence to the ideology does not in itself mean that an individual is necessarily willing to commit an act of violence. At another level, therefore, individuals need to make the step change to being prepared to commit an act of violence.

This ideological indoctrination is an incremental process. The Official Narrative of the 7 July bombings reported that the role of personal mentors and then bonding with a group of fellow extremists appears to have been critical in the radicalisation of many terrorists. The mentors and others doing the indoctrination vary from authority figures, such as Abu Hamza and Abu Qatada, to other rank and file militants. After initial contact, recruiters 'groom' them through subsequent contacts, often privately in small groups until groupthink occurs. Part of this incremental process is to actively draw individuals away from mainstream society and the potentially moderating influences in their lives which serve as protective factors.

After ideological indoctrination mentors gradually move on to what they claim is the religious justification for violent *jihad* in the *Qur'an* and the *Hadith*. If suicide attacks are the intention, the importance of martyrdom in demonstrating commitment to Islam and the rewards in Paradise for martyrs are emphasised (see below). Hassan Butt, a former recruiter for *al Muhajiroun*, revealed, 'We were very well versed in the *Qur'an*, in the verses of the *Qur'an*, in the sayings of the Prophet and show that how it was permissible for people to go around killing innocent men, women and children.'[3]

Propagandists

The Official Narrative of the 7 July bombings reported that the influence of an extremist spiritual leader may be important in the radicalisation process, either through direct meetings and sermons or via video, DVD and written material.[4] During the 1990s and early 21st century, there were a number of extremist preachers operating openly in the UK, including Abu Hamza, Abdullah el Faisal, Omar Bakri Mohammed and Abu Qatada, who may have contributed towards the radicalisation of a number of the dataset and an unknown number of other people.

The role of the propagandist is to spread the ideology of the violent extremist networks and provide justification for acts of terror conducted by violent extremists around the world. Throughout history, race, culture and religion have been used by extremists to advocate violent behaviour. In particular, religious texts, which are often open to interpretation and selective quoting (often out of context), have been exploited by extremists to create a religious justification for violent behaviour. They are generally charismatic individuals who can connect at an intellectual or emotional level with their audience. Operational terrorists would generally steer clear of such public figures for fear of being compromised, but, in the period while they are being radicalised and before they decide to engage in terrorism, they might nevertheless be closely associated with such figures.

CONCLUSION: THE RATIONALITY OF MARTYRDOM

Facilitators

Individuals who want to engage in terrorist violence but are not recruited into terrorist groups or cells by experienced terrorists can form their own cells. These individuals rely on facilitators to arrange training, or arrange access to a conflict zone, and possibly access to weapons or funds. Evidence during the trial of the Ammonium Nitrate cell indicates that Omar Khyam acted as a facilitator for Mohammed Siddique Khan and Tanweer to obtain training in Pakistan. Facilitators are enablers who arrange for individuals who are intellectually and emotionally committed to violent extremism to take the next steps to active involvement in terrorism. Without the services of a facilitator, an individual may not get an opportunity to engage in terrorism. However, the internet has now also become a facilitator, because it carries operational information for conducting terrorist attacks which potentially enables committed individuals to act independently of any established group or command hierarchy, as part of a 'leaderless *jihad*'.

Participation in Overseas Conflicts

Prior to 9/11, an unknown number of British Muslims had fought in *jihad* overseas. The first evidence emerged at the time of the war in Bosnia in the early to mid-1990s. Since then, there has been a steady flow of British Muslims going to fight in *jihad* overseas; the numbers who have done so are unknown but there have been a number of reports of casualties from Bosnia, Chechnya, Kashmir, Afghanistan, Iraq and Somalia. Some groups engaged in violent *jihad*, particularly those that operate in Kashmir, have established strong links to Muslim communities in the UK.

Empathy or sympathy for the suffering of Muslims in conflicts in other countries is a key driver for British citizens to fight in *jihad* overseas. At a superficial level, their motivation was their desire to support the *ummah* in conflicts where Muslims are fighting non-Muslims, particularly if it also reflects their ethno-nationalist background (for example, individuals of Pakistani descent going to fight in Kashmir). For some, this could be driven by a simple sense of idealism generated by heightened politicisation over these conflicts. For others, however, there could be deeper ideological motivations. Consequently, some may be fighting for narrow political objectives, such as liberating Kashmir from Indian rule, while others may have Islamist agendas in seeking to establish Islamist regimes. Therefore, although these individuals clearly believed in the concept of violent *jihad*, it does not necessarily mean that they adhered to an Islamist ideology, and nor does it necessarily mean that all those who fight in overseas *jihad* will return to engage in terrorist violence in the UK.

Training

Violent extremists do not necessarily require training in order to carry out acts of terrorism but most terrorists are trained. Training defines the potential operations that a terrorist can conduct (see below). Among the dataset, there appear to be two levels of training: preliminary training that is used to select individuals for acceptance into terrorist cells or for further military training overseas; and overseas training that provides the violent extremists with the necessary skills to conduct acts of terrorism.

During preliminary training sessions, the recruiters are looking for individuals who meet the criteria they hold for suitable candidates. Training is available throughout the world, although it is easier to acquire specific terrorist training in certain places, such as Afghanistan or Pakistan. Paramilitary training is also available through commercial companies around the world, in particular companies training close-protection operatives. In addition, non-specific paramilitary training can occur in any country during the pursuit of legitimate hobbies and sporting activities. Most terrorist cells are small tight-knit groups of individuals with a common purpose, rather than large organisations like those detailed above. Team building or training of any description will prove useful to these cells as this will reinforce group cohesion. Some sports, such as paintball, airsoft and target shooting, can provide rudimentary paramilitary training, with some clubs and commercial enterprises deliberately selling such training to the public. Historical re-enactment societies can also provide some elements of paramilitary training and differ from sporting activities by also associating this training with specific ideologies, such as Waffen SS re-enactors.

A key milestone in the violent radicalisation of the majority of the dataset was their attendance at overseas training camps. The majority of the members of the dataset spent limited amounts of time in mainly Pakistani and Afghan training camps. The acquisition of skills is a key step in the incremental process towards engaging in violence through providing an increased sense of control and power. It also seems that terrorist recruiters look for individuals who have gone through this training process. In some cases, individuals appear to be attending training camps that are centred on training fighters for conflicts in places like Kashmir or Central Asia, but *al Qaeda* recruiters will 'talent spot' Westerners from these camps and offer them the chance to move on to more specialised terror training.[5] However, there do seem to be a small number of exceptions among the dataset. Only Barot and Jalil of the Gas Limos cell are known to have attended training camps in Pakistan and there have been no reports of Lindsay or Hasib Hussain attending training camps. It also seems that many more people than are in our dataset attend these training camps, which suggests that individuals who attend overseas training camps are not automatically recruited into terrorist cells.

Risk Factors for Violent Extremism

The third phase is the act of terrorism itself. Terrorist violence is best described as instrumental behaviour that is used to coerce the state or groups and individuals within it. Terrorism is used to attain ideological goals and, therefore, acts of terrorist violence are clearly rational. However, as we saw in Chapter 8, the willingness to kill another person is not a universal human trait. The presence of 'killing enabling factors' indicates a high risk of terrorist violence among radical or militant extremists.

Justification

The diffusion of responsibility for violent behaviour reduces the individual's inhibitions about committing violent acts and, in particular, killing. Therefore, individuals, groups and institutions that provide justification for violent behaviour will make the individual feel less responsible for their own acts. British Islamist terrorists receive justification for killing from a variety of sources, including militant Imams, the *emirs* of their individual cells and pronouncements by *al Qaeda*. This justification usually takes the form of revenge or retribution for wrongdoing by the target of the violent behaviour. Hence, the key message in the 'martyrdom' videos of the Airline cell was that the attack was in revenge for British and Western interference in Muslim countries. However, this justification is frequently strengthened by pronouncements or *fatwas* issued by militant Imams, which clothe the justification with theological legitimacy, particularly in terms of killing 'apostates' and unbelievers.

Dehumanisation

One of the most pervasive killing enabling factors is dehumanisation, where the target of instrumental violence is believed to be less than human. Dehumanisation is most obvious in the language used by the individuals concerned, for example, as we have seen, the Hutu extremists in Rwanda referred to the Tutsi minority as 'cockroaches'. This terminology seeks to attribute extremely negative characteristics to the target group with the purpose of excluding them from the rest of humanity. The use of this language is normally emotionally laden (usually contempt or fear) and culturally determined, and emphasises discriminatory rejection of the target group. The phraseology usually incorporates two inhuman categories: animals or other subhuman beings; or superhuman beings, such as monsters, demons and devils. Militant Islamists dehumanise their non-Muslim targets by arguing that, as *kuffar*, they are inferior to Muslims.

Dehumanisation serves several functions for the individual as it explains the conflict, provides a sense of superiority and justifies their violent behaviour. The dehumanisation of the target group undermines the normal moral restraints on the instrumental use of violent behaviour and makes violence towards the target group morally acceptable. This protects the individual from the psychological costs and consequences of their violent behaviour towards the target group. The use of language by an individual or group that dehumanises any other individual or group within society indicates an increased threat of violent behaviour by that individual or group. The use of such language will create the impression that such beliefs are normal and morally acceptable.

Violent Media

Despite the controversy surrounding the issue of violent media in the generation of violent behaviour, there is substantial evidence that exposure to violent media can have a negative effect. Exposure to violent media will reinforce any cognitive distortions that the individual has regarding the instrumental use of violence and desensitises them to its effects. One of the key mechanisms involved in this process of reinforcing cognitive distortions is social learning, where the individual learns how to behave from significant others, such as family, peers and role models. If the individual learns that violent behaviour is normative and appropriate then they are more likely to use violent behaviour when provoked. Examples of the type of media that promote the use of violence would be propaganda material about the activities of insurgents in conflicts overseas, such as Chechnya, Iraq and Kashmir. Members of the dataset are known to have viewed and possessed a wide range of this violent media.

Martyrdom

Martyrdom is common in many cultures and religions and the martyrs are venerated by those same cultures and religions. Achieving the status of a martyr will therefore attract some individuals. As it is the wider community that assigns the status of martyr to the individual rather than the individual themselves, the mainstream discourse within a community creates the conditions for martyrdom. However, within the wider Muslim population of the UK, this is not the case. So-called 'martyrs' are not celebrated within the Muslim population of the UK as they are in the Palestinian territories or Lebanon for instance. In fact, there is widespread renunciation from the majority of the Muslim population for acts of terrorism in the UK. Nevertheless, the groups and networks from which the terrorists emerged provide sufficient social support for the act of martyrdom. British Muslims who die in *jihad* or in terrorist attacks in the UK or overseas have been accorded the status of *shahid* by Islamist ideologues in the UK and the radicalised networks of which they are part. Their deeds will therefore be remembered and celebrated by their successors in those networks, and also in wider *jihadi* networks through the reporting of their 'martyrdom' on *jihadi* websites.

Training

Based on the level of training they received and their operational experience, there appear to be at least three types of terrorist and terrorist cells operating in the UK: (i) existing transnational terrorist cells (e.g. Richard Reid and Saajid Badat); (ii) experienced individuals from existing transnational terrorist groups who recruit individuals in the UK to form a cell (e.g. Dhiren Barot and the Gas Limos cell); and (iii) inexperienced individuals who form their own cell (e.g. the 7/7 cell) or act as individuals (e.g. Abu Mansha). The dataset largely consist of individuals and groups in the latter two categories. This indicates that the Islamist terrorist threat to the UK is not the same as the threat previously posed by the various Irish Republican terrorist groups, such as the Provisional IRA. These groups utilised a cadre of experienced terrorists operating within a larger organisational framework and hierarchical command structure. As these groups had an extensive logistics network and had varying levels of community and foreign support, it was possible for them to obtain, store and use sophisticated weapons and explosives. The level of training received by the dataset would therefore have had a critical impact on the nature of the attacks that they chose to carry out. The less skilled that a person is in performing a particular task, the more likely they are to fail. Consequently, this would tend to encourage terrorists to undertake attacks that are within their capabilities, in order to be successful.

OPERATIONAL CAPABILITIES

Every terrorist seeks to achieve something and their decisions must be analysed with this in mind. The previous chapters have outlined some of the long-term goals of terrorist cells and networks. In particular, defending the *ummah* and re-establishing the *caliphate* can be seen as tangible objectives; for example, Reid's attorneys claimed that he believed bombing the plane was necessary to 'prevent the destruction of Islam'.[6] As we have discussed above, most real-world decisions involve a large degree of uncertainty about the consequences of any decision taken. The decision maker is not in possession of all the necessary relevant information to determine whether any particular course of action is the right one to take. Decisions are therefore inherently risky as there is no guarantee that the desired outcome will occur. The decision maker must therefore take into account the probability of the desired outcome occurring. For some decisions, the terrorist can be almost certain of some aspects of the outcome; for example, if a bomb explodes on a packed commuter train then people will be injured and possibly killed. They cannot be certain of other aspects of the outcome, such as the response of the wider Muslim community to that bomb explosion. If the terrorists rely on, or are seeking the support of, the wider Muslim community then this may prove too large a gamble for them. Similarly, the terrorist must be confident that their attack will succeed in achieving these aims and central to this will be the viability of the plan of attack. In this context, important questions in our analysis of the Islamist terrorist threat and the dataset are how and why they made their operational decisions.

TARGET SELECTION

To date, there have been four distinct categories of targets that have been attacked or discussed as potential targets by the different British-based terrorist cells: mass casualty attacks directed at the population as a whole; economic targets; off-duty members of the security forces; and political targets. One similarity between most of these targets is that they are 'soft targets', in that they are easily accessible and present the highest chance of success. The 7 July attack on the undefended London transport system took place at the same time as the heavily defended Gleneagles G8 Summit was occurring. According to Rational Choice theory, it is a logical plan for the attackers to have followed. As the attention of the security services is directed towards a major event, the attackers have a greater chance of escaping detection. The execution of the attack at that specific moment would also bring the terrorists to the attention of the world's media and hijack the agenda of the world's most powerful political leaders. The benefits of conducting an attack are therefore enhanced by the timing. The nature of the target did not change with the timing but the impact may have been potentially increased. Any potential attack would have to have the highest impact possible due to the low number or one-off nature of the attacks. In making these judgements, terrorist cells will have learned from the outcome of previous terrorist attacks, even those in which they were not involved. This is evident from comments made by Waheed Mahmood a few days after the Madrid bombings in 2004, when he was overheard saying, 'Spain was a beautiful job, weren't it? Absolutely beautiful, man, so much impact.'[7] Similarly, Parviz Khan's plot to kidnap and behead a British soldier was directly inspired by similar incidents involving Western civilians in Iraq which generated considerable media attention in Britain and horrified public opinion. He knew that the impact of such an attack in the UK would be enormous.

Target selection can also be justified and explained by reference to the ideological and religious belief system of the perpetrators. Jawad

Akbar stated that 'a big nightclub in central London, no one can put their hands up and say they're innocent – those slags dancing around'.[8] As a 'place of sin', as identified in some Islamist training manuals, this particular target would have found resonance within the peer networks of the attackers. Similarly, the decisions of Abu Mansha and Parviz Khan to target off-duty British soldiers would directly link their planned attacks to British foreign policy, which according to Islamist ideology is propping up so-called 'apostate regimes' in the Muslim world and oppressing the *ummah*.

Economic targets, on the other hand, were discussed by some of the cells, but never actually targeted. Supergrass Babar Ahmed told the Old Bailey at the trial of the Ammonium Nitrate cell, 'Everybody was talking about operations regarding the loss of life, but in his [Waheed Mahmood's] estimation, they could have a different objective, like economic damage. He started to list operations against utilities where there would have been no loss of life. It would cause millions of dollars worth of damage and affect the economy of the country.'[9]

One reason why such economic attacks may not have been undertaken is the need for a sustained campaign of attacks in order for there to be a significant impact on the economy. As a long-term strategy, it was also likely to fail, just as the IRA's strategy of attacking economic targets failed to undermine the British economy. In addition, the financial impacts of such attacks are easily forgotten by the public yet the cultural impact of the mass casualties is more lasting.

The targets selected by the dataset are consistent with targets suggested in *al Qaeda* and other *jihadi* training manuals, but it is questionable whether all of these cells were directed by *al Qaeda* planners in Pakistan or elsewhere. It is known that Dhiren Barot, Richard Reid and Saajid Badat all discussed their plans with *al Qaeda* leaders so it is likely that they received direct instructions. Other cells were networked with *jihadis* in Pakistan, but it is unclear whether those individuals were members of *al Qaeda*, and whether those individuals directed any members of our dataset. Nevertheless, these training manuals are readily available online, so it is entirely conceivable that the cells in our dataset were acting in accordance with the target selection strategy of the *al Qaeda* leadership. After all, the essence of 'leaderless *jihad*' is that cells which form at grass-roots level will act independently of the *al Qaeda* command structure, but will still be directed by its ideology and objectives, through material that they can access online.

TACTICAL CHOICES

Rational Choice theory ultimately tells us how we should make decisions but in reality very few of us are completely rational in our choices. Most decisions are not based on a thoughtful deliberation on all of the available options. Herbert Simon, the Nobel Prize-winning psychologist and economist, developed the concept of Bounded Rationality to explain this. He proposed that our choices are as rational as they can be, given the limitations of our ability to process information. These limitations are overcome by the development of strategies to balance the cost of searching for and processing information against the benefit of making the absolutely best decision. One such strategy is 'satisficing', where the decision maker aims not to make the best decision they can, but instead opts for one that is good enough to meet their objectives. 'Satisficing' provides us with a step-by-step framework for interpreting how terrorists make their decisions. The terrorists must first identify what the important characteristics of the attack will be for them. Barot claimed that the purpose of his proposed radioactive 'dirty bomb' project was to cause 'collateral' objectives such as 'injury, fear, terror and chaos'.[10] Next, the terrorists would need to set criteria for acceptability on each important attribute. All of the available options for an attack would then be considered in turn until one is found that is good enough and then the search stops. The amount of planning required for 'satisficing' is a lot less than that required if the terrorists adopted a true Rational Choice approach. Using this approach, terrorist plans would be good, but not optimal.

In the UK, we have seen a relatively limited set of plans and methods utilised in terrorist attacks. The majority of the attacks have incorporated an explosive device. Richard Reid and Saajid Badat were both in possession of bombs made of PETN (a commercial plastic explosive) with a TATP detonator concealed in a pair of shoes. These devices were manufactured in Afghanistan and Badat stated that he was handed his device by an Arab while he was there. The 7/7 and 21/7 cells are believed to have used bombs made of TATP which had been made from commercially purchased hydrogen peroxide and other chemicals. The 7/7 cell managed to successfully explode their bombs, while the 21/7 cell mixed the explosive incorrectly and only the detonators exploded. The 'fuel-air' bombs used in the failed 29 June 2007 attacks in London utilised petrol, gas canisters and nails (for shrapnel), but the mixture of fuel to air was incorrect so the bombs failed to detonate properly. There was evidence of multiple attempts to detonate the devices through the use of mobile phones connected to the detonators. The subsequent attack on Glasgow airport involved ramming a Jeep Cherokee containing both petrol and gas canisters into the terminal entrance. Kafeel Ahmed crashed into pillars at the side of the entrance doors and then repeatedly attempted to ram the doors without much success. The vehicle became trapped and Ahmed set it and himself on fire.[11]

Both the attack on Glasgow airport and the 'Gas Limos project' resemble suicide truck bomb attacks from other conflicts around the world, which neatly illustrates the application of Bounded Rationality on the decision making of the perpetrators. The vehicle-borne improvised explosive device is known to work, because there are numerous examples of attacks that have successfully used this method, notably the suicide-bomb attacks on the Multinational forces in Beirut in 1983. Indeed, following other truck bomb attacks including those on the World Trade Center in 1993, the Khobar Towers in Saudi Arabia in 1996 and the US embassies in Kenya and Tanzania in 1998, it could be argued that this is a standard *al Qaeda* method and something that might have been taught to those who had passed through one of its specialist terrorist training camps.

Given the need to enact a plan which can provide a reasonably high assurance of success, Bilal Abdullah and Kafeel Ahmed would have employed the methods in which they had been trained. The devices that were used in both the Glasgow airport attack and the attempted attacks in London the day before were relatively simple as they consisted of propane gas canisters and petrol with nails used for fragmentation. These devices and this plan of attack would only require limited training.

Most of the formal training in weapons and explosives that the dataset received occurred overseas, in training camps run by *jihadi* or terrorist organisations. The amount of time spent in these camps would thus be a crucial factor in the expertise of the trainees. The technical proficiency of some individuals in the dataset was therefore limited and variable, which may explain why the 7 July attack on the London transport system succeeded and that of 21 July failed. The 7/7 cell mixed their explosives correctly, whereas the 21/7 cell mixed the ingredients in the wrong quantities. Given the limited amount of time available for training, it appears that the instructors in the camps attempted to maximise the effectiveness of their training by focusing on one specific type of device only, one which their recruits would have a good chance of making after they returned to the UK. Salahuddin Amin and Omar Khyam of the Ammonium Nitrate cell attended a training camp at Kohat between May and June 2003 where they learned how to manufacture and use improvised explosives using ammonium nitrate fertiliser, one of which was tested in a nearby river.[12] This focusing of the training on one particular type of explosive device would reduce the amount and duration of training required to become proficient. However, if the training is deliberately restricted in this way, it probably reduces the ability to innovate and further restricts the tactical options available to the terrorists.

Most of the dataset had relatively limited operational experience, with only a few of them having served in combat prior to their involvement in terrorism. Compared to other terrorist organisations, such as the Provisional IRA, they also lacked the capacity for direct experiential learning because all of these plots resulted in either the death or capture of the terrorists during their first operational attack. As a result, there was no ability for the cells of the dataset to learn from their experience, and so all of the experiential learning would have to occur vicariously through analysing the activities of others. This would severely limit the acquisition of expertise as there would be very few opportunities to practise their skills. The most sophisticated attacks were planned and carried out by those terrorists with the most extensive training and operational experience. Richard Reid and Saajid Badat both attended Khalden training camp and other terrorist training camps in Afghanistan and their shoe bombs were manufactured in Afghanistan from commercial rather than homemade explosives. Another factor limiting the experiential learning of the terror cells is the success of the security services in locating them and disrupting their activities. Even cells that have been able to escape early detection have been ultimately identified and captured.

Some of the methods that were discussed by these cells were beyond their technical capabilities. Dhiren Barot planned to use a radioactive 'dirty bomb' but lacked the radiation source necessary to construct such a device, and none of his cell was trained in handling radioactive sources. The Ammonium Nitrate cell discussed the option of poisoning beer or burgers at a major football match, but lacked the capacity to manufacture a poisonous substance.[13] Kemal Bourgass had the protocol and raw materials to manufacture the biological toxin ricin, but there was no evidence that he ever actually produced any. Much speculation and anxiety is focused on the use of chemical, biological, radiological or nuclear (CBRN) weapons by terrorist organisations; however, this discussion rarely incorporates an analysis of whether such actions are actually feasible. On paper, the protocols for producing some biological and chemical agents appear to be relatively straightforward for anyone with a science degree. But using this knowledge to engineer a weapon is a completely different and much more complicated undertaking. The example of Aum Shinrikyo in Japan (one of the few terrorist organisations to actually use a CBRN weapon) suggests that an organisation that is seeking to develop and deploy a mass casualty CBRN weapon would need access to skilled engineers, equipment, materials and financial resources, in order to be successful. Maintaining operational security for such a large undertaking seems unlikely in the UK. For example, Operation Crevice, the operation to investigate and arrest the Ammonium Nitrate cell, was initiated after the police were tipped off by the operators of a storage facility about a large quantity of ammonium nitrate fertiliser being stored there. In addition, handling the material once it is weaponised will also pose major safety problems for the terrorists themselves. CBRN weapons may be attractive to terrorist organisations but the difficulty in acquiring, storing and using them is likely to prevent their use.

High-value targets tend to be well defended and this poses serious challenges for any planned attack. A comparison of the Madrid and London attacks illustrates the potential impact of the security environment on the behaviour of terrorists. The cell that carried out the Madrid attack in 2004 were affiliated with *al Qaeda* but did not employ suicide attackers, although some of them did subsequently commit suicide when the police cornered them in a Madrid apartment block. The attack itself consisted of a highly sophisticated and co-ordinated series of explosive devices that used commercial explosives. Renfe, the Spanish rail network, did not attempt to raise public awareness of security by asking passengers to report suspicious behaviour or unattended packages to staff members. It would therefore have been easy to leave the rucksacks containing the bombs on the trains without being detected or challenged. There was no specific requirement for the attackers to remain with their devices as it was unlikely that the bombs would be disturbed. On the other hand, the London Underground is considered to be the largest area of controlled public space in Europe. There is round-the-clock CCTV surveillance and substantial investment in anti-terror measures to reduce the risk of emplaced explosive devices. There are no waste bins, vending machines are sloped so that nothing can be left on top, seats are designed so that nothing can be concealed beneath them, and the travelling public are constantly reminded to be vigilant for suspicious behaviour and unattended luggage. All of these measures would be easily discovered via reconnaissance by the terrorists. Therefore, the physical environment of the London Underground would not afford the same opportunities to leave improvised explosive devices as the Spanish commuter rail system.

The Madrid bombings also demonstrated that the use of suicide attacks is not an automatic feature of the decision making by *al Qaeda*-inspired terrorists and their supporters. The undercover police officer, codenamed Dawood, who infiltrated the Training cell recorded Mohammed Hamid downplaying the carnage of the 7 July attacks, while also telling Atilla Ahmet and another member not to easily give up their lives:

Hamid: 'You know what happened on the tubes, right, how many altogether, four people *shaheed* [martyred].'

Ahmet: 'Allah wa Allah, I have to say this is as well, but four people got *shaheed*, right, how many people did they take out? ... Fifty-two.'

Hamid: 'Fifty-two, that's not even a breakfast for me.'

Ahmet: 'I know it's not.'

Hamid: 'That's not even a breakfast for me, for me in this country, do you understand me? Now, at the same time, how I look at it, I would take my breakfast and I still be with my children and my wife and I'll be looking after them. Remember the Jack the Ripper. Remember this people that never get caught, right, don't let your ego go forward, let your intelligence go forward for the sake of Allah, use your *hikma* [wisdom] and be effective, effective, see how many gets it, see how many you can take at the same time, see how long you can last out, then if you have to go, then you're going for a good reason.'[14]

This strategic thinking is consistent with the decisions of several of the cells in the dataset, including the Gas Limos and Ammonium Nitrate cells.

However, this level of independent strategic thinking is not universal. The 21/7 cell simply attempted to replicate the success of the 7 July attack, even down to the three attacks on the London Underground and one on a bus. In fact, the 7 July attack on the bus in Tavistock Square was probably a target of opportunity following the closure of the Northern Line, but this decision provided the terrorists with what they wanted, an image that would become a lasting symbol of the 7 July attacks. It was not part of the original plan and, given the time between the initial explosions and that on the bus (57 minutes), it is unlikely that it was a prearranged 'plan B'. In all likelihood, it took that long for Hasib Hussain to realise that the others had successfully detonated their bombs and for him to decide on an alternative target that was consistent with the original plan. Given the time pressure, stress and prevailing conditions, it is the most likely 'satisficing' decision that he could have made in order to 'martyr' himself.

CONCLUSIONS

Can our analysis of individuals involved in terrorist activity answer the original question – why did Reid try to blow up an airliner and why did Badat put his bomb in a cupboard? The answer to this seemingly simple question is potentially very complex.

One possible interpretation of our analysis is that Reid had nothing else to live for, and that his life was given meaning and purpose through his involvement with the global Islamist *jihad*. He had no moderating influences in his life that could counter the appeal of the Islamist community. Within this community, acquiring the status of *shahid* would provide him with social standing and a lasting legacy.

CONCLUSION: THE RATIONALITY OF MARTYRDOM

By dehumanising his potential victims and believing in the religious justification of his actions, the rewards of martyrdom may have been more attractive than the rewards of living life among the *kuffar*. If this was the case then Reid may have believed that his life would improve after he was dead. This would suggest that his apparently altruistic suicide was not as altruistic as it first appears. That is, the social status acquired before and after his 'martyrdom' operation may have been the main driver for his decision to blow up the airliner.

Badat, on the other hand, was well integrated into the wider Muslim community in Gloucester and had a certain amount of social status within it as a *hafiz*. This status may have increased within the Islamist community as it did with Reid, but the difference between them was the potential moderating influence of his social support networks. That is, when Badat returned from overseas and was temporarily isolated from the influence of the Islamist community, the protective effect of his social support weakened the influence of the risk factors. Therefore, when it came time to confront the reality of his 'martyrdom' operation, he could not go through with it.

Central to this interpretation of our analysis is that the Islamist community and radical networks confer the necessary social status on the *shaheed*. As we discussed in Chapter 9, the wider Muslim community does not recognise or support 'martyrdom' operations in the UK. Recently, respected Islamic scholars have criticised the killing of innocents, particularly other Muslims, in 'martyrdom' operations. This has led *al Qaeda*'s second-in-command, Ayman al Zawahiri, to publish lengthy rebuttals of these criticisms, which highlights how vulnerable the Islamist *jihad* is to criticisms from other Islamic authorities. When asked, 'Who is it who is killing with your excellency's blessing the innocents in Baghdad, Morocco and Algeria? Do you consider the killing of women and children to be *jihad*?', al Zawahiri responded that 'it was either an unintentional error, or out of necessity as in the cases of *al Tartarrus*'. This latter point refers to a *fatwa* which authorises the killing of innocents who are being used as human shields by the enemy. However, he subsequently goes on

309

to 'emphasise to my brothers the *mujahideen* to beware of expanding the issue of *al Tartarrus*'.[15] This clearly indicates that the killing of innocents is a major problem for retaining the support of individuals within radical groups and networks, particularly if there appears to be no progress in achieving some of the core objectives of those attacks. For example, *al Qaeda* has yet to actually attack Israel, mount a serious challenge to the apostate regimes in the Middle East or make any progress in establishing the *caliphate*.

Does this indicate that, with each successive attack which results in the death of innocents, support will drain away from *al Qaeda*? The available evidence is that *al Qaeda* in Iraq is losing the support of the *Sunni* population. It would be premature to assume that this has real significance for violent extremists in the British Muslim population. A close parallel would be the defeat of Nazi Germany in the Second World War; despite the overthrow of Hitler and his regime, they have remained potent symbols for successive generations of violent neo-Nazi extremists. It would not be too far a leap of faith to assume that bin Laden and *al Qaeda* will also remain potent symbols, regardless of what eventually happens to them.

Despite this, the prognosis for the spread of violent extremism in the British Muslim community is actually quite promising. The police and security services have been successful in preventing most cells from conducting acts of terrorism. The numbers of individuals involved in terrorist activity are low, and there is no widespread community support for their actions. If our interpretation of the dataset is correct, then superficial engagement with radical groups and networks will not necessarily translate into violent extremism, particularly if there are protective factors present. The continuing threat from violent extremists within the British Muslim community is very real, but the threat must be put into perspective.

One huge problem is the assumption that all violent extremists are actually prepared to commit acts of violence. As we discussed in Chapter 8, killing people is not easy and not everyone can bring themselves to do it. Even with all the passive and active risk factors we have identified, some violent extremists may be unable to override the cultural taboo against killing, although this may not be apparent until the moment at which they must take another's life. It may be simply that the most important protective factor for preventing violent extremism is the sanctity of life itself. The reality of actually killing people may be something that only a select few are able to cope with, which represents a natural barrier to the spread of violent extremism.

Notes and references

[1] Zimbardo PG & Boyd JN, 'Putting time into perspective: A valid, reliable individual differences metric', *Journal of Personality and Social Psychology*, No. 77, 1999, pp 1271–88.

[2] Anecdotal evidence indicates that a significant number of the dataset were considered to be devout Muslims. Shahid Butt was regarded by those who knew him as a strict Muslim, and a Birmingham cleric claimed that both Ahmed and Harhara were 'religious kids'. Naveed Bhatti was also noted to be a very devout Muslim, as are his family. This was partially confirmed by Ghulam Hussein's wife who reported that he had turned back to religion. Tanvir Hussain was a devout Muslim by 2003. 'Suspects in the Aden "bomb plot"', 13 February 1999, http://www.al-bab.com/yemen/hamza/suspects.htm; 'Yemen: The British link', *Observer*, 19 January 1999, www.al-bab.com; '"Led astray" by Al Qaeda general', *Harrow Times*, 21 June 2007, http://www.harrowtimes.co.uk/display.var.1488240.0.0.php; 'The eight in the dock', *The Times*, 9 September 2008, http://www.timesonline.co.uk/tol/news/uk/crime/article4707712.ece.

[3] CBS News, 25 March 2007, http://www.cbsnews.com/stories/2007/03/23/60minutes/main2602308_page3.shtml.

[4] Report of the Official Account of the Bombings in London on 7 July 2005, HC1087 (London: The Stationery Office), 11 May 2006.

[5] 'Al-Qaeda resurgent six years on?', BBC NewsOnline, 11 September 2007, http://news.bbc.co.uk/1/hi/world/middle_east/6988356.stm.

[6] 'Exchange between Reid and judge follows life sentence', CNN, 6 December 2003, http://www.cnn.com/2003/LAW/01/31/reid.transcript/.

[7] 'Profile: Waheed Mahmood', BBC NewsOnline, 30 April 2007, http://news.bbc.co.uk/1/hi/uk/6149800.stm.

[8] 'Suspect "had nuclear bomb plan"', BBC NewsOnline, 22 March 2006, http://news.bbc.co.uk/1/hi/uk/4832740.stm.

[9] 'Profile: Waheed Mahmood', BBC NewsOnline, 30 April 2007, http://news.bbc.co.uk/1/hi/uk/6149800.stm.

[10] 'Muslim was planning dirty bomb attack in UK', *Daily Telegraph*, 13 October 2006, http://www.telegraph.co.uk/news/main.jhtml?xml=/news/2006/10/13/nterr13.xml.

[11] *Jane's Terrorism and Security Monitor*, May 2008, pp 16–18.

[12] 'Accused "helped make test bomb"', BBC NewsOnline, 24 July 2006, http://news.bbc.co.uk/1/hi/uk/5210870.stm.

[13] 'Accused "talked of poison plot"', BBC NewsOnline, 24 March 2006, http://news.bbc.co.uk/1/hi/uk/4841314.stm.

[14] 'Hamid, Ahmet and their associates may well have been the last graduates of Abu Hamza's Finsbury Park terrorist finishing school', *The Times*, 26 February 2008, http://www.timesonline.co.uk/tol/news/uk/crime/article3441588.ece.

[15] *Jane's Terrorism and Security Monitor*, May 2008, pp 16–18.

Bibliography

Abbas T (ed), *Muslim Britain: Communities under Pressure* (London: Zed Books, 2005).

Ajzen I, *Attitudes, personality, and behaviour* (Homewood, Illinois, Dorsey Press, 1988).

Alam MY & Husband C, 'British-Pakistani men from Bradford: Linking narratives to policy', Joseph Rowntree Foundation, November 2006.

Alexiev A, 'Violent Islamists in the UK and Europe', *Internationale Politik* (Berlin), September 2005.

American Psychiatric Association, *Diagnostic and statistical manual of mental disorders*, 4th Edition Text Revised (*DSM-IV*) (American Psychiatric Association, Washington, DC, 2000).

Ansari H, *The Infidel Within* (London: C. Hurst & Co, 2004).

Bartone PT & Kirkland FR, 'Optimal leadership in small army units', in Gal R & Mangelsdorff MD (eds), *Handbook of Military Psychology* (John Wiley & Sons, 1991).

Begg M, *Enemy Combatant: A British Muslim's Journey to Guantanamo and Back* (London: The Free Press, 2006).

Bloom M, *Dying to Kill: The Allure of Suicide Terror* (New York: Columbia University Press, 2006).

Brown R, 'Intergroup relations', in Hewstone M, Stroebe W & Stephenson GM (eds), *Introduction to Social Psychology* (Oxford: Blackwell Publishers, 1996).

MARTYRDOM

Burke J, *Al-Qaeda: The True Story of Radical Islam* (London: Penguin, 2004).

Buunk BP, 'Affiliation, attraction and close relationships', in Hewstone M, Stroebe W & Stephenson GM (eds), *Introduction to Social Psychology* (Oxford: Blackwell Publishers, 1996).

Comer RJ, *Abnormal Psychology* (5th ed) (NewYork: Worth Publishers, 2004).

Commission for Racial Equality, Briefing on Islamophobia.

Dill KE & Dill JC, 'Video game violence: A review of the empirical literature', *Aggression and Violent Behavior*, No. 3, 1998, pp 407–28.

Durkheim E, 'Suicide: A study in sociology', summarised in Shneidman ES (ed), *Comprehending Suicide: Landmarks in 20th-century Suicidology* (American Psychological Association, 2001).

Dutton DG, Boyanowsky EO & Bond MH, 'Extreme mass homicide: From military massacre to genocide', *Aggression and Violent Behavior*, No. 10, 2005, pp 437–73.

Dyer G, *War: The Lethal Custom* (New York: Carroll and Graf Publishers, 2004).

Glenn RW, *Reading Athena's Dance Card: Men against Fire in Vietnam* (Annapolis: Naval Institute Press, 2000).

Grossman D, *On Killing: The Psychological Cost of Learning to Kill in War and Society* (Boston: Back Bay Books, 1996).

Hafez MM, 'Dying to be martyrs: The symbolic dimension of suicide terrorism', in Pedahzur A (ed), *Root Causes of Suicide Terrorism: The Globalization of Martyrdom* (Oxford: Routledge, 2006).

Hall JR & Benning SD, 'The "successful" psychopath: Adaptive and subclinical manifestations of psychopathy in the general population', in Patrick CJ (ed), *Handbook of Psychopathy* (New York: Guilford Press, 2006).

Harik JP, *Hezbollah: The Changing Face of Terrorism* (London: IB Taurus, 2006).

Haslam N, 'Dehumanisation: An integrative review', *Personality and Social Psychology Review*, No. 10, 2006, pp 252–64.

Hewstone M & Fincham F, 'Attribution theory and research: Basic issues and applications', in Hewstone M, Stroebe W & Stephenson GM (eds), *Introduction to Social Psychology* (Oxford: Blackwell Publishers, 1996).

Horgan J, *The Psychology of Terrorism* (Oxford: Routledge, 2005).

BIBLIOGRAPHY

House of Commons, Home Affairs Select Committee, Terrorism and Community Relations, 6th Report, 5 April 2005.

Husain E, *The Islamist* (London: Penguin, 2007).

Intelligence and Security Committee Report into the London Terrorist Attacks on 7 July 2005, May 2006.

Janis I, *Victims of Groupthink* (2nd ed) (Boston: Houghton-Mifflin, 1982).

Kirby A, 'The London bombers as "self starters": A case study in indigenous radicalization and the emergence of autonomous cliques', *Studies in Conflict and Terrorism*, No. 30, 2007, pp 415–28.

Lévy B, *Who Killed Daniel Pearl?* (NewYork: Melville House, 2003).

Maher S, 'Campus radicals', *Prospect*, September 2006.

Malik S, 'My brother the bomber', *Prospect*, June 2007.

Malik S, 'Society NS Profile – Omar Sharif', *New Statesman*, 24 April 2006.

Marshall SLA, *Men Against Fire: The Problem of Battle Command* (Norman: University of Oklahoma Press, 2000).

Nadelson T, *Trained to Kill: Soldiers at War* (Baltimore: Johns Hopkins University Press, 2005).

Packer DJ, 'On being both with us and against us: A normative conflict model of dissent in social groups', *Personality and Social Psychology Review*, No. 12, 2008, pp 50–72.

Pape R, *Dying to Win: Why Suicide Bombers Do It* (New York: Random House, 2005).

Pedahzur A (ed), *Root Causes of Suicide Terrorism: The Globalization of Martyrdom* (Oxford: Routledge, 2006).

Phillips M, *Londonistan* (London: Gibson Square Books, 2006).

Report of the Official Account of the Bombings in London on 7th July 2005, HC1087, London: The Stationery Office, 11 May 2006.

Riek BM, Mania EW & Gaertner SL, 'Intergroup threat and outgroup attitudes: A meta-analytic review', *Personality and Social Psychology Review*, No. 10, 2006, pp 336–53.

Ronson J, *Them: Adventures with Extremists* (London: Simon and Schuster, 2002).

MARTYRDOM

Sageman M, 'Radicalization of global Islamist terrorists', Evidence to the United States Senate Committee on Homeland Security and Governmental Affairs, 27 June 2007.

Sageman M, *Leaderless Jihad: Terror Networks in the Twenty-First Century* (Philadelphia: University of Pennsylvania Press, 2008).

Sageman M, *Understanding Terror Networks* (Philadelphia: University of Pennsylvania Press, 2004).

Shneidman ES (ed), *Comprehending Suicide: Landmarks in 20th-century Suicidology* (American Psychological Association, 2001).

Sikand S, 'The origins and growth of the Tablighi Jamaat in Britain', *Islam and Christian–Muslim Relations* 9:2, 1998.

Silke A (ed), *Terrorists, Victims and Society* (John Wiley & Sons, 2003).

Silke A, 'Cheshire-cat logic: The recurring theme of terrorist abnormality in psychological research', *Psychology, Crime & Law*, No. 4, 1998, pp 51–69.

Staub E, 'The roots of evil: Social conditions, culture, personality, and basic human needs', *Personality and Social Psychology Review*, No. 3, 1999, pp 179–92.

Stephan WG & Stephan CW, 'An integrated threat theory of prejudice', in Oskamp S (ed), *Reducing Prejudice and Discrimination* (The Claremont Symposium on Applied Social Psychology) (New Jersey: Lawrence Erlbaum Associates, 2000).

Stephan WG & Stephan CW, 'Predicting prejudice', *International Journal of Intercultural Relations*, No. 20, 1996, pp 409–26.

Taseer A, 'A British jihadist', *Prospect*, August 2005, http://www.prospect-magazine.co.uk/article_details.php?id=6992.

van Avermaet E, 'Social influence in small groups', in Hewstone M, Stroebe W & Stephenson GM (eds), *Introduction to Social Psychology* (Oxford: Blackwell Publishers, 1996).

Wilke H & van Knippenberg A, 'Group performance', in Hewstone M, Stroebe W & Stephenson GM (eds), *Introduction to Social Psychology* (Oxford: Blackwell Publishers, 1996).

Wilson M & Daly M, 'Competitiveness, risk taking, and violence: The young male syndrome', *Ethology and Sociobiology*, No. 6, 1985, pp 59–73.
Zimbardo P, *The Lucifer Effect: How Good People Turn Evil* (New York: Random House, 2007).

BIBLIOGRAPHY

Zimbardo PG & Boyd JN, 'Putting time into perspective: A valid, reliable individual differences metric', *Journal of Personality and Social Psychology*, No. 77, 1999, pp 1271–88.